FIREFLY

A Skyraider's Story About America's Secret War Over Laos

Richard E. Diller

First published by Dog Ear Publishing
4010 W. 86th Street, Ste H
Indianapolis, IN 46268
www.dogearpublishing.net

ISBN: 978-1-4575-1969-7

This book is printed on acid-free paper.

Printed in the United States of America

To the families
of the men
who were killed
or missing in action
while flying
A-1 Skyraiders
during the war in
Southeast Asia

Attack. It designated that realm devoted to the obliteration of enemies *on the ground.* An attack pilot was a bomber. And a rocketeer. And a strafer. Attack pilots were the mud-fighters, the guys who flew down in the weeds and delivered fire on the heads of the enemy. And who took fire in return.

Being an attack pilot had always implied a certain *expendability.* Losses were expected. It was like walking into a barroom brawl: you always hoped to land a lucky first punch and take the guy out, but you *knew* you'd probably take a few hits yourself. That's just the way it had always been for attack pilots.

—Robert Gandt, *Bogeys and Bandits,* Viking Press, 123.

Table of Contents

PREFACE

During the time of the Vietnam War, the neighboring country of Laos was a battleground of two wars: one was in northern Laos between Hmong people who were being supported by clandestine American forces against the Pathet Lao, and the other was the effort to interdict the traffic of southbound supplies along the Ho Chi Minh Trail in southern Laos. Those supplies were for support of North Vietnamese Army (NVA) activities in South Vietnam. By early 1969, the battle pattern was well established.

This book is about a part of those wars, especially the night mission over northern Laos and the Ho Chi Minh Trail and how it was conducted by A-1 Skyraider pilots in coordination with forward air controllers (facs). To my knowledge, no one has written about the night mission over Laos until now.

The main reason propeller-driven A-1s were still being used in the jet age was because of their usefulness in recovering aircrew members who had been shot down over Vietnam and Laos. Skyraiders could stay over the target (or survivor) for an extended time, they had three communication radios (UHF, VHF, and FM), they could carry a lot of ordnance and deliver it accurately (especially from low level), and they could take a lot of punishment.

While the sun was up, O-1 Bird Dog pilots with the call sign Raven flew out of Lima Site 98, the "secret CIA base" in northern Laos (called Barrel Roll) and provided facing service for the friendlies and high performance fast mover jets. But the Ravens didn't fly at night, which meant the Barrel Roll night mission was left to Skyraiders.

In daylight, A-1s were too slow and vulnerable to the many guns used by the enemy along the Trail (southern Laos was known as Steel Tiger), so the only times they were allowed to enter the area was at night or when an airplane was shot down and a survivor was in need of rescue.

The 609th Special Operations Squadron, which flew A-26s and had the call sign Nimrod, covered nights in Steel Tiger until it was phased out in November of 1969. At that time A-1s picked up the night Trail mission in addition to going north. Because of that, for approximately the first half of my tour I flew nights only over northern Laos. Later I flew over the Trail as well. The enemy had big guns in northern Laos, but the main hazard was high terrain—mountains, as well as the guns—and in the south the hazard was ground fire.

Although the search and rescue mission was the main reason low and slow A-1s were still being used in the jet age, I specialized—by choice—in night missions. Therefore, that is what this book is mostly about. However, I do cover one SAR written from my perspective—that being Boxer 22.

America's wartime involvement in Laos was not acknowledged by the United States government until 1997. Pilots were advised not to talk in our letters home of where we were flying. The location of awards earned as a result of heroics was listed as Southeast Asia, not Laos or Vietnam. Because of this, A-1 pilots perceived a lack of recognition and credit for our efforts, which was an ongoing irritation.

The events related here are recalled from my flight log and audiotapes I sent to my parents over the course of the year. Many times I picked up the recorder just after returning from a mission, so the recall is very fresh in many cases. None of this is fiction.

Names have not been changed except in a couple of places when I tell about people doing stupid things. In those instances, I changed names to protect the guilty.

This book is about many things, including how weather affected operations and how pilots lived their lives in a combat environment.

I hope you enjoy it.

Sincerely,

Dick Diller

ACKNOWLEDGEMENTS

Several people have contributed to this book, and without their efforts the story would be lacking important information. No one A-1 pilot experienced it all, and the contributions of others add depth to the story.

Jim George told stories only he can tell.

Jack Hudson told of several experiences that shouldn't be lost because no one recorded them.

Don Combs contributed the details of his shoot-down and recovery.

Fighter pilots George Marrett and Mike McCarthy and navy helicopter pilot Tom Phillips are authors who advised and encouraged me to continue this to completion.

The "anonymous A-1 pilot" who added his point of view of Boxer 22 and Christmas deserves recognition.

Thank you to Robert Gandt for the use of his words about attack pilots.

I'm not the one who invented this saying, but if my grandchildren ever ask me if I was a war hero, my answer will be, "No, but I flew with a lot of guys who were." That will be a reference to Jim, Jack, Don, Jim Monk, Jon Ewing, and many others with whom I flew. I learned a lot from them, especially humility.

Thanks to Emily for always being there for me, and for her contributions to the story. Thanks to my son Chris for maps, daughter Cori for ongoing never-ending help with the technical part of computers, and daughter Angie for her work right after graduating from the University of Iowa.

I also want to recognize Nancy Payne-Olewiler, who edited my work and kept me from embarrassing myself by straightening out literary missteps. Nancy was a valuable sounding board who made me defend passages and justify why I said certain things the way I did.

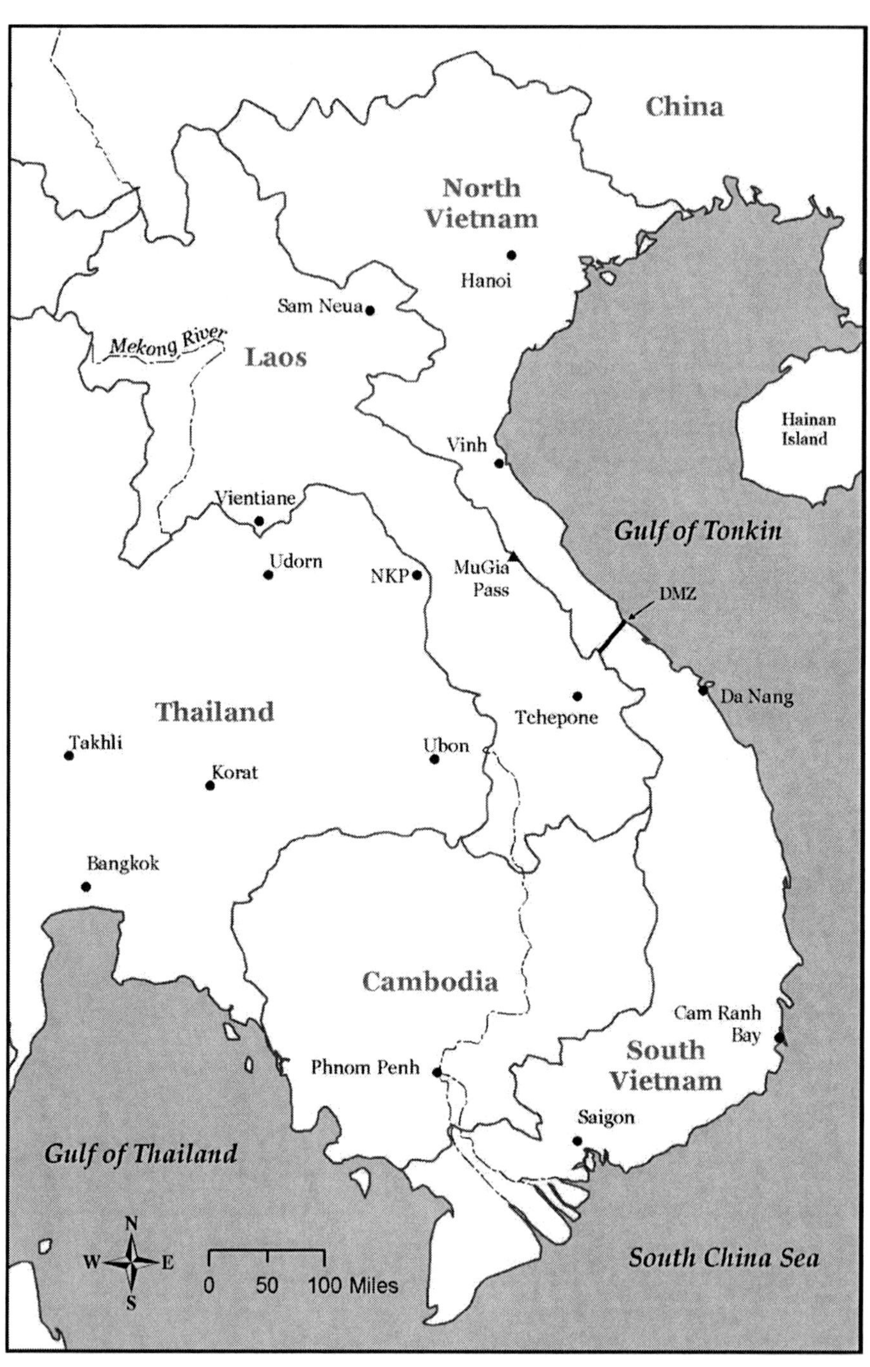
China
North Vietnam
Hanoi
Sam Neua
Mekong River
Laos
Hainan Island
Vinh
Vientiane
Gulf of Tonkin
Udorn
NKP
MuGia Pass
DMZ
Da Nang
Thailand
Tchepone
Takhli
Ubon
Korat
Bangkok
Cambodia
Cam Ranh Bay
South Vietnam
Phnom Penh
Saigon
Gulf of Thailand
N
W
E
S
0
50
100 Miles
South China Sea

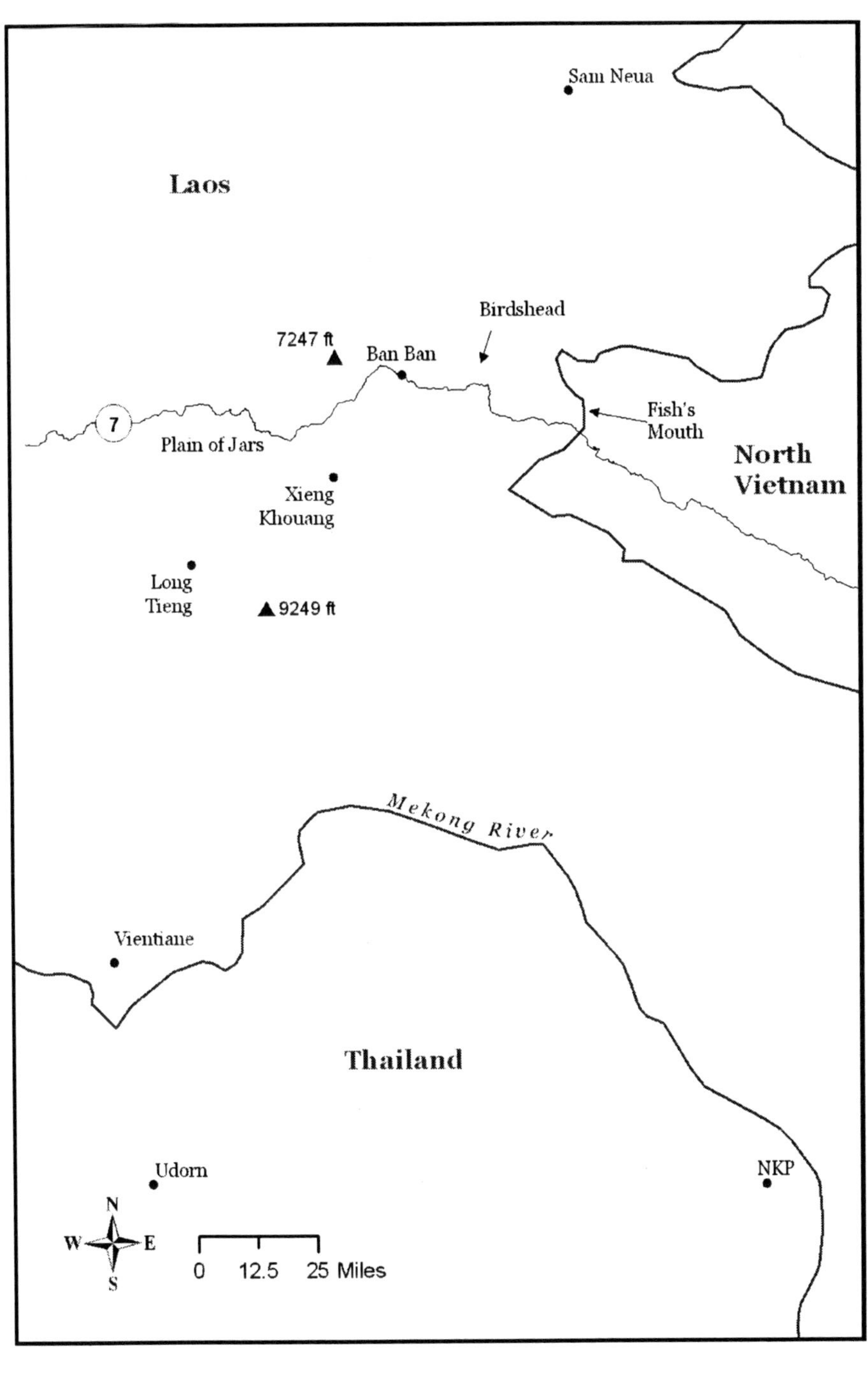
Sam Neua
Laos
Birdshead
7247 ft
Ban Ban
7
Fish's Mouth
Plain of Jars
North Vietnam
Xieng Khouang
Long Tieng
9249 ft
Mekong River
Vientiane
Thailand
Udorn
NKP
N
W
E
S
0 12.5 25 Miles

INTRODUCTION

From April, 1969, until March, 1970, I flew A-1 Skyraiders as a United States Air Force pilot from Nakhon Phanom Royal Thai Air Force Base, Thailand, on missions over Laos. Nakhon Phanom was commonly called NKP and sometimes was known as Naked Phanny. The base is near the Mekong River about 300 miles northeast of Bangkok.

Many Skyraider pilots came directly from pilot training, but most, like me, came from other flying squadrons in the air force and so had varying experience levels. We ranged in age from about twenty-four years to somewhere around forty, with a few commanders and more senior people a little older. In the late 1950s, the air force instituted a requirement that all new officers have a college degree. So as a group, my fellow pilots were well educated. Some had graduate degrees.

A-1 pilots were excellent pilots, well trained and dedicated to accomplishing the mission to which they had been assigned. That's a testament not only to them as individuals, but to the system from which they came, the education they had received, and the pilot training system of the United States Air Force. They were taught to be aggressive and safe, and to respect one another and the mission.

Within our group of pilots we were very matter-of-fact about what we were doing. We were all A-1 pilots and no one did anything above or beyond what anyone else did or thought he could do, so events related in this book weren't anything remarkable to an A-1 pilot. But whenever we were with people who weren't fighter pilots or attack pilots, there was a feeling of superiority—you can't do what I do—that is probably an essential part of being a fighter pilot or attack pilot. When we were in the company of pilots of other aircraft, A-1 pilots carried a great deal of prestige because of the aircraft we were flying and the job we did.

Four months prior to my departure for war I got married. During my year in Thailand, my wife, Emily, lived in an apartment in Bangkok for about nine months and I was able to get to Bangkok about every six weeks for crew time off (CTO), leave, and rest and relaxation (R&R).

This is a day-to-day account of flying in combat and how it affected me and of how my previous experiences shaped my ability to do what I did. It is also a description of life on the base, the life and death encounters of pilots flying in the war, what flying combat missions was like, some of the preparation required to become a combat pilot and preparation for daily missions, and the sadness, happiness, and frustrations combat pilots must deal with on a daily basis. Dealing with combat losses is never easy. I found a need to develop an emotional numbness to the loss of fellow pilots who had become my friends.

Life goes on, but sometimes I wanted to stop and reflect and that wasn't built into the schedule. So we pressed ahead.

I am blessed to be able to share my story and the story of the men with whom I had the privilege to fly.

FIREFLY

A Skyraider's Story About
America's Secret War Over Laos

Chapter 1

The Physical

My favorite toy when I was a little boy belonged to Beverly Kasbeer, a girl in my kindergarten class whose grandparents lived across the street from our house. It was a silver-colored pedal-powered go-cart in the shape of an airplane that I thought was about the neatest thing I had ever seen. Beverly's grandparents lived next to the hospital and our street was busy, so I wasn't allowed to go across just any time I pleased. I can remember many times when that airplane was in front of their house, and all I could do was look longingly at it. Only once was I allowed to ride in that airplane for oh, so short a time, but it was a moment of magic. I could imagine myself flying way up into the clouds as I pedaled along the sidewalk.

*

My mother noticed I couldn't see objects in the distance very well when I was in first grade, so she took me to an optometrist and sure enough, I needed glasses. Not only that, but my right eye had a tendency to turn in—I was cross-eyed. Not many people had seen a kid so young wearing glasses, and I frequently received comments about how little I was to be wearing them. At age six, I thought that was pretty neat. I had always wanted to fly, but everyone knew a pilot had to have perfect vision, so that eliminated me.

Sometime in grade school I discarded the glasses because I no longer needed them, but I still carried the perception that my eyes were weak and that one day soon I would need to wear them again to see properly.

*

In the late 1950s and early 1960s at the University of Oklahoma, Reserve Officer Training Corps courses were mandatory for all male students for the first two years, with female students attending physical education courses. OU had both air force and army ROTC courses available for the boys and a small naval ROTC attachment for those who had been accepted into the navy's four-year course before they even enrolled as students at the university. If an applicant was accepted for advanced ROTC for his last two years, the air force paid ninety cents per day, and he was expected to accept a commission in the air force as a second lieutenant and a four-year active duty commitment upon graduation. The air force was my choice for my ROTC obligation because my brother had gone through the AFROTC program at Southern Methodist University, and he was an air force officer when I entered college. Also, the air force seemed to be a nice, clean, safe way to meet my military obligation when I compared it to the army. The romance of airplanes was an influence even though I knew I could never fly because of my eyes. I envied the guys who were in the aviation part of the program.

The United States still had a military draft at that time, and although not everyone was drafted, the possibility of having to serve two years in the army as a grunt did not appeal to me at all. So I applied, took a lot of tests, and was accepted into the advanced AFROTC program.

*

I went to OU in the first place because when I was in high school, I thought I wanted to be a petroleum engineer, and they had one of the best schools in the nation for that. I hadn't been in college very long when I discovered engineering was not for me. About then, I saw an article in a magazine about hospital administration, which seemed like a good field, so I decided to pursue that for a career.

A master's degree in hospital administration was needed to be successful, but practically any undergraduate degree was an acceptable prerequisite with business courses being preferred. The stock market and the structure of corporations interested me, so I switched my major to finance at the start of my sophomore year.

When the air force asked what field I would like to pursue while on active duty, my answer was hospital administration, and I received that as an assignment. My first duty station was to attend the fifteen-week Basic Course in Medical Service Administration at Gunter Air Force Base in Montgomery, Alabama, in the fall of 1963, with a follow-on assignment to Paine Field, Washington.

The class had sixty-three students, most of whom were pharmacists with direct commissions. That is, they had not been commissioned through ROTC or officer candidate school (OCS), but just signed up as second lieutenants. One of them was Chuck Zwiers, who was from Seattle and whose sister was in a large sorority at the University of Washington. Marilyn was engaged to be married, but Chuck said she would be willing to get dates for me with her friends. She did, and my time at Paine Field was very pleasant indeed, with the university only twenty miles south of the base.

The Gunter AFB Recreation Services Department sponsored a flag football league and our class entered a team. I was the organizer/coach, as flag or touch football was one of my passions. The class team had some good athletes, and we won the base championship. Maxwell AFB, which was just across town, also had a football league, and they challenged our team to a game. A lot of hype went into the buildup to the game. On game day, we discovered the Maxwell crowd had brought an all-star team of the best players from their league. The game was close and hard-fought, and it ended in a tie. Best of all, no one got hurt.

*

On October 30, 1963, a message came that my parents had been in an auto accident the day before on US Highway 40 near Roosevelt, Utah. They were on their way home from a farm equipment dealers' convention in Seattle when an oncoming car hit a horse in the road and slid broadside into the front of their car. My dad was in the front passenger seat with another man driving, and my mother was in the back seat behind him. Dad was wearing a seat belt, but shoulder harnesses weren't in cars in those days, and his head had been cut very badly by the windshield. His ankle was broken when another car hit them from behind, and the door, which was open from the collision, came down on his leg.

Cars also didn't have seat belts in the back seats in 1963, and Mom's legs had been shattered in some twenty places above her knees. Her injuries weren't life-threatening like Dad's were, but they were very painful and potentially crippling. My first reaction was to try to get a flight to Utah, but there really wasn't much I could do to help and my brother, Bill, was en route, so I stayed at Gunter. They eventually recovered, but five people and the horse were killed in that crash.

*

November 22 of that year was a bright, sunny Friday in Montgomery and a few of my classmates and I were walking up to the front of the school building after lunch at the Officers' Club when news came that President Kennedy had been shot in Dallas. One of the guys had a portable radio, and we gathered around in the classroom to listen to coverage of the event. But our instructor came in the room and told us we had a syllabus to cover and we could hear what happened on the evening news. So we had to turn the radio off and get to the lesson of the day.

*

I arrived at Paine, which is eight miles south of Everett, on December 31, 1963, and reported to work on January 2, 1964. Paine Field was a small base whose only mission was to support a squadron of F-102s. It had a four-bed dispensary for which I was the medical supply officer.

Paine Field's medical supply officer (USAF photo)

My boss, the dispensary administrator, was Captain Frank Mugford. One of the first things he told me was that I was scheduled to go to the air force disaster control school at Lowry Air Force Base, Colorado, the last two weeks of March and the first two weeks of April. Denver. Ski season. Not bad!

My classmates at Lowry were a couple of majors, three captains, a first lieutenant who was the only other medic in the class, and me, a brown bar. The majors and captains were pilots, one of whom had been an instructor pilot at an undergraduate pilot training (UPT) base. We were a small class and we got to know each other well. One evening at the O Club I was having a beer with one of the captains and a major and confided how much I wanted to fly.

"Well, why don't you?"

"Because my eyes aren't good enough to pass the physical."

"You aren't wearing glasses. Have you tried to pass it?"

"No."

"You ought to at least give it a try. You might pass."

Yeah. Why not at least try? I can see pretty well.

When I got back to Paine, I applied for pilot training. Passing the physical presented some pretty high hurdles, but what did I have to lose? Part of the eye test was a check for astigmatism, and for that I had to see an optometrist at the hospital at McChord AFB, about eighty miles south of Paine. I thought it would be a good idea to meet him before I took that part of the exam, so one day, with Frank's blessing, I concocted a medical supply excuse to go to McChord, and invited the optometrist to the Officers' Club for lunch. He was a Japanese-American first lieutenant who seemed sympathetic to my situation, and I felt good about having met him before I saw him officially.

The day of the exam, he put drops in my eyes to dilate the pupils, which I didn't like at all but knew had to be done. Then he put a machine before my eyes and flipped back and forth between a lot of lenses, always with the question, "Which one is clearer, this one or this one?" Over and over. Then with a light he peered deeply within my eyes to the retinas.

At the conclusion of the exam he said, "You have a little astigmatism, and your eyes are right on the border of meeting the qualification, but I'll give it to you." I passed! Fantastic! Thanks! Pilot training, here I come!

I soon received orders to UPT, and I was about to begin one of the most exciting parts of my life.

*

Upon arrival at Laughlin AFB in southwest Texas to begin pilot training in the middle of April, 1965, the first order of business was a physical. I didn't have to do the astigmatism exam again; hence, no eye drops. The night before the physical, I rented a motel room off base so there would be less chance of my rest being disturbed. I pushed the physical out of my mind and slept well.

A part of the eye exam that I hadn't seen before but had heard about was the red lens test that I knew was potential trouble. The exam looked for any tendency of an eye to turn inward, just like my right eye would do on occasion if I wasn't careful.

Technical Sergeant Congleman turned the lights out in the room and told me to hold my head still. He covered my left eye with a red lens and then moved a small light to my right and then to my left and watched my eye follow the light. Far to the left was my potential trouble spot because my eye had a tendency to follow, follow, and then bury itself into the corner as the light passed from my field of vision. It was part of my legacy of being cross-eyed as a youngster. Intuitively, I knew what he was looking for, and as the light went around to my left ear, I followed it with my right eye until it passed the bridge of my nose, and then looked at that. He looked and looked at my eye and then said, "OK, I've got just one more thing," something I wasn't prepared for.

He covered one eye with a cardboard patch and moved his pencil around. "Follow my pencil." Left eye covered, right eye following, no problem because when he removed the cover from my left eye, it was where it was supposed to be—looking at the pencil. But when he covered my right eye, moved his pencil, and removed the cover, my right eye was not where it was supposed to be. It had wandered off somewhere. Not very far, but just enough. "I can't pass you on this, Lieutenant. You'll have to come back Monday morning and see the flight surgeon."

*

Oh, to be so close and yet not there. I spent a very anxious weekend wondering if I was going to make it. One of the class members, a first lieutenant named Eric Levins, had failed the test because of the color portion of the eye chart. He could see eight of the twelve numbers on the charts, but nine were required, and he just couldn't see them. Others were concerned about hay fever or high blood pressure. It seemed like everyone had *something* he was worried about, but that didn't help me much.

I didn't sleep well on Sunday night, and blundered my way through a retest of most of the eye exam. An optometrist put some letters on the wall and asked me to read them. I could barely see 20/25 and my heart really sank. "It's over," I thought. But he said, "You passed this on Friday, so I know you can do it. We won't worry about it."

It was time to see the flight surgeon, a friendly captain from Selma, Alabama, named H.M. Sanford, Jr., who had three weeks left on active duty. He looked at my chart, then said, "Look at that spot on the wall." I looked at the wall, didn't see a spot, and was just about to say, "What spot?" when better sense said, "Find something and look at it."

He moved his pencil around a couple of times, looked at my eyes, and then said, "There's nothing wrong with your eyes. You can fly these airplanes, can't you?"

My heart took a leap. "Yes, sir, I can!"

"I'll sign you off. Sgt. Congleman! He's OK."

Sgt. Congleman came around the corner. "But sir," he sputtered, "his eye isn't right. He didn't follow the pencil like he should have. You can't pass him." My emotions were now really on a roller coaster.

"Sergeant, I'm signing him off. There's nothing wrong with him." Case closed. Wow! Was I ever grateful to Dr. Sanford. He saved my career as a pilot that day.

Chapter 2

Pilot Training

The bachelor officers' quarters (BOQ) at Laughlin in early 1965 were pretty basic, with two students assigned to each room. The rooms were water-cooled instead of air-conditioned, which worked well in a dry desert environment. The heat of midsummer hadn't arrived yet, so we were comfortable until newly remodeled and air-conditioned BOQs opened for our use in May. The new quarters were very nice. My suite-mate was Jim Watkins, one of my classmates whom I had known in college and who had received his commission through OCS. We each had a bedroom and shared a bathroom and common living area. We didn't have a kitchen and hot plates weren't allowed.

A few days after we arrived at Laughlin, the area was struck by a huge hailstorm, which put dents in everyone's car, including mine, and in the airplanes. Laughlin had just received new T-38s to replace T-33s as the primary trainer for the last six months of the course. T-38s have a honeycomb structure in the wings, which allows for strength and light weight, but they weren't designed to withstand large hailstones, so just like our cars, they were dented. Ironing dents out of airplane wings was an expensive procedure, and the wing commander, Colonel Mosher, lost his job over it. The big shots at Air Training Command headquarters decided he should have had the airplanes moved into hangars before the storm hit, but they didn't say how he was supposed to know it was going to be such a bad storm far enough in advance to move them inside. Severe thunderstorms in that part of the country in the spring aren't unusual. I guess they just needed a scapegoat to keep from being blamed themselves, and he was it.

Once I got past the physical, the pilot training regimen was very demanding, but the flying and ground school courses weren't too difficult, and I had every confidence I was going to do well. Some of the courses, such as weather and navigation, were almost identical to courses I had had in ROTC, so they were like a review. Almost half the class washed out—two at first because they were afraid of flying and got sick whenever they went up, but most because their flying ability was limited.

My first flights in the T-37, called the Tweety Bird because of the extremely loud ear-piercing sound of its engines, and especially the T-38, which we students called the Great White Rocket, were about the most exciting and thrilling things I had ever done. The only experiences that might compare were my first flight in an F-102 and the first one in an F-106. I was living a dream, and I appreciated it all the more because of my near-miss with the flight physical.

Laughlin AFB is seven miles east of Del Rio, Texas, and 150 miles west of San Antonio. The town is on the banks of the Rio Grande, which forms the border between Texas and Mexico. In 1965 Del Rio was a sleepy border town that had no McDonald's or any other fast food restaurants, no Holiday Inn, and not much of anything else. It was a desolate place for a single guy, so on most weekends a few of my classmates and I went to San Antonio looking for relief from the boredom of life in Del Rio. San Antonio had several military bases, and we tried the quarters at most of them. It didn't take long to determine the visiting officers' quarters (VOQ), the Officers' Club, and the location of Fort Sam Houston offered about the best accommodations, so that's where we went most of the time.

In mid-June, I had a reason to go to the base housing office and noticed a very attractive young lady and called her for a date. She said, "Yes." She was the daughter of the owner of the local dairy and was a student at Texas Western University in El Paso. Del Rio and its sister city of Ciudad Acuna, which was just across the river, weren't so bad when there was a girl around to share it with. We had several weekend dates, usually at a honky tonk across the river in Mexico. One of the popular songs of the day was The Rolling Stones' "Satisfaction." She had girlfriends who were home for the summer, so she and I played matchmakers with her friends and mine, and we had a fine time.

El Paso is 400 miles from Del Rio, and when she went back to school, my social life really slowed down. One of her friends was Ellen, a member of one of the top sororities at the University of Texas in Austin. Ellen was eager to arrange dates for us as long as she got to go out too, so Austin, which is about 220 miles from Del Rio, became one of our favorite weekend destinations.

*

A pilot's first assignment after UPT was determined by how many positions in different airplanes the air force needed at the time, and by the ranking of each pilot within his class. Class rank was determined by a combination of academic grades and flying grades. By the time we got to T-38s, everyone had a pretty good idea of what his class rank was going to be, and we speculated about what kind of airplanes we'd be flying next. Century series fighters (F-100, F-101, F-102, F-104, F-105, and F-106) were the choice of many of my classmates because, along with the F-4, they were the hottest fighters the air force had at the time. A few wanted to fly C-141s, and some hoped for assignment back to the training command as instructors. A B-52 assignment to Strategic Air Command was the least popular, but every class had some of those, and some guys in our class were going to fly B-52s. I had had a non-flying job in the air force before pilot training and had a good understanding of how fantastic it was to get to fly, so I reminded my classmates, "*Any* flying job is better than any non-flying job even if you end up in the right seat of a C-47." That put things into perspective, and I got a lot of agreement with that philosophy. It took some of the pressure off the aircraft assignment sweepstakes.

In 1965 McDonnell Aircraft Corporation was mass producing two-seat F-4 Phantoms for the air force, which meant a lot of F-4 pilot jobs were available. The problem was the commander of Tactical Air Command wanted pilots for the back seats of TAC F-4s instead of the navigators they were designed for, and those back seats were filled by new UPT graduates. It was not the type of job I wanted as a pilot. Complicating things was the fact that the Vietnam War was really heating up, and both F-4s and F-105s were getting shot down all too regularly over North Vietnam.

*

The T-37 formation check ride sticks out in my memory. Formation flying required great precision and oh, so little movement on the stick to stay in position on the wing. My T-37 instructor, First Lieutenant Ray Ditterline, said the key to smooth formation flying was not to *move* the stick to maintain your position on the leader's wing, but to just *think* about moving it, which is about all it took.

Prior to my check ride, I had been only an average formation pilot, but that day it was like I was glued to the leader's wing. I stifled the urge to say, "I've never flown formation *this* well before." And I hadn't. I was right where I was supposed to be on all the maneuvers, in perfect position. I tried not to think about it, just do it. It was the first time I had flown with that particular check pilot, and he was quite impressed. It's a good thing he hadn't flown formation with me before.

I got the second best grade in the class just a fraction behind Travis Vanderpool, a Horny Toad from Texas Christian University who was called Possum. Possum was one of the guys with whom I went to San Antonio and Austin and who benefited from my finding dates for him. He lucked out and finished just ahead of me in class standing and got an F-100 assignment. He was a member of Delta Tau Delta fraternity at TCU, the same fraternity of which I had been a member at Oklahoma.

Another flight that stands out in my memory of UPT was a T-38 formation flight. The T-38 formation working area was northwest of the base and northeast of Big Bend National Park in West Texas. I had two T-38 instructors, First Lieutenant Wendell Green and Captain Don Garrett. I was with Captain

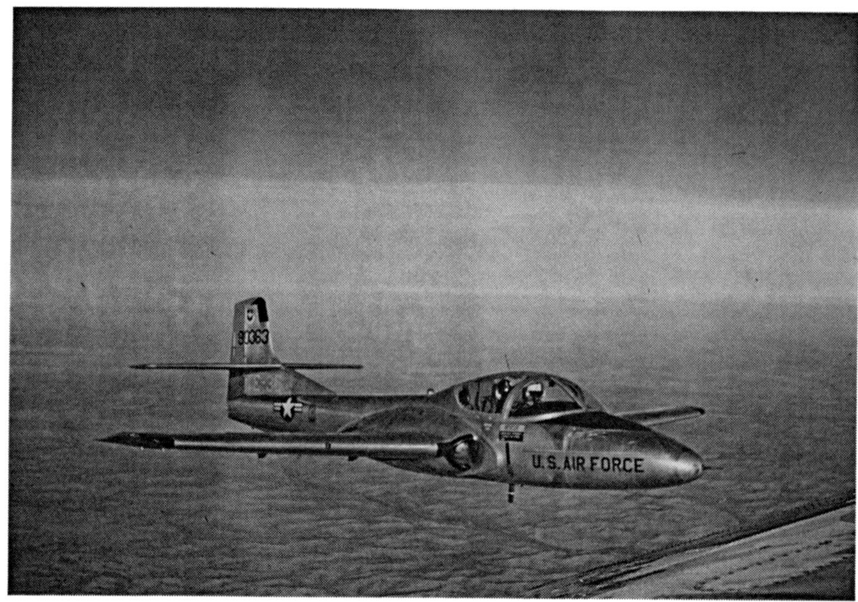

T-37 in formation over west Texas

Garrett that day and since I had led the formation on departure and first part of the mission, I was on the wing on the return. We were in the designated departure and arrival corridor, descending on the leader's right wing, when all of a sudden I saw another flight of T-38s pass just above us going in the opposite direction.

"Did you see that?" I asked.

"Yeah, that was too close," Captain Garrett said.

He followed up on it with a near-miss report, but I don't know what became of it and why we were so close to disaster. A few days later, two two-ship flights of T-38s collided in the working area about 200 miles west of the base. Three airplanes were destroyed, three pilots were killed, two were injured, and one ejected and was recovered uninjured. The fourth airplane was not hit.

*

Navigation was a course that was easy for me because it was the same stuff I had in ROTC and it was all so logical. Each course had mid-term and final exams and every mid-term exam counted in the final score except, for some reason, the mid-term navigation exam. It was the only one I failed. It was so easy for me, I was so confident, and it meant so little, that I didn't pay attention during the exam and made several careless wrong marks on the answer sheet. They were easy questions. I just blew it. Even though the exam didn't count in the final overall score it counted in a way that was very important to me, which was in my planned weekend trip to San Antonio. Those who were struggling academically were required to attend Saturday morning study hall. The navigation instructor, Captain Larry Cotton, gave me the bad news—my presence was required at the study hall.

"I know that stuff," I protested. "I just made careless errors."

It didn't do any good. I had bombed the test and had to go to study hall and miss a weekend in San Antonio. It was a good lesson. Be careful on exams. A bad score can hurt.

On the final exam I missed only one question—something about a Mercator projection map—and tied Bob Johnson, a former navigator, for the best grade in the class. For the sake of my grade and overall standing in the class, I was fortunate the mid-term navigation grade didn't count.

*

When we were in the T-38 portion of the class, the BOQs became full and Jim and I got another roommate—Scotty Roberts, a second lieutenant who was just starting pilot training. Scotty was a handsome guy from Shreveport with blond hair, a winning smile, and a happy disposition, and he was a good addition to our quarters. His bed was set up in the living room because the bedrooms were too small for two. As our class got close to graduation, the pressure became less and less and we had more time to spend at happy hour at the Officers' Club after flying or after class. We alternated flying in the morning and class in the afternoon, and the other way around each week.

Fortunately, Scotty was a good sport because we had a tendency to harass him at times when we got in late from the Club. One night Scotty had his turn. He came in from the Club after having a snootful of beer and was ready to turn the tables. Possum's room was just down the hall on the upper level, and Scotty decided he wanted to call Possum to give him some well-deserved grief for all the times Possum had harassed him.

I said, "Possum's asleep. You should leave him alone."

"I want to call Possum. What's his number?" he insisted.

After a couple of times around that circle, I realized I wasn't going to talk him out of calling Possum, so when he went into the bathroom to get rid of some beer, I looked in the phone book for the number of the sheriff's office and gave Scotty that number.

The conversation went something like this:

"Val Verde County Sheriff."

"I want to talk to Possum."

"There's no Possum here."

Scotty thought Possum was trying to trick him, so with a more determined tone in his voice he said, "I want to talk to Possum."

"I'm sorry, sir, but we don't have any possums here."

"Well, where is he? I want to talk to him."

"I'm sorry, but I don't know where he is."

Gradually it dawned on Scotty he had been had, and he gave up. Possum's sleep went undisturbed that night.

*

I had no intention of returning to Del Rio as an instructor, so I entered "UPT instructor" as my last choice for assignment out of pilot training. "UPT instructor" could have been at any one of the eight UPT bases and might even have been a T-38 assignment, but it sounded too much like T-37s at Laughlin to me, so I put B-52s ahead of it.

The day I received my F-102 assignment to Perrin AFB, Texas, I felt pure elation. F-102s were my first choice and my goal throughout the entire year, and I was really excited to be going to Air Defense Command (ADC). Possum, who thought he was a big shot because he got an F-100 assignment, teased me by saying, "All you have to do (in an interceptor) is follow what the GCI (ground controlled intercept) controller tells you to do. That's no challenge!" But it was a whole lot safer than going to Vietnam in an F-100.

Since the F-102 interceptor course was longer than 179 days, I received a permanent change of station (PCS) to Perrin instead of a temporary duty (TDY) assignment, and it was understood I would get a follow-on assignment either to a squadron flying F-102s in Alaska or to the Philippines or, more likely, to F-106s, as Perrin was only a training base for the F-102.

Graduation date for UPT Class 66 G was May 13, 1966. At midmorning on April 5, shortly after I received my F-102 assignment, I was playing basketball in the base gym in PDC (physical development and conditioning) class. I jumped up for a rebound and the inside half of my left foot came down on half of Dale Miller's right foot. I came down full force on my left leg with my foot turning inward, twisted my ankle, and severely sprained it. I lay on the floor in a great deal of pain, and when I got up I could walk only with a lot of difficulty and a severe limp.

The PDC instructor wanted me to go the base hospital for an x-ray to see if a bone was broken. I knew that might jeopardize my F-102 assignment because I might wash back to the next class and have to go through the aircraft selection process again, so I said no. I had my F-102 assignment and wasn't about to let a sore ankle take it away from me if I could help it.

The next item on the PDC schedule was judo training and we were expected to toss our training partner over a shoulder and to be tossed over his shoulder. If I had been thrown over a right-handed person's shoulder, I would have landed with my left ankle down first, smack on the mat, and I just couldn't do that. So I was paired with a left-hander and landed with my right leg down first. It was still a jolt to my left ankle, but it was bearable.

To complete the required training, I had four check rides in the next two weeks, which I accomplished. My ankle was still sore, so I agreed to an x-ray after my last check ride because I knew I wouldn't wash back to the next class with all of them completed.

The next morning, a message came to the class that the doctor wanted me to come back to the hospital for another x-ray. It showed a break of the lower tip of the inside of the tibia of my left leg, and they thought maybe they had my x-rays mixed up with someone else's because I shouldn't be able to walk with a broken leg. The second picture showed the same thing and the doctors didn't know what to do about it. The only pain was on the outside of my ankle where the ligaments had been so severely stretched.

What should be done? The doctor at Laughlin called ATC HQ and a decision was made to send me to Wilford Hall Hospital at Lackland AFB in San Antonio for further consultation. Wilford Hall was a 1,000 bed hospital, the largest in the air force. They had specialists who would know what to do about this.

When I arrived at Wilford Hall, another x-ray was taken and the ankle was still broken, so they put me in a walking cast. Because it already had been two weeks since the break occurred and the standard cast time was six weeks, the doctor said I had to wear the cast for only four weeks. If I had known all this was going to happen, I never would have gone in for the x-rays, because my sprain was getting better and walking had become much less painful.

Even though I had completed all my check rides, a few flying hours still remained in the syllabus. I wanted to fly them, so I received permission to have the cast cut off for about four days while I flew those flights after which they recast my ankle. I didn't understand the logic of having a cast at that point, but I had to do as I was told. The only time I had pain in the area of the break was when the cast was cut off.

They were fun rides. The pressure was off because I had no more check rides and I flew them all solo. I had a T-38 all to myself! One flight in particular was enjoyable. It was a formation flight with one of my classmates and we went to an abandoned airfield at Eagle Pass, which was along the Rio Grande about sixty miles southeast of Laughlin. We made low approaches, sometimes with the landing gear down and sometimes at high speed with the gear up. I had a feeling of freedom and excitement I hadn't had before, because the syllabus was tight, with goals to be met on each mission. This was just for fun.

After that, the cast was reapplied and at the graduation ceremony, I clunked across the stage, but I didn't care, because I had my wings and was going to fly F-102s. Life couldn't get much sweeter!

Chapter 3

Fighters

The airplanes flown by Air Defense Command in the 1960s were the F-101 Voodoo, F-102 Delta Dagger, and F-106 Delta Dart, which were considered all-weather interceptors. The mission was to protect the skies above the United States from invaders from the air, with nuclear armed Soviet bombers the most serious threat. The instrument flying capabilities of all-weather interceptors were only as good as the pilots who flew them, so the first part of the training when I arrived at Perrin AFB was to sharpen my instrument flying skills.

The commander of the instrument training flight had a questionnaire to fill out about each student before we began training and one of the questions was, "Can this student fly a raw data ILS (instrument landing system) approach?" His response on my questionnaire was, "No." I had flown ILS approaches in T-38s and thought I did it pretty well. And besides, I hadn't even flown at Perrin yet, so how did he know whether I could fly an ILS approach? I questioned him about it.

"You flew ILSs in T-38s with a flight director and here you have to shoot raw data ILSs. I haven't had a student come out of T-38s yet who can shoot a raw data ILS without more training," he said.

The instrument training was done in the back seat of T-33s with a hood up to simulate actual instrument conditions. Most of the time we went to Carswell AFB at Fort Worth and Sheppard AFB at Wichita Falls where I made approach after approach and learned a lot about flying instruments. He was right. I had a lot to learn about how to fly a raw data ILS among other things.

*

The Convair F-102 was designed in the early 1950s and was a fine-flying airplane. The weapon and electrical systems were very complicated though and took a lot of studying to learn. The instructors demanded that we know those systems well.

The TF-102 was the trainer version and it had a wide cockpit to accommodate side-by-side seating with the instructor on the right and the student on the left. The instructors called it the Tub because of its shape and its diminished performance compared to the F model, but it was a very stable airplane for flying instruments.

After a few rides in the TF, I was ready to solo in the F and what a thrill that was! A single-seat century series fighter at last. I had no fear, just excitement. Here I was ready to go in an F-102 by myself and this was for real! The F cockpit was small compared to the TF cockpit and when I lowered the canopy at the end of the runway just prior to takeoff I realized I was all alone in an F-102! I had soloed in pilot training, of course, which was pretty special, but here I was in a single-seat, single-engine fighter! The TF seating arrangement being side-by-side meant that in the F model I was flying a new airplane with a completely different picture.

*

Pilots learning to be interceptor pilots needed targets to intercept—something besides the commercial airliners that passed near the Perrin AFB training area (and it was all too easy to lock the radar on to one of those by mistake). The training squadrons had T-33s assigned to the target mission and students were assigned to fly them. In 1965 and 1966 some of the UPT bases were still using T-33s for primary training and the new pilots who had trained at those bases were required to fly those target missions. Those of us who had trained in T-38s were not qualified in T-33s, but we were offered the opportunity to fly in the back seat in order to build flying time and as additional eyes to help keep track of what was going on. Because I was eager and looking for a challenge, I flew several target missions in the back seat of T-33s. It wasn't as demanding as the instrument training I had just completed in those same back seats, but I was getting flying time and flying time opened doors of opportunity to a young air force pilot as his career progressed.

Much of the time was spent orbiting and waiting for the interceptors to show up. While doing that, I learned an ADF (automatic direction finder) radio has the capability of receiving the broadcasts of commercial radio stations. I especially remember one morning in an orbit about sixty miles east of Perrin just north of Paris, Texas, when news came over the radio of the murders of eight young student nurses in an apartment in Chicago.

*

The class consisted of seven pilots: Jim Thomes, a Naval Academy graduate who had an F-101 assignment and who was expected to check out first in the F-102; Ed Davis, a Notre Dame graduate; Grier Cooper, who had graduated from UPT a couple of years earlier and was just now coming to interceptor training with an F-101 assignment; three air national guard pilots; and me. Ed and I had received F-102 assignments from UPT with the understanding that the assignment was likely to change to F-106s while we were at Perrin.

Standing in front of an F-102 L-R: Len Johnson, Dick Diller, Bob Bater, Grier Cooper. Front row: Ron Murphy, Jim Thomes, Ed Davis (USAF photo)

In mid September, 1966, Ed and I were called in to the squadron commander's office. He said, "We just received a message from ADC that they need another F-101 pilot out of your class and you are the only ones who can do it, since everyone else is either already going to F-101s or is in the guard. Which one of you would like to fly F-101s?"

If someone had asked me that question a year earlier, I would have been absolutely elated at the prospect of such a choice. The thought of having a choice of flying F-101s or F-102s and maybe even the F-106 would have been far beyond my expectations. Anything would have been just fine back then. The F-101 had a reputation for being a fine airplane, but it had a two man crew with a radar-observer—a navigator—in the back seat and the F-102 and F-106 were single-seaters. It didn't take me long to say, "Not me."

Like an echo, Ed said, "Not me." We were really getting picky to turn up our noses at flying F-101s.

The squadron commander said, "You two are the same rank and I have no way to determine who gets what, so I propose we flip a coin. Is that OK with you?"

We both agreed. If I had to fly the F-101 it wouldn't be so bad, but I still wanted to fly a single-seater. The F-101 had two engines and could out-accelerate an F-106 at low altitudes, but at high altitudes and in high maneuvering situations, the F-106 was aerodynamically superior and it had a higher maximum airspeed. They both were among the hottest fighters of the day.

The coin was flipped, and I won. I became the only pilot in the class who would be flying F-106s.

On September 30, 1966, my follow-on orders finally came. I was assigned to the 95th Fighter Interceptor Squadron at Dover AFB, Delaware, with TDY scheduled at Tyndall AFB, Florida, from January to mid-March for F-106 training. I had never been to Delaware and had been hoping for an assignment to the west coast, but I had a big smile after getting those orders. F-106s were based at some remote, very cold-weather bases like Loring AFB in northern Maine and Minot AFB, North Dakota, to name just a couple, so Dover sounded pretty good to me.

Ed Davis received an F-101 assignment to Glasgow AFB, Montana, the location of which made Minot seem uptown. Glasgow was one of those places for which the word remote was invented. He eventually received an O-1 assignment to Vietnam about the same time I went to A-1s.

*

One sunny afternoon in November of 1966 the class was close to the end of the F-102 training course. I was scheduled for a front snap-up mission in an F model in formation with classmate Len Johnson, who was from the Idaho Air National Guard, leading in a TF with an instructor. F-102 front snaps were flown in training at 29,000 feet with the target coming in the opposite direction at 39,000 feet. The idea was to lock onto the target with the aircraft's radar, pull the trigger, light the afterburner, and pull up sharply to keep the steering dot on the radar screen in the center of an ever-decreasing circle until an X appeared indicating the fire control system had shot the radar-guided missile toward the target. The missile firing was only simulated of course, but the rest of the exercise was quite realistic. The intercept portion of a front snap was flown with the wingman about three miles behind the leader.

The demands of the pass required the interceptor pilot to keep his attention and eyes concentrated on the radar screen, which, when I made my intercept, I did. But the fire signal was delayed. I had the dot in the circle (referred to as having the rabbit in the hole) and it got smaller and smaller, but no fire signal. I didn't want to lose the intercept, so I hung on and hung on until the weapon system signaled fire about the same time the airplane ran out of airspeed with the nose pointed seventy degrees up.

The F-102 airframe and its J-57 engine were not a happy combination, as the engine was known for compressor stalls if things didn't go just right, and things weren't going just right at this particular time. Spins were forbidden in F-102s because of the difficulty of recovery with the external fuel tanks mounted under the wings, but we were required to know the spin recovery emergency procedure just in case, and just in case was quickly approaching. As the nose fell over to almost straight down, two things went through my mind: "Don't compressor stall the engine," and the spin recovery procedure that came to me as clearly as if I was looking at it on a printed page, step by step.

As the nose pitched down, the first thing I did was move the throttle inboard to turn off the afterburner to decrease thrust. The engine was still producing full military power, but at least the AB wasn't lit. I was afraid if I pulled the throttle back the engine would compressor stall, possibly causing the EGT (exhaust gas temperature) to over temp and destroy the engine. One problem was taken care of, but I still had another.

I was not sure what was happening in terms of aircraft attitude because the nose was sharply down and the airplane was pitching back and forth from side to side. It didn't seem like a spin, but something definitely was not right. The spin recovery procedure: Throttle idle, jettison external fuel tanks, deploy the drag chute, pitch control full down, rudder in the opposite direction of the spin, neutralize the flight controls when the spin stops, apply engine power, and fly out of the resulting dive.

My altitude was about 37,000 feet when I entered the dive, so I had some room in which to recover, and I certainly didn't want any instructors to know about this little excursion. Things might have gotten messy if I had jettisoned the fuel tanks and the drag chute over somebody's farm along the Red River, so I elected to try to ride it out for a while to see what would happen. Altimeters couldn't keep up with the rapid rate of descent, so we had been instructed to eject when it read 10,000 feet if ever we found ourselves in an uncontrollable situation—which I was going to do if I fell that far.

Gradually the sharp oscillations to either side began to moderate and airspeed began to build up. As I saw the altimeter unwind past 25,000 feet I also saw the airspeed was high enough to pull out of the dive. The engine was still producing a lot of power and I pulled back on the stick until the attitude was level. I was at 21,000 feet and a long way behind the lead airplane.

The GCI controller called and said, "I show you way out of position behind your leader. Is everything OK?"

"Yeah, I've just got to catch up here," I replied, hoping Len's instructor wasn't paying too much attention. He wasn't. I lit the burner and caught up to where I was supposed to be and the rest of the mission went as planned. The radar film (called NESA in F-102s) showed an extra long time to get the fire signal, but I got credit for a successful intercept and a good grade. I was expecting a question, but the instructor was in a hurry to get home at the end of the day and nothing was said.

After debriefing, Len and I walked to the parking lot together and I turned to him and asked, "Did you wonder why I was three miles behind you going into the first snap and fifteen miles behind when we came out of it?"

A mystified smile came over his face and he said, "That's right. I didn't think of that! What happened?" I told him my story.

When I looked it up in the aircraft flight manual, called the Dash One, to see what it said about my maneuver, the closest description was a post stall gyration. It wasn't a spin and it got my attention, but no harm was done.

*

Upon graduation from UPT, I had a commitment to the air force of four years starting from the date I completed F-106 training, which was ten months after my UPT graduation date. About the time I arrived at the 95th at Dover, the air force changed its requirement to a four-year commitment from the time I completed pilot training and made it retroactive to include me.

One of the first things I did when I arrived at Dover was go to the squadron personnel officer to request a date of separation (DOS) that reflected the new rule before Someone changed his mind. My new flight commander, Major Mike Howard, didn't appreciate that first move and, while he was not a vindictive man, I never did completely remove myself from his dog house for the whole nineteen months I was in the 95th. But he always treated me fairly regarding the alert schedule and scheduling leave.

*

I hadn't been in the 95th very long when the decision was made that another T-38 pilot, First Lieutenant Jack Wojnaroski, and I would be required to check out in T-33s, of which the squadron had four. In addition to being used for target missions in the same way they were used at Perrin, the squadron used them for parts and personnel delivery and pickup missions. The squadron commander, the executive officer, Jack, and I were the only pilots in the squadron who weren't T-33 qualified.

Even though I was not enthusiastic about flying T-Birds, Jack and I soon found ourselves at Andrews AFB, Maryland, for three days of ground school. Compared to T-38s, the T-33 represented a major step backward to what seemed to me to be the Stone Age of aviation. The T-33 was one of the first jets ever built, and its systems and performance reflected that. Captain Frank Walters was the instructor pilot for my T-33 check out, and we flew a cross-country flight—first to Memphis Naval Air Station because Frank liked its flight line snack bar. We continued on to Ent Air Force Base at Peterson Field at Colorado Springs because Frank wanted to check his records at ADC headquarters. He signed me off at Pete Field and I flew back to Dover solo.

For a pilot who wanted to fly to different places, T-33s provided an advantage. They had been around so long and the air force had so many of them, every base had a mechanic who knew how to fix them if something was broken, which didn't happen very often. The F-106 was a one-of-a-kind, and if a pilot should venture away from an F-106 base and something on the airplane broke, the chances of finding a mechanic and parts to fix it were not very good. So cross-country trips in an F-106 to other than F-106 bases were discouraged, but T-33s could go just about anywhere.

Being single, I was always ready to go on parts-delivery or pick-up flights or to help other squadron pilots by taking them when they needed a one-way ride. I also flew target missions involving overnight trips to places like Bagotville, Quebec, or Loring AFB, Maine, when the married guys would rather stay home.

*

In 1967 and 1968 the war in Southeast Asia (SEA) was in full bloom, pilots were needed for combat, and the major air force commands were tasked to supply them. The ADC personnel office in Colorado Springs made a list of their pilots who were most eligible to be assigned to SEA based primarily upon who had the most recent overseas return date. I had not had an overseas tour of duty, and because I had been on active duty prior to going to pilot training, I had a longer time of no overseas duty than the other young pilots in ADC who had entered pilot training directly out of college.

The ADC code name for the list was Palace Cobra, and when it came out about a year after I arrived at Dover, my name was near the top. Going to war was not something I wanted to do as I liked the F-106, the 95th, and Dover, but with my name so near the top of the list the inevitability of a combat assignment was overwhelming, so I accepted the challenge and vowed to make the best of it.

No dates or airplane assignments were attached to the Palace Cobra list, so I knew those decisions were still to be made and I might have some influence in what would come next in my life. I called the ADC personnel officer, who was a major, to try to influence his decision.

"I'd really like to fly F-105s, sir. Do you have any F-105 slots available?"

"Yes, I do, and I'll put your name on one right now," he replied as he shuffled some papers. I was amazed at how easy it was to get the assignment I wanted. "Oh, wait a minute," he said, "you have a DOS (date of separation) in about two years don't you? I can't give you an F-105 because the training incurs a commitment of four years and you have less than two to go."

I knew that, but thought maybe I could get a Thud assignment and have my training completed before anyone figured out I had a DOS that would take precedence. All jet training schools had a four-year commitment and all reciprocating engine airplane schools had a one-year commitment.

I already knew the answer to my next question: "What airplanes can I fly with the time I have remaining?"

"A-1s, O-1s (Bird Dog, a single engine light plane used for forward air control), and C-123s," he said. They all had reciprocating engines and therefore incurred a commitment of one year, which would be satisfied by spending a year in Southeast Asia.

"My choice of those would be the A-1. Do you have an A-1 assignment you could assign me to?" I asked.

"I do, and I will give you one," he said. It must have made his job much easier to have a pilot call in with a specific request rather than have to arbitrarily assign names to aircraft slots with no idea of what a man would like to do. I wasn't very enthusiastic about going to fly A-1s, but it seemed like the best of the choices that were presented to me.

Not long after that conversation, I received my orders to Hurlburt Field, Florida, to begin A-1 training.

Chapter 4

Introduction to Combat

April 20, 1969. Sunday. "Hey, Dick, you're on the schedule for tomorrow."

After all the training and preparation, it was finally time to go to war for real. The first ride was going to be in an A-1E, a two-seat model of the Skyraider, and I was to be in the right seat for my orientation ride, commonly referred to as a dollar ride. The pilot in the left seat was to be Captain Jerry J. Jenkinson. I was glad to be flying with Jerry because we had met and had dinner at the Dover AFB Officers' Club about a year and a half before, and I felt like I at least knew *some*body.

I had looked forward to the first flight for a long time with mixed emotions. On the one hand, I was a bit frightened because of the unknown and the danger of actually being at war. But on the other hand, I had a certain amount of eagerness to see what it looked like across the river and to see an actual target where real bad guys needed to have bombs dropped on their heads.

The briefing in the Tactical Unit Operations Center (TUOC) building took about an hour and included a weather briefing, the latest information about what was happening in Laos, who controlled what territory this morning, and a discussion of tactics between the pilots. The TUOC building was the nerve center and command post for the American flying operations at the base. It was clean and air-conditioned and seemed like a nice safe place to be, but we couldn't stay long because we had work to do.

The first stop was the personal equipment building to get our gear. The building had recessed fluorescent lights, no windows, a shiny gray-painted floor, and rack upon rack of personal equipment for every USAF crew member on the base. I had been briefed on all the equipment in survival training and what it was for and had been fitted with my own vest, helmet, and parachute. I marveled at how much was stuffed into the vest. Among other things, the vest had detailed maps of the terrain over which we would be flying that were intended for use in case we found ourselves on the ground, a quart of water that was to be used for survival purposes, a knife, a signal-smoke generator, a pen gun with flares, a first aid kit, food rations for a day or so, insect repellent, a signal mirror, matches, our own personal parachute and helmet, two survival radios with extra batteries, and a .38 revolver with extra rounds that was the last thing we got before going out the door. I felt like I wouldn't get very far if I had to try to evade the enemy wearing all that stuff.

The plane we were assigned to that Monday was normally used for night flying, so it was painted black. We got to the flight line about 12:45 p.m., and April is the hot season in Thailand. Nakhon Phanom is located at 17° north latitude, so the broiling tropical sun was directly overhead and the temperature was 97° F. To say I was sweating profusely was an understatement. I had never been so hot in my life.

I accompanied Jerry on the walk around and he pointed out a few things, which I appreciated because my last flight in an A-1 had been six and a half weeks ago at Hurlburt Field, Florida. So not only was I hot, I was a little rusty. It was also the first time I had seen a Skyraider fully loaded with 250- and 500-pound bombs, two different kinds of rockets, and cluster bomb units (CBUs). In training we used bomblets, which were intended to simulate the trajectory of an actual bomb but not the size or weight. The airplane also carried 200 rounds of 20mm shells for each of the guns mounted two to a wing. The gun shells did not have tracers as they did in training, so it would be hard to tell where the bullets were going.

After strapping in and just before starting the engine, the crew chief gave us each a quart canteen directly from the freezer. The water was frozen into a solid block of ice, and boy did it look good! The breeze from the prop was sweet relief from the oppressive heat. My day was definitely starting to look up except for one little detail: We were headed for enemy territory, and if we were mad enough to drop all this nasty stuff on them, I hated to think about how mad they were at us for dropping it!

Jerry handled the plane like the veteran he was. He had only a week to go until his last flight and I kept thinking, "I wonder how long it'll take me to do the job as well as he does it?" I watched his hands and marveled at how they knew just where to go and what switches to flip at just the right time. He was a career officer, about six feet tall, slender and handsome (Gene McCormack told me much later that the Thai waitresses at the Officers' Club called him Sweet Eyes), and he had the relaxed manner of someone who knew his job well. I wished I looked like that and had only a week to go until my last flight!

The maximum takeoff weight for a fully loaded Skyraider was 25,000 pounds, 10,000 pounds of which hung under the wings and the cockpit. It had a 300-gallon (1800-pound) fuel tank mounted under the mid-section, which left about 8,200 pounds to be divided between two stub stations six feet either side of the centerline and six external stations on each wing. Armor plating protected the underside of the cockpit. A-1s could stay over a target for an extended time if necessary because the reciprocating engine used a lot less fuel than a jet. The airplane was ideally suited to its assigned mission. The Skyraider's Curtis-Wright R3350 radial engine produced 2700 horsepower with a four blade propeller that stretched over thirteen feet from tip to tip. It had two circular banks of nine cylinders each. It was a big, tough engine with an unfortunate flaw—its tendency to quit with little or no warning at almost any time. Pilots who made it back after an engine failure said the sump light, a red light on the instrument panel, had illuminated just before the engine failed. Sump lights were designed to come on when metallic cylinder shavings in the oil system closed an electrical circuit. It was only an indication and not the cause, but a sump light usually meant engine trouble.

Takeoff was at 1:15 p.m. on NKP's brand-new asphalt runway that had opened a week earlier. The original runway was made of pierced steel plank (PSP), which was a temporary surface being used until a real runway could be built. PSP was slippery when wet and was still being used for taxiways and parking areas.

A heavy airplane on a hot day is normally not a good performer, and this one was no different. The trees at the perimeter of the base passed barely a hundred feet under our wings and then Jerry turned us to the right for the shortest distance to the Mekong River and Laos, nine miles away. Once we crossed the Mekong, we made a left turn to a heading of 330° and paralleled the river for about seventy nautical miles until it made a sharp turn to the left away from where we wanted to go. Our target today was in an area the American pilots called Happy Valley, which was not too far from the big bend in the Mekong. It was surrounded by beautiful mountains that were covered by the lushest green foliage I'd ever seen. And this was the dry season.

Major J. B. East was in the lead airplane and he and Jerry seemed to be enjoying themselves, but I was still not sure this was for me. For one thing, I had drunk all of my survival water shortly after we crossed the Mekong and was eagerly anticipating when more of the canteen would be thawed so I could drink it, too. And what if the engine quit about now? Although I had learned as much as I could about survival and what to do in case of a nylon let down, the whole process had a high degree of uncertainty. Hurtling my body at the ground at a 40° dive angle as we did most of the time when dropping ordnance while someone down there was shooting back, wasn't very inviting. "What'm I doin' here, anyway?"

The strike mission turned out be a relatively short one—only two hours and twenty minutes total for the flight and soon we were on our way back to the base. The forward air controller (fac) said Jim and Jerry had blown up one bunker and damaged six buildings. Daytime facs who found targets for us in northern Laos used the call sign Raven and flew Cessna O-1 Bird Dogs.

When I pulled up a chair in the Sandy Box that evening and popped the top on a beer, I felt for the first time a little like I belonged with the rest of the guys.

*

The check out procedure for a new pilot called for a total of five dual rides, the last four in the left seat with an instructor pilot (IP) in the right, and if he passed his check ride on the fifth, he went out on his own. After twenty-five missions as wingman, he would get checked out as flight lead by flying five flights in the lead with an IP as his wingman. The procedure was the same for the night check out—one ride in the right seat followed by four more in the left with an IP.

J. B. East was getting checked out as a flight leader at the same time I was getting my initial check out. He had been in the class ahead of me at Hurlburt and arrived at NKP about six weeks earlier. Because his lead check coincided with my initial check out and one instructor pilot could accomplish both goals at once, I flew with him quite a bit that first week. We became friends from daily briefings, riding the TUOC bus to and from the flight line and PE buildings, flying, and debriefing. His room was just a few doors from mine.

*

Twenty-two days elapsed from the time I left Travis AFB until I got my first flight at NKP. Palm Sunday, 1969, was about four hours long for me as we crossed the dateline en route from Travis to Anchorage to Yokota, Japan, and on to Clark Air Base in the Philippines. I arrived at Clark on Monday, March 31, and had to wait until Thursday to begin jungle survival school, known to the pilots as snake school. After two days of ground school, the class was sent to the jungle for forty-eight hours. The time in the jungle was intended to be an acquaintance lesson and not truly a survival experience. We were taken to a hilly area with very big trees, well-worn paths, and tents made of nylon parachutes already set up. All we had to do was move in and get comfortable. We each had a machete and had the opportunity to hack down a few banana trees, which were not woody, but were tall, slender plants that grew wild in the forest. The wild fruit tasted like cultivated bananas, had large seeds, and it was hard to get more than a sample of the flavor when eaten.

*

<u>April 6, 1969.</u> Easter Sunday. Still in the jungle. Some of the guys amused themselves by firing pen gun flares into the air. Early April is the end of the dry season in the Philippines and the vegetation was parched, so the inevitable happened—a flare started a fire that quickly began to spread and soon we were in real danger. An evacuation route was selected to a helicopter landing pad where we would be in an open area and away from the burning brush and trees for the duration of the fire. If worse came to worse, we could be evacuated via the choppers. But the fire was soon extinguished, and we were allowed to

return to our tent area. For me, the fire was a lighthearted diversion from life in the jungle that hadn't taken long to become boring.

April 7, 1969. Monday. We returned from the jungle in the back of open trucks about 7:00 a.m., tired, dirty, unshaven, and glad to be back in civilization. Not one of us had even seen a snake, which was probably the biggest confidence-builder we could have had.

April 8, 1969. Tuesday. The Officers' Club at Clark was very nice. If any place could be considered a crossroad of air force pilots during the Vietnam War era, the Clark O Club was it. I thought if I could hang around for a while I'd eventually run into just about everyone I knew. Though the club had a certain genteelness to it, it had an underlying feeling of business and it was understood that any stopover would be brief and was the precursor of an adventure that would be different from anything I had ever experienced—the end of which I couldn't even guess.

*

April 9, 1969. Wednesday. I left Clark on a Capitol Airways flight to Tan Son Nhut Air Base near Saigon, where we off-loaded passengers. Through passengers weren't allowed to leave the DC-8, and my step onto the top of the portable drive-up aircraft steps was as close as I ever got to setting foot in Vietnam. Soon we were on our way around the southern tip of Vietnam and Cambodia and on a direct route to Don Muang Airport, Bangkok, Thailand. My flight to Nakhon Phanom wasn't scheduled until the afternoon of April 12, so I had in excess of two days to explore Bangkok. So far, this war business wasn't too bad.

*

April 12, 1969. Saturday. I arrived at NKP on flight Klong 902B, a C-130, about 5:30 p.m. Five lieutenant colonels met me upon my arrival, which made me feel like a big shot until I realized it probably meant they were short of pilots and just couldn't wait to get their hands on the new guy.

The 56th Special Operations Wing (SOW) at Nakhon Phanom Royal Thai Air Force Base had three A-1 squadrons: the 1st, which used the call sign Hobo; the 22nd, call sign Zorro; and the 602nd, the Fireflies. Historically, the 1st had been a general purpose squadron that operated mostly in the daytime. The 22nd's mission was night attack, and the mission of the 602nd was search and rescue, at which time the squadron call sign was Sandy.

I was assigned to the 602nd with no input from me. Even before I flew my first mission, I decided I wanted to fly nights, so I requested an assignment to the 22nd. I was told the wing commander had decided to blend the missions of the squadrons, so every squadron would fly some of each and if I wanted to fly nights I'd have the opportunity to do so no matter which squadron I was in.

I was given ample time to get signed in to the base and situated. A new pilot needed to get acquainted with a full menu of items including being outfitted with personal equipment, getting settled into a room, and reading the local flying regulations. It would be nine days before I would get to fly. Maybe they were just being nice.

All the hooch rooms were said to be full until someone remembered Major Harry Dunivant had an empty bed in his room, so I moved in with him. Harry was a West Point graduate, Class of '53, who was a very pleasant, quiet, and capable career officer. He was a good roomie because he was considerate and we got along well. I was told the bed in Harry's room had been vacant since his previous roommate had been shot down and killed a few weeks ago. Welcome to the war!

Nakhon Phanom RTAFB

*

April 16, 1969. Wednesday. An F-4 was hit over Steel Tiger today. The pilot managed to get back to NKP, but at the slower traffic pattern speeds it just wouldn't fly, so both crew members had to eject and were picked up uninjured. I continued to check in to the base and to read the local flying regulations.

Someone on the base had a remote controlled model airplane that he flew in the late afternoons in an open area between the Firefly squadron hooches and the base exchange. Some guys had extra flares for their pen guns and tried to shoot it down. It was fun to watch, but no one ever hit it.

*

April 22, 1969. Tuesday. Today I flew my first left seat mission with Lieutenant Colonel Dave Andrews as my IP in the right seat and the commander of the 602nd, Lieutenant Colonel Walt Stueck, in the lead. I must have seemed awfully slow to Colonel Andrews, but I don't think I've ever worked so hard in my life, trying to keep ahead of things and remember everything I was supposed to do at the right time. We struck southeast of the Plaines des Jarres (PDJ) in Barrel Roll about thirty-two miles from Lima Site 98 on the zero-eight-eight degree radial (088/32) and were up for three hours.

April 23, 1969. Wednesday. We struck east of the PDJ with Captain Jim Jamerson in the right seat doing double duty as an IP for J. B. East, who was still getting his lead check out, and me. It was much easier today, which was a good thing because it couldn't get much harder than it was yesterday. I had dinner at the Officers' Club with J. B. and Major Jim Monk and really enjoyed their company. Jim had been a classmate in A-1 training at Hurlburt Field a couple of months ago and had moved in right next door. He had arrived about a week before me, so we all were new guys in the squadron. He had attended Southern Methodist University in 1952 and 1953, the same years my brother had been a freshman and sophomore there, and J. B. had been a member of Delta Tau Delta at Oklahoma State. Both Jims were easy-going guys with nice personalities and pleasant to be with.

April 24, 1969. Thursday. I had a three-hour mission over the Ban Ban Valley along Route 7 with Major Bud Cass in the right seat and J. B. getting his lead check ride at the same time. It was amazing how much more comfortable I felt in the airplane compared to just three short days ago. It was like that first flight was just a dream. But it *had* really happened, hadn't it?

The Raven said our target was a truck and howitzer in Ban Ban. We beat up some trees and destroyed a structure, but he wasn't so sure of what the target was after we hit it. A lot of dust and smoke rose up as a result of our bombs.

Being the wingman was easy because all he had to do was follow the leader and do what he said. The leader navigated, told the wingman what to drop on each pass, and ran the mission.

At this point, I felt like the missions were kind of fun and I was enjoying them. Part of the reason for the feeling of enjoyment was that I had yet to see any ground fire, and as far as I knew I still hadn't been shot at.

*

April 25, 1969. Friday. This was a big day for two reasons. First, I had my initial check ride with Captain Don Dunaway in the right seat. First Lieutenant Rex Huntsman got his lead check on the same mission. I hadn't flown with Rex before, but he turned out to be a good pilot and a good guy. Rex was short and had a bushy blond mustache. Some of the guys thought he resembled the comic strip character Yosemite Sam, so of course he was called Sam about as often as he was called Rex.

The other reason this was a big day was that my mail finally caught up with me. I had left Travis AFB on March 29, so I had a lot of reading to do.

*

April 26, 1969. Saturday. A-1Es and A-1Gs had side-by-side seating with a big blue-room behind the cockpit that was originally used by navy crewmen when they were flown off aircraft carriers. The air force used them with the pilot in the left seat and the right seat unoccupied unless an instructor pilot was required. The pilot seats in E and G cockpits seemed to be lower in the fuselage, and seeing out the right side was difficult. Two-seater cockpits were wide, which allowed a lot of elbow room, but they didn't handle nearly as well as the single-seaters.

The single-seat A-1Hs and A-1Js had different cockpit layouts. The pilot sat right up on top center of the fuselage and the cockpit was narrow, like that of a true fighter. They handled crisply and were fun to fly. The pilot could see out the right side just as easily as he could the left.

For those reasons, Colonel Stueck required a new pilot to have a ride in a single-seater on a noncombat mission—one without all the extra weight of the ordnance. He could just go fly and familiarize himself with the airplane. Today's mission had an H model assigned to it and, since I hadn't had my H check out, I was removed in favor of another pilot. It was my first day off the flying schedule since I started, and I welcomed the time to catch up on a few things including additional duties at the squadron building.

*

Even in a combat squadron in wartime, pilots had additional duties, some so insignificant that the junior officers retaliated with a job title that could be assigned to one of them, which came with an official-sounding acronym: SLIJO. The SLIJO was the silly little insignificant jobs officer. And the junior officer (or officers) with the silliest, most insignificant additional duty could wear the title.

I was a SLIJO at my previous duty station: assistant information security officer. The information security officer, First Lieutenant Dick Colby, and I had the responsibility every three months to tour all the squadron sections that had a need to maintain classified information. Together we inspected the records of security safes where classified information was kept when it was not needed to make sure someone had initialed the form when the safe was opened and that it had been initialed when it was closed. The air force and the information security officer and his assistant had to assume that if the forms were initialed properly, security had not been breached. The breadth of that assumption was broad indeed.

Usually more than one officer in a squadron qualified for SLIJO, which brought up the possibility of a club composed only of SLIJOs!

As long as I had to have additional duties, it was to my advantage to have input as to what they would be. Because I had attended the disaster control school and I knew the air force's approach to disaster control pretty well, I volunteered to be squadron disaster control officer wherever I went. Disaster control in the air force was mostly concerned with how a base would protect itself in the event of a nearby nuclear attack in which most people survived the blast, but were subjected to radioactive fallout. It was a job no one else wanted. The person whose place I was taking would sometimes say, "You mean he *wants* to be disaster control officer?" So I earned the good will of everyone in the squadron who dreaded the possibility of seeing his own name typed next to "disaster control officer" on the squadron assignment sheet. The good will of fellow pilots in a squadron was nice to have. I volunteered for the job because I knew the field and it was easy for me, but I was pleased by the fact that, due to an oversight, the record of my having attended the school was never entered on my personnel record.

Another advantage of being disaster control officer for the squadron at Nakhon Phanom was that most disaster control functions of the base were handled at the wing level, so all I had to do was to attend a monthly meeting and report to the squadron commander what had happened. I had the feeling that was about all he wanted to know about disaster control, anyway.

It was possible that I was the only officer on the base who had been to the school at Lowry, and I might have known more about air force disaster control than anyone else. If my attendance at the school had been on my records and Someone had happened to notice, I could well have been assigned the disaster control job for the entire wing, which was not the sort of thing I had in mind.

There were far more additional duties than pilots, so I was also assigned to be squadron mobility officer because Someone decided mobility and disaster control were somehow related. They weren't, but I didn't mind that one either because mobility was also handled at the wing level. I didn't have much of an idea what it was all about other than preparation for a hasty departure should it become necessary.

In addition, when I first arrived at the squadron, I was assigned to be COMSEC (communication security) officer and squadron athletic officer. SLIJO qualifiers, all.

*

After I got back to the hooch that sunny Saturday afternoon, April 26, word came that J. B. East had been killed north of the Plaines des Jarres. I was stunned. It felt like someone had ripped part of my insides out. How did it happen? No one was sure, but the theory was he had been shooting his 20mm guns and a shell had blown up and somehow damaged the wing beyond his ability to control the airplane.

Our 20mm ammunition was known to be old stock—the suspicion was that some of it may have been left over from World War II—possibly making it unstable. Some of the guns had been known to jam when the empty casing didn't clear the chamber in time for the next one to get into proper position before the bolt slammed shut, resulting in an explosion. Maybe that's what happened to J. B.

At any rate, he was dead, and I had lost a friend and was very upset about it. Just when I was starting to feel like I knew what I was doing and was beginning to get comfortable in the cockpit, my friend Jim was killed. He had a wife and three young children. I had gotten to know, respect, and like him and Jim Monk more than anyone else during my short tenure, and now he was gone. If it could happen to him, it could happen to me or anyone else. It was so unexpected, but then I guess combat losses are never expected. But to have it happen to J. B.!

His death upset me and severely shook my confidence and eagerness for the job. Maybe I wasn't cut out for this. First Lieutenant Clint Ward was the leader of J. B.'s final flight.

*

April 28, 1969. Monday. I had my H model check out today and then had mobile control duty in the tower.

Five guys had their last flights today and the squadron party for them was in the evening. Boy, it must have felt good to them to have completed a year of this. I could only imagine how they felt, because looking from here with eleven months to go, it seemed to be a long way—an almost impossible mountain to climb.

J. B. East (USAF photo)

Chapter 5

Sandies

Flying A-1 Skyraiders was a big change for me. In pilot training, I started in jets and flew only jets in subsequent assignments. From T-38s in pilot training, I went to a comparatively old airplane, the F-102 Delta Dagger, for my next assignment. It was still a Century Series fighter, a single-seater, and as such commanded the respect of those whose opinions counted—other air force pilots. Before I was even fully qualified in the Deuce, I received my assignment to the F-106 Delta Dart. Now that was something important: Air Defense Command's front line fighter and a real hot rod. The Convair F-106 was one of the fastest and highest-flying planes of the late 1960s. It was capable of flying twice the speed of sound (mach 2) and reaching altitudes that seemed to be on the fringes of the earth's atmosphere.

In order to demonstrate the airplane's capabilities and so we would be confident of its abilities, one of the first things demonstrated to students new to the plane was a speed run. It was interesting to see the rate of acceleration didn't slow as it approached mach two. The mach meter needle just kept inching upward, faster and faster until the magic number was reached. An eye had to be kept on the skin temperature gauge to make sure the fuselage didn't melt away because of air friction at very high airspeed. Other than that, there was very little sensation of speed and no untoward noise in the cockpit to indicate anything unusual was happening.

The biggest shock of all was when I brought the throttle inboard from the outboard afterburner position and felt the loss of thrust. Because of the extremely high drag, the immediate deceleration caused my head and body to thrust forward for an instant. I was traveling at a speed near the outer limits of where man had ever traveled and near the outer limits of the airplane's capabilities. Very little margin for error existed if anything went wrong. And then the sudden deceleration. A moment of panic raced through me until I saw the airplane was safely slowing through mach 1.5 and finally subsonic, so I could bring it down for a landing.

I made speed runs several times in F-106s and went over the top at the service ceiling of 65,000 feet. The sky was a darker blue than what we see from the surface of the earth because not much atmosphere remained above that altitude to reflect the sun's light.

The F-106 had an air-conditioned cockpit, modern instrumentation, radar to run intercepts on the target, a computer, a flight director, one seat, and one engine.

The A-1 had a reciprocating engine. About half our A-1s had one seat and because of the length of the assignments (one year), a proportionally larger effort went into training new guys—first for day missions, then to be flight leader, and finally for night missions. Once I gained proficiency, I spent a large amount of time in the right seat as an instructor pilot and not flying missions—which was the primary reason for being in the war in the first place.

In F-106s we referred to speed much of the time in terms of mach number. The first time a new pilot experienced a mach two speed run, he received an M2 lapel pin that could be worn proudly. A-1s didn't have a mach gauge; all speeds were referred to as indicated air speed (IAS). When a new pilot soloed in the A-1, he was given a lapel pin shaped like a radial engine with the words "mach nix" written on the bottom. Stick it up your noses you hot-shot jet fighter pilots.

The A-1 cockpit was not air-conditioned. Indeed until the engine fired up to create airflow and relief from the tropical heat at mid-day it was one of the hottest places I'd ever been. A-1s were dirty. The sides of the fuselage were usually covered with engine oil and it was impossible to get in or out without getting it on the soles of boots and tracking it onto the seat, the floor, and eventually flight suits.

The A-1 engine had cowl flaps—I had never heard of them before—and it had a mixture lever. In a jet, fuel mixture is controlled automatically by the fuel control. A-1s had wing flaps that were an advantage because takeoffs and landings could be flown at slower speeds due to the greater lift provided by the flaps. That meant less runway was required for takeoffs and landings, providing a greater margin of safety.

The F-106 had a delta wing and so had no place to put flaps. Flight controls were called elevons, a combination of elevators and ailerons. The final approach speed for F-106s was 173 knots plus more speed for any extra fuel weight. It was not unusual for final approach target speed to be 180 knots—about 207 mph.

When A-1s were light after a mission, the speed on final was a little more than half that. The joke about the A-1 was that we took off at 140 knots, climbed out at 140 knots, cruised at 140 knots, rolled in on the target at 140 knots, and flew final approach at 140 knots. It wasn't too far off.

On takeoff the F-106 had so much power that after rotation speed was reached, the stick could be pulled back and the airplane would fly enthusiastically. A pilot really had to be incompetent to get into trouble by pulling back too much. Not so with the A-1. Takeoff at maximum gross weight, which was routine, was a delicate maneuver. Skyraiders lifted their load grudgingly into the air instead of leaping off the ground like they really wanted to fly. At the end of the runway the tall trees of the jungle seemed to reach up to try to grab the airplane as it passed just above them. The whole thing depended upon that big engine. If it failed at the wrong time, as it was known to do, Big Trouble arrived in a hurry.

The mission was totally different, too. The job of an interceptor pilot was—with the help of ground-based radar—to locate targets that were intruding into United States airspace or other sensitive areas, identify them, and turn them away from their course or destroy them. The mission was defending American airspace from air attack by hostile forces.

The A-1 mission was attack—air to ground. It provided close air support for friendly forces or interdiction of enemy supply lines that required different skills from those required for air-to-air interception. Attacks involved diving at the ground at a 40° angle in order to deliver the ordnance as accurately as possible. A-1s did not have an on-board computer to assist the pilot, who used the intervalometer to select which ordnance was to be dropped on each pass. A visual sight projected an image on the windscreen to line up the target. If there was a wind, the pilot had to compensate for it. The gunsight was the projected image of an illuminated dot on the windscreen that moved up or down as the pilot made recommended adjustments for different ordnances. It was only a reference point with no input from a computer and the accuracy of its projection was dependent upon such things as the height of the pilot's seat, whether the correct amount of rudder was being applied, the speed at the moment the ordnance was pickled (released or fired), whether the wind was blowing, how accurate the 40° dive angle was, and how high above the ground the release was made.

The adjustment to the projection of the dot was known as mil setting. If the terrain was a little higher or lower than the pilot thought, it might throw his accuracy off. In a 40° dive, the airplane picked up speed quickly. With a large propeller, a big change in airspeed produced a change in rudder trim that needed to be offset by pressure on the rudder pedals to keep it going straight. If the pilot didn't compensate, weapon delivery accuracy would be off.

Flying A-1s was considered by pilots to be real flying—stick and rudder stuff like it used to be done. As a result, many pilots wanted to fly them—or said they did. It was one of the last chances in the air force to feel what flying a "real airplane" was like—to use rudders almost as much as ailerons.

Other recips were still flying that provided the feel of real flying, but none that carried much ordnance. If an A-1 pilot was shot at, he could shoot back with a vengeance. He was unlikely to get picked on by a bully who might think he was an easy target.

The primary reason the air force was still using an old, slow, out-of-date airplane was that it was still the best one for a very important mission—the search for and rescue of crew members who had been shot down over enemy territory. In addition, it was useful for close air support of ground forces, was versatile in the types of ordnance it could carry and deliver, could stay over a target for an extended period, and had relatively simple systems for maintenance to repair. It had three radios for communication—UHF, VHF, and FM.

So it was that a very old airplane was used in a very modern war.

By the left wheel. Note the minigun on the stub.

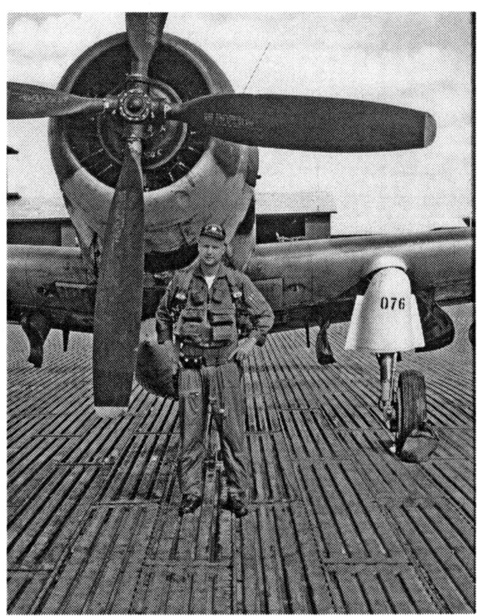

Dick Diller in front of Kawliga. Note the PSP and the size of the airplane and propeller

*

May 1, 1969. Thursday. I was not scheduled to fly again until today. I had had five days off the schedule, which was to prove to be the longest I wouldn't fly for the entire year with the exception of when I got crew time off visits to Bangkok for four days at a time, or when I went on leave and R&R. During those days, I had been assigned to be mobile control officer in the control tower twice and had worked on my additional duty assignments.

Today's flight in aircraft #141, a Hobo E model, was my first solo mission, and it was a strike in Happy Valley, where I had had my first mission only ten days ago. It seemed like a lot longer. J. B. East was on my mind as I went through the motions of the day and I was beginning to wonder how I was ever going to make it through an entire year. Life seemed so fragile, and there was nothing between me and whatever fate would await if I should ever find myself on the ground—nothing except my own ability to fly this airplane and its ability to hold together under sometimes very trying conditions and get me safely back to base.

*

I began to find myself thinking about The Closet. The Closet was in my room at my parents' house when I was in high school in Princeton, Illinois. My thought of The Closet was a fantasy—an escape—wherein I would imagine myself in a closet, living in it with the door shut for the rest of this entire year. The clothes were still hanging in The Closet, so there would not be much room for me, but I didn't need much room. Just enough to sit on the floor. The only time I would leave The Closet would be to use the bathroom. Food would be brought to me and I would eat it in The Closet. I would sleep there and I had very little light, so I couldn't read. No TV or radio. Just sit in The Closet for another eleven months. It would be a very boring year, a total loss of time from my life with absolutely nothing accomplished. The Closet had only one redeeming feature—at the end of that time I'd still be *alive*, even if I had accomplished nothing and no one could take that away from me. Flying A-1s at NKP did not provide me with that assurance. It seemed like just the opposite was likely to happen, and I was having a hard time dealing with it.

*

Once I was airborne and on the way to the target, my fears subsided and I began to enjoy myself. It was my first solo mission. Happy Valley was sometimes referred to as the Raven's Playground and was a relatively safe place to strike as the area had no known big guns and wasn't too far from the base. When we arrived, a Raven was working with a flight of two F-105s and we were instructed to hold out of the way. We climbed to 12,000 feet and began circling the area with me following the leader by about 400 yards. I looked alternately at the leader and the target area, where I could see the concussions of exploding bombs. I got a good view of the shock waves as they rapidly spread out in a perfect circle from the point of impact for a couple hundred yards. They didn't flash, but it was easy to see the explosion. Then it was gone, like it never happened.

All of a sudden I saw an F-105 on a bombing run in a steep dive pass directly between my flight leader and me! The leader didn't see it because the F-105 passed behind him and the thud pilot was unaware because he was busy making his pass and because of the camouflage paint on our airplanes. So much for Happy Valley or anywhere else being relatively safe! I called the leader and suggested we move farther out.

When we finally got to work the target, I dropped four bombs on each of two passes, three 250-pounders and one 500-pound Mark 82 per pass, and then made two passes shooting a pod of nineteen rockets on each pass. The rockets fired instantly when I hit the pipper and made a quiet whoosh sound as they streaked toward the target. A steady stream of sparks fired out the aft end of each rocket that was more fun to see at night. I could never see where they hit, though, because as soon as they were gone, I had to pull off the target to keep from flying into it, which was disappointing. Then I made a pass shooting my 20mm guns until one of the guns in the left wing jammed.

The Raven needed to leave the target, so he set us up to fac in two flights of F-4s. The object of this three hour and fifteen minute mission was to support friendly troops against the communist insurgent army, known as the Pathet Lao, and the North Vietnamese Army (NVA).

*

Even at that early date in my tour, it began to seem to me that, in the long run, the chances of the good guys winning was pretty low, at least as far as the war in Laos was concerned. Geographically, Laos was very important to both sides because it was in the center of Southeast Asia and was a buffer between Vietnam and Thailand. But for the direct interests of the United States, its location was remote, it had a small population and no important natural resources. The only reason we were there was to support the effort of the United States in Vietnam. Laos was much more important to the North Vietnamese because it was right next door, so they were willing to support their interests with ground troops, which the United States was not. Sending ground troops to Laos was a drain on the resources of North Vietnam, but that was nothing compared to what the political drain in the United States would be if American ground troops were to be deployed in Laos. Our near total superiority in the air over Laos was important to the support of the ground forces, but it was not enough to win a war over a committed enemy.

*

When I returned from the mission, a party was under way in the base picnic area for the pilots who had flown their last mission four days ago. Because such a large group was all going home at once, including several of the squadron's enlisted men who were leaving about the same time, a party was organized for everyone. Someone had gone to Udorn for T-bone steaks and filets. A lot of guys were unable to attend because they were flying or working. I arrived too late to get a T-bone, but plenty of filets were still left, so I ate four.

May 2, 1969. Friday. Today I had my first combat ride in an H model, aircraft #569. Our target was a bridge the bad guys were building fifty-seven miles almost straight north of Channel 89, the NKP tacan (tactical air navigation). The Raven fac marked it with a smoke rocket and told us to hit the smoke, so we tried but my accuracy wasn't good. We couldn't see the bridge, the road, or the stream because they were under trees. Captain Rich Hall was the leader.

May 3, 1969. Saturday. I had another mission in an H model with Clint Ward leading. The good guys had just recently captured Happy Valley and were pushing the bad guys out the west side. The target was 57mm recoilless rifle positions on top of a hill on the west side of the valley. Clint and I both made nine passes dropping bombs and CBUs and we each made five passes covering the other while he was making his passes. When Clint came in from one direction, I came in from another shooting my guns to try to keep their heads down while he was making his pass and he did the same for me. I had the feeling we were ganging up on them and had fun doing it. In contrast to yesterday, we both were accurate with our ordnance. Maybe I was getting better with practice.

*

About 6:00 p.m., Jim Monk and I went into town for the first time with Don Dunaway, who was close to the end of his year. It was after dark when we left the base, which disappointed me because I was hoping to see things in the daylight. About three miles of the road was gravel, and at the end of the dry season it was very dusty. The rest was paved road. Downtown stores were dimly lit with fluorescent bulbs that lent a gloomy atmosphere to the entire business district. We were the objects of mild curiosity to the local people, as our caucasian features stood out.

One of the things any well-dressed A-1 pilot needed at a squadron party was a party suit. Party suits for the 602nd were orange, the same color as flight suits worn by Air Defense Command pilots. A properly decorated party suit was worn proudly and had patches of the squadron, a patch that said "Yankee Air Pirate" (which was meant to thumb our noses at the North Vietnamese who called the POWs yankee air pirates), an A-1 patch, and maybe a patch or two of a previous assignment or squadron so others would know where a pilot came from without having to ask or be told. They weren't meant to be subtle and were in sharp contrast to the usual camouflaged flight suits, sometimes called goatskins, which we wore during daily activities and on missions.

Jim and I wanted to order a party suit from one of the town's tailors, most of whom were from India. We went to an Indian shop named "Hong Kong Tailor" to get measured. The Indian tailors weren't very good at their craft, but they had a certain style and flair, and if we needed a ride somewhere in town, they were happy to provide customer service in a big Mercedes-Benz. If the clothes didn't fit quite right, well, we were pilots, not clotheshorses, and no one would notice until we got home and our wives wondered where we got *that* suit. And you have *how* many shirts?

The next thing a well-dressed A-1 pilot needed was a pair of boots, the tops made of calf skin and the bottoms, we were told, made of elephant hide. The boots were custom-made, and our sizes were measured when we stood on cardboard while the boot maker traced the outline of our feet with a pencil. Jim was also interested in a bicycle to get around on the base, so we went to a bicycle shop. The prices were pretty reasonable, but a bicycle presented problems I decided were more than I wanted to deal with. Where would I store it?

It would get wet in the monsoon and I probably would, too. It would be subject to theft and I would have to keep track of it. The base had no racks and wasn't set up for bikes.

What I really wanted was a motor scooter, but that required a Thai license to use off base and an air force license to use on base, and the problems of storage, theft, and getting wet in the monsoon still remained.

We were entertained by the displays of Asian art in many of the stores. Trips to town weren't complete unless we ate at one of several restaurants that appealed to us Americans. It was a welcome break from the food available on base. All the restaurants served Thai, Chinese, and Laotian cuisine, so we picked one for our meal. Just don't drink the water.

To get back to the base, we found a taxi and rode back for forty baht—about two dollars.

*

May 4, 1969. Sunday. The call sign for the 602nd Special Operations Squadron was Firefly except when we were assigned to fly in a search and rescue mission (SAR), at which time the call sign was Sandy. Sandy missions were an integral part of the 602nd, and everyone was expected to become qualified. Sandies had an alert shack at the end of the runway and were required to be on alert from dawn until mid-afternoon when they would takeoff. Two would go southeast to the Steel Tiger operating area of eastern and southern Laos and the other two would go north to Barrel Roll. Then if anybody went down in the late afternoon, Sandies would be near the scene and a rescue operation could quickly begin. They were called November orbits. Jolly Green Giant helicopters also took off and were nearby.

If no one went down, the Sandies expended their ordnance just before dark and returned to base (RTB).

Jollies had two kinds of helicopters. Sikorsky HH-3Es, called little Jollies, had a maximum takeoff weight of 21,500 pounds, and the Sikorsky HH-53B Sea Stallion, Super Jolly Green Giant, or big Jolly, had a maximum takeoff weight of 42,000 pounds. The little Jollies were based at NKP and the big Jollies at Udorn.

On this bright, hot Sunday I was scheduled to fly a Firefly mission, but early in the day an F-100 from the New Mexico Air National Guard flying out of Danang went down in Steel Tiger at 120/86 from NKP and Sandies were launched to look for him. The Sandy mission was to locate the survivor, scout out the area for enemy guns or other activity, and, when Sandy Lead thought it was safe, escort the helicopters in to pick him up.

Sandies operated in flights of two with the leader working low in order to see as much of the area around the survivor as possible. Sandy One also offered himself as bait for enemy gunners, trying to get them to shoot at him so he could identify their locations and knock them out before calling in the choppers who couldn't shoot back and who were sitting ducks for gunners. The helicopters had to be protected.

Sandy Two's job was to fly about 2,000 feet above the ground, which was a very dangerous altitude in a high threat area. His mission was to support Sandy One in locating the survivor, relay radio messages, identify the location of enemy guns, and take over as Sandy low lead if Sandy One went in. Both Sandy One and Sandy Two were very dangerous jobs, but pilots were eager to do the mission because of the tremendous thrill and satisfaction derived from a successful rescue of a fellow American pilot from the forbidding jungles of Southeast Asia and an unknown fate at the hands of whoever might capture him. Sandy One was the on-scene commander and he gave the orders as to what he needed to soften up the guns and when to bring in the helicopters, even if he was a lieutenant and the one taking the orders was a major. It was not a mission for the fainthearted.

Because of the SAR, the rest of the squadron schedule for the day got scrambled and Captain Jack Hudson and I were assigned to Sandy alert duty. The first duty for a pilot assigned to alert was to get set for immediate action, which meant putting on everything required for a mission—parachute, helmet, survival vest—taking it out to the airplane, getting in the cockpit, adjusting the seat and seat belt, dialing in radio and navigation frequencies, and getting everything ready to go in a hurry if the need arose. Then he unstrapped and left it all in the cockpit, so if the call came he could just run out of the alert building, strap in, and go. The set-up procedure included an external walk-around inspection to check for fluid leaks and for any obvious external damage and to check the ordnance load. I had pulled a lot of alert duty at Dover while flying F-106s in the 95th, so it was an exercise with which I was familiar.

The temperature was 100° F with high humidity as we set up for alert just before noon. As soon as Jack and I returned to the air-conditioned alert shack, we were told our airplanes had been changed, so out we went in the heat to do it all over again.

As soon as we got back in, we were directed to takeoff on a Sandy mission for the downed pilot. So out we went again and started our engines. We were in the arming area at the end of the runway when we received a message the recovery had been made. Unfortunately, the F-100 pilot was dead when rescuers reached him. We once again resumed our alert status until 3:15 when we took off for the November orbit.

Like all holding patterns, the orbit was boring, just drilling holes in the sky, and it was comparatively safe as long as no one went down. It was all combat time (for whatever that was worth) and counted as a mission. We hit a target just before dark.

The ordnance load for a Sandy mission was all rockets, CBUs, and miniguns, with no bombs or napalm. This mission was two hours and fifty-five minutes long.

*

May 5, 1969. Monday. I was up at 2:30 a.m. for the dawn patrol in Barrel Roll. Since I had flown late yesterday evening, I had gotten to bed late and didn't sleep at all. Why was I scheduled for the early mission after a late one yesterday? My body's clock didn't flip the schedule very well and I was tired! Takeoff was at 6:00 a.m. and we hit what intelligence said was a truck park along a road west of Sam Neua (also spelled Xam Neua) in far northeastern Laos. It looked very much like a bunch of trees to me, no different from all the other trees in northern Laos. First Lieutenant Jon Ewing was the leader. We hit the target well but had no secondary fires or explosions.

Sam Neua is almost exactly 200 miles straight north of NKP and about 120 miles from Hanoi. We were over the target for only about fifteen minutes. This was my tenth mission and it lasted three hours and twenty-five minutes.

I learned more about our operating area today. Sam Neua, even though it was very much in enemy territory, was off limits for airstrikes. It was by far the largest settlement in northeast Laos, but was still quite a small town with only a few thousand people. Close to North Vietnam, it reportedly had a Chinese consulate and there were rumors that a few American pilots were being held as prisoners of war (POWs) somewhere in the area. It was the only visible settlement of any kind in any of the territory the enemy held in northern Laos.

The good guys had recently taken the town of Xieng Khouang, located on Route 4 southeast of the PDJ, for the first time since 1964. They captured several 37mm antiaircraft guns and other weapons and quickly withdrew.

As of this time, I still hadn't been shot at as far as I could tell.

*

Even though I thought it was a good idea to become familiar with our operating area by flying daytime missions at first, I still wanted to fly nights and decided it was time to again make my wishes known. The other guys in the squadron thought I was crazy to want to fly at night when there were perfectly good missions to be flown in daylight. Each of the three A-1 squadrons at NKP were assigned night missions—usually two flights of two per squadron each night. If I would take a night slot on a somewhat permanent basis only three other cockpits had to be filled from our squadron.

To me, night flying made a lot of sense for several reasons. First, it wasn't so miserably hot. I well remembered the heat of the flight line on my first mission. Second, I figured if the gunners couldn't see me they would have a much harder time hitting me. Third, there was much less supervision by the commanders at night. They didn't like to fly nights any more than the next guy and they had the horsepower to influence the schedulers to stay off the night schedule. A few of the colonels flew at night, such as deputy wing commander Colonel George Morris, Colonel Daryle Tripp, and squadron commanders Lieutenant Colonels Walt Stueck, Dick Michaud, and Lucky Lowman, and they were well respected by the junior pilots for doing so. Fourth, I could get my body's internal clock on one schedule and keep it there instead of switching back and forth. Fifth, I could become the squadron expert at a particular mission.

*

I hadn't been flying very much in May because so many new pilots were getting checked out there wasn't enough flying time to go around.
<u>May 6, 1969.</u> Tuesday. I didn't fly today. I received orders for my first CTO.
<u>May 7, 1969.</u> Wednesday. The CTO didn't officially start until tomorrow, but since I wasn't on the flying schedule I was allowed to leave on the afternoon C-130 flight to Bangkok, which left at 3:15. We arrived at Don Muang Airport in Bangkok about 8:15 after a stop at Ubon. The flight was nearly full of people and cargo and if I didn't get on, I would have had to wait until tomorrow.

When the plane arrived at NKP, I was in the passenger waiting area and stood by as the inbound passengers got off. I was mildly surprised to see one of them was Airman Doug Scroggs whom I had been expecting although I didn't know when. Doug was from Princeton and had grown up literally across the back yard from me. Our parents were friends and we had known each other most of our lives. He was about four years younger than I, an enlisted man, and a weapons loader. We were to share most of our year at NKP. I just barely had time to say hello and give him a phone number where I could be reached on base, as he was going one way and I the other.

The uniform for the flights to Bangkok was known as 1505, light tan pants and matching shirt with an open collar. The seat on the C-130 was webbing placed along the side facing inward and would not be considered luxurious by anyone.

*

My wife, Emily, left Chicago on May 3 and flew on a Pan Am flight to Anchorage and Tokyo where she had a twenty-one hour layover before resuming her journey. The flight from Tokyo to Bangkok was via Japan Air lines and she arrived on May 5. An epidemic of Asian flu was making many people sick in the spring of 1969 and Emily caught it during her trip to Bangkok. She also experienced some severe air turbulence on the flight from Anchorage to Tokyo, which didn't help things at all.

Upon her arrival at Don Muang Airport in Bangkok she got a ride to the Bangkok YWCA via an airport limousine service for twenty baht—about one dollar—and arrived just before they closed the gates for the night. The air-conditioned room cost five dollars per night and the girls took good care of her. It was a good place to rest up from the long flight across the Pacific Ocean. The Y was close to JUSMAG—Joint United States Military Advisory Group—so its location was convenient and it had a snack bar. JUSMAG was the location of most of the United States military's advisory activities in Bangkok. Emily had worked at Neiman Marcus in Dallas, Texas, for a while after she graduated from Drake University and she said it was more difficult getting settled in Dallas than in Bangkok.

After my 8:15 arrival at Don Muang, I took a taxi to the YWCA and arrived about 9:15 p.m. just after the gates had closed for the evening. The rules were very strict: Once the gates were closed no one could go in or come out. I asked the taxi driver to translate what I wanted. I wasn't going to just go away because the gate was closed. They kept saying, "Come back in the morning," which wasn't a very good option. With a good deal of persistence I finally persuaded them to summon a supervisor to make a decision and I was allowed in.

Emily and I stayed at the Manhora Hotel, which was top notch with a European trained staff for the military rate of twelve dollars per night. The normal rate was fifteen dollars.

<u>May 8, 1969.</u> Thursday. An F-4 was shot down near Saravane in southern Laos today and both crew members ejected. One talked briefly on his survival radio and then there was silence. A SAR was mounted to look for him, but after his radio went silent, it was assumed he had been killed or captured and the SAR was called off. The location was difficult in terms of enemy guns and several of the rescuers were hit by groundfire.

*

The contrast between the activity of Bangkok with its modern hotels, fine restaurants, traffic jams, schools, businesses, and friendly people, and the barbarousness of war, with its guns, sweat, bombs, napalm, and injury or death within a few hundred miles was stark. News of the war was in the English language newspapers in Bangkok and presumably in the Thai language media, but everyday life of the citizens seemed to be untouched. The presence of Americans was an accepted part of life in the city and most of the people with whom we came into contact spoke English and seemed genuinely glad to see us. Tourism was a significant part of the economy and Bangkok had plenty of things to see and do, including tours of the city.

The American military was well represented in Bangkok, with JUSMAG, a commissary, a small United States Army hospital, and the leasing of an entire hotel, the Chao Phya, as a BOQ for United States military officers who were passing through.

The Manhora Hotel's restaurant was named Botan and it had Italian cuisine, European-trained waiters, a pianist, and excellent food. For our noon meal we ate veal with asparagus and a sauce that included spinach. It cost six dollars for both of us.

We went to the Chao Phya Hotel where we rented a taxi and driver for the afternoon, took Emily's medical records to the Army hospital, and went to the United States military base exchange. I was impressed with how Emily already knew her way around the city. The streets were terribly crowded with vehicles.

May 9, 1969. Friday. We continued to explore Bangkok, which had many sights of interest. We had heard one of the better restaurants in the city was The Two Vikings, which was operated by two Danes, so we went there for supper and weren't disappointed. The first course was a choice of twelve different kinds of herring. The salad had water cress, which was a delicacy to us. The main course was Chateaubriand for two with two kinds of wine and goose liver gravy. The whole meal cost twenty-five dollars, which was a lot of money, but well worth it.

After we ate we went out to the front of the restaurant and asked for a taxi. The doorman blew his whistle and a cab came right up to the door.

"How much to go to the Manhora Hotel?" I asked.

The cabby said, "Twenty baht."

I thought I was well versed in bargaining for services in the city. "Too much," I said, so he backed up to where he had been parked. I was surprised he wouldn't even discuss it. We walked out to the street, hailed a cab, and got a ride to the Manhora for ten baht.

May 10, 1969. Saturday. I bought a Seiko watch for Emily and a TV for me. We ate lunch at an excellent French restaurant, which cost five dollars and fifty cents. For supper we went to a German restaurant in another hotel and the food was really good.

Chuck and Ethel Everett, who were living in Bangkok, were friends of Colonel Stueck, who connected us, and they became our contact people. Chuck was a civilian fuel supply expert who worked at JUSMAG, and they were very helpful in getting Emily settled. Chuck let me use his mail box at JUSMAG as an address for letters to Emily, which was a big help. Otherwise we would have had to use the Thai mails, which we weren't familiar with, and we weren't confident of their speed and reliability. Chuck and Ethel were always ready to extend a friendly helping hand whenever we needed it.

May 11, 1969. Sunday. This was the last day of my CTO, and in order to be back when I was supposed to, I had to leave on the morning flight to NKP. Emily was on her own in Bangkok again and I had to go back to the war after a wonderful respite in the city.

*

When I arrived at NKP, a SAR was being conducted in southern Laos for an F-4 crew. They were in a comparatively safe area with no bad guys nearby and both were picked up unharmed. One of the survivors was standing on his parachute in the middle of a field waving at the helicopters to come pick him up.

I went to church in the evening.

May 12, 1969. Monday. I was duty officer this morning and went to Don Dunaway's going-away party this evening. One year from today is my DOS.

May 15, 1969. Thursday. I had my first mission to Steel Tiger today and it was short and easy—we were back on the ground in only an hour and a half. The target was at 096/55 from the base, which was very near the guns of the Trail, but still relatively safe. I had good bombs and rockets. Colonel Andrews was the leader.

May 16, 1969. Friday. Early this morning an F-4 took a hit over the Trail and the back seater panicked and ejected before the pilot had a chance to determine if the Phantom was flyable. He turned toward NKP and managed to land safely.

A SAR was mounted for the man who had ejected. When the helicopter rescue team got to him he was found dead in a tree with his parachute lines so badly entangled they had to leave his body because the ground fire was intense. Normally an attempt would have been made to recover the body, but when the environment was too bad, it was judged to be not worth the risk of further loss of life and the possible loss of an entire helicopter and its crew.

I was duty officer in the afternoon.

*

The 602nd had a major project underway with the Zorros, whose hooch was located across a small grassy area with doors facing ours. We needed a place to call our own as combat pilots where we wouldn't be subject to the rules of the Officers' Club; a place close and convenient where we could go in our shorts and shower shoes for a beer and a game of ping pong. The grassy area between the Zorro and Firefly hooches was a perfect location, so permission was received, plans laid, and construction begun on our playroom, or party hooch, called the Sandy Box. The catch was that no government funds were allocated for our project. So it had to be done using "midnight supply" sources and "volunteer" labor. Some guys were well trained as carpenters or electricians and were able to be of great benefit to the project. Others had very limited construction talents and felt very conspicuous in their inability to contribute anything meaningful to the project.

My dad was an International Harvester farm equipment dealer and I had worked for him in the summer when I was in high school, so I could have been helpful if the project had been assembling a grain wagon, a combine, or a corn cultivator. But I had never done carpentry, so I fell into the second category and genuinely felt envious of those who could score a few points by putting in some high profile time working on a project of benefit to all.

Today I tried to be helpful to the cause. I hung around and watched some of the other guys work, trying to pick up pointers and be as useful as I could, but generally I succeeded at getting in the way. So I spent more time on the cleanup crew than I would have liked (which was another skill I learned working for my dad).

Chapter 6

Night Flying

May 18, 1969. Sunday. I was scheduled for a 2:30 a.m. takeoff on my first night mission. The night check out procedure was much the same as it was for day flying and came after a dozen or so rides. The first ride at night was in the right seat, just like the first day mission, so a new pilot could get familiar with the procedures. First Lieutenant Jim Beggerly was my instructor pilot in the left seat. Rich Hall was the flight leader and we struck near the area of Khan Kai in the northeastern PDJ.

Night flying was different, and I had a lot to learn. Pilots had to know where the mountains were and where the other airplane in the flight was in order to avoid a midair collision. We carried flares that had a million candle-power of illumination. CBUs looked like harmless fireworks sparklers when they detonated. Napalm canisters varied in size from 550 to 610 to 750 pounds and looked like they splashed across the ground when they hit. A 500-pound bomb would flash and be gone, but napalm continued to burn, so it was useful for marking a target as well as a fearsome weapon.

Instrument flying skills were required at night immediately after takeoff and when pulling off the target because spatial disorientation was a constant hazard, especially on moonless nights. Fighting between ground forces during the day was usually light in northern Laos but frequently would heat up at night resulting in the friendlies' need for close air support.

Truck traffic under the cover of darkness brought supplies from North Vietnam to the bad guys, and A-1s were used for interdiction much like A-26s were used over the Trail. Even if we weren't successful, we were capable of making their job more difficult and hazardous. Nighttime skies over northern Laos belonged mostly to Skyraiders, but we frequently had to share our airspace with a flight or two of F-4s, at which times we were assigned forward air control duties to direct them to the target. Sometimes we'd see an AC-47 making its rounds. They were known as Puff the Magic Dragon and had three Gatling guns, each of which shot 6,000 rounds per minute mounted in the left side cargo door. As the airplane circled the target, it could put down a lot of fire. It was an impressive sight.

Locating a target in the dark was different too, but I saw nothing that first night to shake my resolve. I knew it would be tougher than flying day missions, but I welcomed the challenge.

*

The entire country of Laos is slightly smaller than the combined area of Illinois and Indiana. Its population was estimated to be four million people, less than the city of Bangkok. The Plaines des Jarres, known by the acronym PDJ, got its name from large jars the French found scattered about. Archeologists speculate they may have been used as funeral urns long ago, but no one knows for sure. The PDJ is diamond shaped, about thirty miles by thirty miles, and is one of the largest relatively flat areas in the country. It is part of what is known as the Tranninh Plateau and the elevation is about 3,600-3,800 feet MSL with surrounding mountains rising to 5,000-6,000 feet, with some terrain to the southeast significantly higher. The PDJ is not completely flat, but has gently rolling hills covered with green foliage and a few small trees. Much of the country looked like a washboard from the air. For a downed pilot the only possible rescue from the terrain and the enemy was by helicopter.

*

While en route up the Mekong at night the flight leader maintained an altitude of 6,500 feet and the wingman 500 feet higher in order to maintain positive separation between airplanes. When we reached the bend in the river (called the fence), we climbed to 10,000 and 10,500 feet respectively in order to cross a mountain range. Then as we neared the target area, we extinguished external lights, hoping to become invisible to any bad guys on the ground. The mountain range had several peaks as high as 8,600 feet with one, Phou Bia or Mount Bia, the tallest peak in Laos at 9,249 feet. North of Phou Bia a 7,247-foot mountain was the only terrain higher than 7,000 feet. As long as I knew where it was from my position and stayed above 7,000 feet at the bottom of a pass in Barrel Roll at night I knew I would have terrain clearance. A horizon was not visible most of the time, which made reference to instruments, especially the attitude indicator, indispensable.

*

A-1 pilots flew two distinct kinds of missions in northern Laos at night. One type was when a specific target was assigned. We were given a picture that had been taken a day or two before by a reconnaissance plane, we were told why the target needed to be hit, and we were expected to find it using map coordinates.

Friendly outposts in northern Laos were known as Lima Sites (Lima standing for Laos). The largest one, known by the Americans as Lima Site 98 and Long Tieng by the Laotians, was the headquarters of General Vang Pao and his army of Laotian fighters. LS 98 was in a mountainous area southwest of the PDJ and had a tacan radio beacon named Skyline, channel (frequency) 113 that was used for aerial navigation. The transmitter was about twelve miles southwest of the PDJ and seventy-three nautical miles northeast of the capital, Vientiane. Although Long Tieng and Skyline were not far from the PDJ, they were behind a range of mountains, and an aircraft antenna requires a direct line of sight to receive the signal from the transmitting station. The mountains were high enough that they blocked the signal for aircraft operating below about 13,000 feet over the eastern part of the PDJ and areas to the northeast.

Because we were almost always flying below 11,000 feet, Channel 113 was not useful for navigation for most A-1 missions in Barrel Roll. In the daytime or when we had a moon, locating a target wasn't a problem because terrain features were easily identifiable. But on moonless nights, navigation had to be done by dead reckoning (DR), which was difficult when a small target was located in a remote area. Precise navigation was required to find just the right spot along just the right bend in a road. Even though reception of the signal was frequently not possible, Channel 113 was often used as a reference point from which to identify where a strike was made. The radio signal was useful to F-4s who flew high enough to gain line-of-sight reception.

A-1 pilots then, from a little north of the bend in the Mekong northward, navigated mostly by dead reckoning and by whatever could be seen in the moonlight. When flying nights in the Skyraider, I always knew what the moon cycle was because even a little moonlight was a tremendous help to navigation.

We didn't get just one target on this type of mission. Frequently three or four targets were assigned along with two flights of F-4s to fac, which was an area of training I didn't receive at A-1 school at Hurlburt Field. So we had to learn in the real world where a lot of people on the ground didn't like us. Why couldn't we at least learn to fac in daylight when we could see? Well, the Ravens were already doing that. At least those guys had enough sense to put their airplanes in the barn when the sun went down. "So that leaves you, GI." Holy cow! And I *wanted* to fly nights. No one told me about this!

The first time I was delayed because of a mechanical problem I found out how important the scheduled takeoff time was because when I arrived in the target area about fifteen minutes late, F-4s were waiting for us. "Hang on for a few minutes," I said, "so I can find the target."

All too frequently the reply was, "Hurry up, because we're getting near minimum fuel."

Is this any way to run a war?

So I had to find a target quickly, any target, and let them dump their bombs.

After the strike it was the fac's responsibility to let them know what the bomb damage assessment (BDA) was. In other words, how much damage had they done to the bad guys and the bad trees they had been assaulting at my direction. The first time I had the responsibility to do that I didn't see much. How could I? I had to get out of the way so the bombs didn't fall on my head and yet somehow keep the target in sight at all times.

So I said, "Zero observed BDA."

The reply came back into my headset dripping with sarcasm. "Thanks a lot, Firefly," as if my manhood were somehow in doubt because trees don't explode.

I made sure from then on to give at least *some* BDA even if it only amounted to one small secondary explosion perhaps caused by a delayed blast of the ordnance and one small secondary fire even if that was probably only the jungle brush or a tree that somehow ignited. That way I could send him on his way with a song in his heart and I could move on to the next guy.

Faccing the fast movers was the first item of business on this type of mission. Faccing in an A-1 when I wasn't rushed was tough enough. We had a full load of external ordnance that provided drag and weight. The first thing to do was to locate an ill-defined target using dead reckoning for navigation *at night.* One zig in a road looked like another zag just a mile or two away when the area of illumination was too narrow to get a proper perspective. On dark nights with no moonlight, it was often necessary to pop a flare or two in order to pin down an exact location. If my DR navigation had been accurate, I might be close to the road I was looking for and then I could begin to look for the specific target. But if I were to one side or the other of the assigned road, the flare would illuminate over trees with no indication of which direction to go to the target. This all took time and to have the fast movers saying, "We're getting low on fuel," didn't help.

When (or if) I was lucky enough to find the assigned target, I had to get into position to put a mark on or near it, so the Phantom pilots knew where I wanted their ordnance. While exiting the area, I somehow had to keep an eye on the target to see if they hit it and got any BDA. All this in a heavy, sluggish airplane.

It didn't take long to discover that if I was faccing C model F-4s they were likely to scatter their ordnance all over the area. The E models were usually quite accurate with F-4Ds somewhere in between. It wasn't an indication of the skills of the pilots, but rather newer technology and a superior weapon delivery system that made the difference.

The F-4 guys might have been airborne a total of about forty-five minutes when they were on their way safely back home again. I still had another hour and a half or so over the target where the bad guys didn't like me, in an airplane whose engine was known to quit from time to time, and each airplane was issued only one. Somehow it seemed like I screwed up somewhere in getting this assignment.

The next picture target was usually in an entirely different area from the first one, so we would go to where we thought it might be, pop a flare to try to identify it positively, and then fac in another flight of F-4s.

After the F-4s were sent on their way back home, the next assignment might be to fly armed reconnaissance (referred to as armed recce) on the road from the Ban Ban Valley to Sam Neua looking for trucks. The road, which was not much more than a dirt path, was winding and twisting over its entire length and was obscured from aerial observation by trees that arched over it. In order to see the road, it was necessary to get down low, fly slowly, and twist and turn the airplane from side to side constantly. Without an external load, it would not have been very difficult, but we were usually still almost completely loaded at that point with thousands of pounds of bombs and napalm except for the fuel we had already burned and maybe a couple of rockets used to mark a target for the F-4s. Flares were contained in a pod on the far outboard station, and we usually brought the pods back because the base had a limited supply and no one was making replacements.

If a truck was spotted, we'd have to climb back up to 10,000 feet, arm the weapons for an attack, and go after it. Meanwhile, if the truck driver had any idea we were present, he would pull over and turn off his lights. Relocating the target truck might be impossible under those circumstances. In other words, trying to armed recce and fac for ourselves at night over that route was not very productive.

Then if no trucks were spotted and we still had ordnance to expend, we had a picture target of our own upon which to bestow our attention.

It didn't take long to realize those missions weren't getting any easier with experience. It was not a very productive mission and I began inserting comments to that effect in my flight reports in the hope that the guy in Saigon who was dreaming up that stuff would get the message that we needed full-time facs at night. Or at least the picture targets could be attacked just as well in the daytime when they were much easier to locate.

Someone must have been listening, because those types of missions became less frequent as time went by.

*

The other type of Barrel Roll night mission was more productive and provided me with a greater sense of satisfaction. It involved working with friendly locals who acted as ground facs for us. They were Hmongs who were fighting for their land, initially against the Pathet Lao and later against the NVA. When they were recruited to fac for the Americans they were taken to the base at Udorn where, among other things, they received instruction in English. Even after the English course, they sometimes didn't understand our language very well if the conversation strayed very far from basic phrases, but they did learn important things like "one hundred meters," "bad guys," "good guys," "my position," etc.

Sometimes it seemed like they just wanted to see the show we put on which must have been quite a sight from the ground. Presumably they also were sending a message to any bad guys who might be in the area.

*

Barrel Roll was the name given to the area in northern Laos in which we worked, and southern Laos was called Steel Tiger. Alleycat was the call sign of the C-130 that controlled the action at night in Barrel Roll, and the night control ship for Steel Tiger was Moonbeam. An EC-121 airborne radar picket ship with the call sign Ethan kept track of our location and was supposed to keep us from straying over the border into North Vietnam. Crossing the border was not hard to do because it wasn't marked with a string of lights or a river or anything else.

En route to the target area the procedure was to check in with the control ship to see if they had an assignment for us. Alleycat was in contact with the friendlies who might have been actively engaging the enemy or who might have a target spotted and be in need of air support. He would then give us the location of the ground fac, and we'd make our way to his area. Communication with other United States military units and the base was done on the UHF radio. We communicated with each other and sometimes other flights on FM and with the ground facs on VHF. Skyraiders also had ADF receivers, which allowed us to receive the American broadcasts of Radio Saigon at night when things were quiet in the target area.

The location of the outpost needing help might be supplied accurately, but it was not always easy to find because of the limits of dead-reckoning navigation. Usually we were reasonably accurate, and as we got closer to his position, we would call on the assigned frequency.

If we were in his area, he might reply he could hear our engines and tell us what kind of identifying mark he had, such as a strobe light or small campfire that was easy to see from the air.

After we had positively identified his location, he would direct us to the target. If we had any doubt about his location, we could pop a flare, and if we were within twenty miles, he could see it and direct us in. We had the option of working with the light of the flares if we wished. They could be helpful if we had a specific feature on the ground to look for, but once the target was positively identified, I preferred to work without them.

The wind was usually light at lower levels of the atmosphere in northern Laos, but sometimes—especially in the monsoon—it was stronger, which made using flares to find the target a little tricky. If the flares were popped over the target and the wind blew them away before a mark could be put down, they weren't very useful. So when the wind was blowing and the fac said the flare was over the target, I had to hurry with a mark because it wouldn't be blown away.

A typical direction from the ground fac would be, "The target is 200 meters north of my position." The pilot might then put a log in the area and if the fac got excited, we knew we had the target. Log was the name given to the LUU-1/B and was so called because it was shaped like a log, five feet long and eight inches in diameter. When logs hit the ground, they burned with a bright glow for about thirty minutes with at least 1,000 candlepower and were easy to see.

If the log was too close to enemy troops, they might shovel dirt on it. If a better mark—such as a nape—wasn't quickly put down, we might lose the exact location of the target and have to start over. Whenever the fac said, "That's where the bad guys are," it was best to hurry and get a nape down, because they couldn't cover 550 pounds of napalm even if they could get near it. The tactic then was to continue to make passes over the target dropping ordnance on each pass. After the leader had made his passes, the wingman had his turn.

*

May 21, 1969. Wednesday. Today was the first day in which I flew two missions, even if that only referred to the twenty-four hour period of one midnight to the next. My first takeoff was at 1:20 a.m. with Jim Beggerly in the right seat. It was my fourth night ride, and up until now I had hardly demonstrated I was cut out to be a night fighter. In terms of accuracy of weapons delivery, I had really stunk up Laos. After all, the name of the game was to put the bombs on target. This was to be my last ride before my night proficiency check ride, and I hoped to show Jim I was at least a *little* better than I had shown up to this point.

On this mission, we had a combination of the two types of night Barrel Roll missions, in that we worked with a ground fac named Hot Dog and also facced some F-4s against a truck park that Hot Dog helped us find. The area was along a part of Route 7 east of Ban Ban known as the Birdshead, so named because the shape of the curves in the road in this mountainous area when displayed on a map were reminiscent of the shape of the head of a bird. I managed to get two trucks with one nape (that's more like it!) and the jets damaged five more. I saw the tracers from a gun Jim identified as a ZPU on this part of the mission, which was the first time I had been shot at as far as I knew. The shells didn't come very close and I thought, "If this is all there is to being shot at, it isn't too bad."

We were about finished with Hot Dog when we received a call that the ground fac Pogo needed help at Lima Site 19, about thirty miles south of our location and just southeast of the PDJ. An AC-47, call sign Spooky, was on the scene when we arrived, but he was almost out of ordnance and ready to RTB. Pogo said the bad guys were only fifty meters from him, he was under attack, and they were advancing.

We could see a lot of ground fire in the area, but first we had to locate Pogo's position so we didn't hit the wrong place. He was at the crest of a ridge and the attack was coming up the hill from the south. We had expended most of our ordnance with Hot Dog and were getting low on fuel, but we had a flight of F-4s at our disposal, so I put down a mark and directed them to hit the target. Within a few minutes they had expended all their ordnance. No other Skyraiders or jets were in the area and the next flight wasn't due for at least twenty minutes.

The only ordnance we had left was our 20mm guns and CBU-14s on two stations. Guns were not the weapon of choice because of what had happened to J. B. East, so we were left only with CBUs, the acronym for cluster bomb unit, which was a nasty antipersonnel weapon. CBU-14s normally were loaded on outboard stations because they were not heavy and allowed stations further inboard to be loaded with denser weapons such as bombs and napes. Each CBU had six tubes that could be dispensed individually, and each tube had nineteen bomblets about the size of a baseball surrounded with BBs that would explode on contact and spray shrapnel in all directions. As ordnance goes, I would have preferred a few napes or 500-pound bombs, but CBUs were OK for what we were up against, and since that was all we had, we used them.

CBUs were usually dropped while the airplane was passing directly over the target while in level flight, but CBU-14s drifted to the right as they descended. The amount of right drift depended upon how high the airplane was over the target, so a pilot had to be careful about how it was dispensed in a close air support situation with friendlies near by, lest it drift into their position. It was a subject covered in training but without much emphasis, so it was possible for a pilot to be less than proficient in his delivery. In this situation, it was important to be careful, because if I didn't offset enough on an east-to-west pass, my CBUs could descend into the good guys. On the west-to-east passes, we were almost directly above the friendlies when I released the ordnance.

I didn't see any bad guys or ground fire, so the concept of danger and being afraid didn't register. In my mind, heavy-weight takeoffs with an unreliable engine were far more hazardous and scarier than this. Beggerly was directing me on how to deliver the weapons, and I was busy flying and dispensing the ordnance. I was more concerned about our low fuel situation.

The sky was beginning to get light by this time with fog and haze. We could just start to make out the ridge and how the terrain dropped off to the south. Being more experienced in the Skyraider, Jim would have been the logical choice to make the passes, but all the weapon controls including the gun sight were mounted on the left side of the cockpit, so I just armed it and made the passes as Jim directed: low over the target and one tube of CBUs on each pass, hopefully offsetting the correct amount to the left. We were low enough that the right drift wasn't a huge factor, but we were close enough to Pogo that we had to be careful about where he was.

I remembered the story of when Skyraider pilot Major Bernie Fisher earned the Medal of Honor at Ashau Valley in Vietnam in 1966 and how the other A-1s made dry runs over the target because they were out of ordnance. The VC didn't know their ordnance was gone and respected the ability of A-1 pilots to do the job, so they had to keep their heads down when the A-1s made their passes. We weren't making completely dry runs yet, but we weren't doing a lot of damage either, and soon we would be completely out of ordnance as well as fuel.

After several passes, we made a couple of dry runs, which amounted to only distracting the attackers and making ourselves a target. We were low, so we must have been a big target to shoot at. To the bad guys we must have looked like an airborne tank and they had only small arms with which to shoot back. If they had had a 12.7, the whole equation would have been changed.

Finally we got word the next flight was approaching and we could leave Pogo in good hands. It was just in time because our fuel situation was close to being critical and the NKP weather was bad. The base had gone on a weather hold twenty minutes after we took off and stayed that way for much of the rest of the night, which was why we were the only Skyraider in the area.

We turned directly for home and I leaned the engine fuel as much as possible. The weather at the base was reported to be 300 feet overcast and raining with a huge cloud right overhead. I was thankful for the instrument training I had received at Perrin AFB because it made me confident of my ability to make an instrument approach. I was just keeping my fingers crossed that we had enough fuel.

We declared an emergency for fuel, and after a long straight-in ground controlled approach (GCA) through the clouds, we finally broke out underneath and could see the runway in the rain and gloomy early morning light. Was that a welcome sight! We touched down with 300 pounds of fuel showing on the gauge, which was about fifteen minutes' worth for that big R3350 engine—provided the fuel gauge was accurate.

When we inspected the airplane carefully on the ground, we found bullet holes in the right flap and in the elevator from small arms fire. Some bullets may have bounced off the underside, but we didn't see evidence. The flight had lasted five hours and five minutes. It was my fifteenth mission.

I was pleased to learn several weeks later that because of what we had done early that morning, Jim and I each received a Distinguished Flying Cross.

*

The bad weather moved off to the east and it was a pretty, sunny afternoon at NKP.

I slept about four hours, then got up to brief for a 5:00 p.m. takeoff for my night check ride. The takeoff was well before sunset, but it was dark by the time we reached the target area, so it counted as a night flight and for my check. Jack Hudson was the check pilot, and we struck a fragged target, which was the term for a picture target. We struck a truck park and storage area west of the Birdshead where I had been this morning while working with Hot Dog. I also facced in some jets, and they silenced a gun and got two secondary explosions. The flight lasted three hours and fifty-five minutes, making a total of nine hours of flying for me today. It was a pretty routine mission compared to the first one.

<u>May 22, 1969.</u> Thursday. A five-day period of intensive air activity began today to press hard on the bad guys. A lot of fast movers were scheduled and some facs had five flights assigned. All of a sudden, there was a lot of optimism and we were told the good guys were in their best position in Laos in fourteen years.

<u>May 24, 1969.</u> Saturday. The maximum effort was still ongoing. I had a 9:00 a.m. takeoff and went to Barrel Roll where I was facced in by a Raven in poor weather. I had to strike through a hole in the clouds and then had a rocket pod that wouldn't fire, so I had to bring it back. The target was hooches on Route 7 in Ban Ban Valley. After we finished our strike, we stuck around long enough to watch a flight of F-105s make a strike near Xieng Kouang.

<u>May 26, 1969.</u> Monday. I took off at 12:25 a.m. and air aborted nineteen miles north of NKP because my external fuel tank wouldn't feed. I received credit for a combat mission because I crossed the river and was over Laos before returning, but I had to make a very heavy-weight landing. Upon inspection after landing, tape was discovered over the vent hole of the newly-painted external tank, which prevented the flow of fuel.

<u>May 27, 1969.</u> Tuesday. My scheduled midnight takeoff was put on weather hold after I got into the cockpit. So I went back to the TUOC building, which had a large briefing room with a stage and screen like a movie theater where briefings for large scale missions such as big search and rescue operations were conducted.

It was late and we were not released from duty and not much was going on, so I looked around for something to do. About all I could find was the old John Wayne movie *War Wagon*. Several years ago an old major had some wise words of wisdom for me regarding life in the air force. He said, "Never learn to operate the movie projector because if you do, you'll always be on call for any dumb program that may come along." I always adhered to that advice.

So I had to go find someone to operate the projector so we could watch the movie. Unfortunately for our viewing pleasure, the projector was not equipped with a wide angle lens, so John Wayne appeared to be about half as wide as he normally was, and the film was very scratchy, but it beat doing the next best thing, which was nothing.

Heavy rain fell for a long time. All of Laos was covered by clouds and the mission was finally canceled.

I took off at 7:35 p.m. with Jim Beggerly leading my first solo night mission and we were assigned to Red Tiger in the southern PDJ. When we got to Red Tiger's location, another fac called and said, "We're under attack and need help!" So Jim left me with Red Tiger while he went to help the other fac. It required a quick OJT (on the job training) lesson for me in how to work with a ground fac. I managed to find Red Tiger's position and put six napes on his target. I also had a flight of two F-4s from Udorn with the call sign Sorehead to put in on the target. All the while, the weather was going from poor to worse as a deck of clouds was moving in from the southwest. I wasn't sure if I could get Sorehead in or not because of the weather, but we managed to before it got too bad. The weather became unworkable just after we finished. I had good results with my ordnance and with the F-4s. Red Tiger said we "killed many bad guys." I wonder how Sorehead got the name.

Having my flight leader leave just as I got to the target area on my first solo night mission meant I had to get proficient in a hurry. It's a good thing I had paid attention in the briefing. I was getting tired of four-hour missions, but I supposed I might as well get used to them.

*

An OV-10 came in to the base today all shot up. The radios were out and the pilot was wounded in the leg. Since he didn't have a radio he just showed up and landed. His landing was so hard that he sheared off one of his main landing gears, but at least he made it back to NKP. He was air evaced out to a hospital.

<u>May 29, 1969.</u> Thursday. I took off at 12:40 a.m. with Beggerly leading again. Once we got to the target area Jim was called to Rainbow who was having trouble again, and I stayed with the scheduled mission. On my first two night solo flights, I began to see a pattern of Beggerly leaving me to fac

F-4s on a picture target so he could have some fun with Rainbow. It was not a good deal for me and I didn't like it very much. We had been assigned a picture target using map coordinates, and I had to dead reckon navigate to get into the area. When I got to about where I thought I was supposed to be, I found some nape fires on the ground from the previous flight. I didn't really know where I was or what I was hitting, but I had a flight of F-4s coming in and I had to think of something fast. I popped out a flare and looked around but couldn't see any roads or distinguishing marks that looked familiar. I really had no idea where I was, but I could see a stand of trees just south of where the napes were burning from the previous guys' strike. I thought, "That's a likely looking bunch of trees. I can't hurt anything putting the F-4s in there." So I said, "Hit the trees."

On the third pass they got three secondary fires. One fire was still burning when I left the area twenty-five minutes later. It was a bright yellow fire that must have been a storage area.

I left to return to base (RTB) before Jim got back from Rainbow. As I approached the Mekong River, I turned on my transponder only to find it wasn't working. Neither was the tacan on the airplane, so I had to come in on raw data on the approach radar at the base. I got to bed at 8:30 a.m.

*

The wing altitude restriction safety rules for night flying in Barrel Roll began to make a lot of sense to me. We were to roll in over the target 7,000 to 9,000 feet above the terrain, line up the target and pickle the ordnance by 5,500 feet above the terrain, and bottom out no lower than 4,500 feet above the terrain. I decided to simplify things. In most areas where we worked in Barrel Roll, if I rolled in at 10,000 feet above sea level (MSL), pickled at 8,000 feet MSL, and pulled out at 7,000 feet MSL, I would be above the high terrain almost all the time. Ten. Eight. Seven. Never deviate from that rule when flying night missions in the mountainous terrain of northern Laos. Then I wouldn't have to constantly try to figure out exactly where I was in relation to the lower mountains, and I could keep track of the higher ones because there weren't as many of them.

A problem was the tendency to press the target, which meant to go a little lower than the recommended altitude in order to get the target better lined up to be more accurate. Even in ideal conditions, the amount of time available to locate and identify the target while going 40° downhill in 2,000 vertical feet is fleeting. Another second or two seemed so important to accuracy. Then another and another, until the airplane became a much bigger target for a gunner to hit from below, or at night a mountain could come up out of nowhere and put a sudden end to the flight.

Maybe my apprehension was good because it caused me to be more alert and aware of what was going on. But it surely took a lot of the fun out of it. I wondered if any of the other guys felt as I did. If so, they didn't show it!

*

May 30, 1969. Friday. I took off at 4:05 a.m. on the dawn patrol with First Lieutenant Rex Huntsman leading. The weather was so bad that we got lost and Rex had to call Ethan to ask where we were. Clouds covered almost everything except for a few breaks with no landmarks we could identify. The east side of the PDJ was a free strike zone, meaning we could hit anything we wanted to in that area, so we found a road just east of Roadrunner Lake and hit it. It's unlikely we did much good.

May 31, 1969. Saturday. I was scheduled for a 1:00 a.m. takeoff, but it was canceled because of bad weather.

Chapter 7

Monsoon

In May the hot season began to give way to the monsoon in Thailand and Laos. The change was caused by a shift in the upper air winds from the northeast to the southwest that brought moisture-laden air from the Bay of Bengal and the Indian Ocean that lies west and southwest of the Southeast Asian Peninsula. My prior thoughts of a monsoon were of a time of year when the weather did nothing but rain. But while a lot of rain fell, many days had sunshine and the extreme heat of the dry season gave way to weather not nearly as hot. Many days brought a light drizzle, and the cooler temperatures felt good. It was not unpleasant to be outdoors, but a person had to be careful to not get caught in rain showers that could be very heavy at times. The air was more humid and the water level of the Mekong was higher. No rain fell at all during the hot season and the jungle vegetation became very dry in the extreme heat. Among the effects of dry versus green vegetation was the burn time of napalm that was put down to mark a target. In the dry season, we could count on it burning for at least as long as we needed to be over a target, but in the wet season, it might burn only long enough to make a few passes with 500-pound bombs before another one was needed to keep the target identified.

Low level clouds frequently covered our entire operating area and obscured all the targets, making it impractical to launch airplanes. Other times had very few clouds and finding a target was easy.

The weather was usually poor to marginal, which meant we would takeoff anyway even with a very small likelihood of having a productive mission. Sometimes we would go just to check the weather and end up flying over northern Laos for an hour and a half fully loaded for nothing. During the first few months of my tour, if we couldn't find a target, we would make a radar strike, called combat sky spotting. Controllers directed us to a track at an assigned airspeed and altitude and told us when to release the ordnance. The area to be bombed was known enemy territory and we were just trying to get lucky. It was an easy way to expend ordnance, but estimating the amount of damage was not possible. So Someone decided it would be a good idea to designate an area north of Vientiane as a drop area that was used when we couldn't expend the ordnance on a target. After a while, that came to be seen as wasteful, and we were told to bring it all back so it could be saved and used again.

When the idea was brought up at a pilot meeting one day, I raised my hand and pointed out if we brought it all back, we would be landing at more than what the Dash One listed as the maximum gross landing weight. The reply was we had been doing just that for some time and it could be done safely, so we were to do it.

"Well, then," I said, "how about putting it in writing that we are directed to make landings over the max gross landing weight, so if something bad happens, we'll have a document to rely on for support."

That idea didn't get very far even though it made a lot of sense to me, so I decided whenever I had to make a heavyweight landing I would do so *very* carefully.

It also seemed to me to be nonsensical to send two fully-loaded Skyraiders to do weather recce when two partially-loaded ones could do the job just as well. That would eliminate the heavy weight landing problem. Better yet, why not send one fast mover from Udorn? He could cover the area in a very short time with significantly less risk than we could in our heavily-loaded airplanes that had an engine reliability problem. Unfortunately I wasn't running things, so I flew several completely useless missions.

<u>June 1, 1969.</u> Sunday. I took off at 1:40 a.m. on one of those useless missions. We flew around northern Laos for a couple of hours looking at the tops of clouds with no holes anywhere. At the end, we went to the Mu Gia Pass area, combat sky spotted our napes, and brought the rest back. Landing was through a low ceiling on a wet runway and nothing was accomplished at the cost of considerable risk to my leader and me for being out there.

<u>June 2, 1969.</u> Monday. Today was my twenty-eighth birthday and I celebrated by flying twice. The first takeoff was at 2:10 a.m. and we flew around in the clouds the entire time and couldn't deliver the ordnance anywhere, so we finally came home. Jim Beggerly was the leader.

On the second mission of the day, I took off in the evening with Jim Monk leading. Jim was an F-106 pilot from Air Defense Command and was a top pilot who made the transition from high-performance jet to low and slow attack missions easily. I was always confident when I was with him, because I knew he would do a good job. We tried to work with a fac named City Hall northwest of the PDJ against enemy troops near a river. City Hall was new and presented problems since he wouldn't mark his position because he was afraid the bad guys would find him. An American in a different location on the ground was also on the frequency, and he was very frustrated with City Hall. The American said he had called City Hall's commander and demanded that he mark his position, but he still wouldn't do it. He said, "I personally took the marks to him and showed him how to use them."

We knew we were close to being in the right area, so Jim put a nape down next to a river that I could see in the night light, and when City Hall got excited about it, he facced in a flight of F-4s, and then we hit the same area ourselves. City Hall liked the show, but I don't know how much good we did.

*

June 3, 1969. Tuesday. The Sandy Box project needed a top for the bar and, since NKP had no suitable material, someone had to go to Bangkok to find some and bring it back. Major Bob Bohan decided to assign the acquisition chore to me, which I was happy to do. He asked if I would like to go to Bangkok for it. Would I? I'll go to Bangkok any time.

At the NKP passenger terminal today while on my way, I saw Captain Bob Karre. Bob was a T-38 instructor at Laughlin when I was a student, and we were in the same A-1 class at Hurlburt three months ago. He was now based at Pleiku in the central highlands of South Vietnam and was very impressed with how nice NKP was. He said Pleiku was much worse and Da Nang was worse yet. His quarters weren't air-conditioned at Pleiku because it is in the highlands and supposedly has a cooler climate. He had found a five-foot snake in his bed in a new BOQ. NKP hadn't struck me as being that nice, but I had heard people say that anywhere in Thailand was better than anywhere in Vietnam, and Bob's testimony confirmed that. I was glad I didn't have to go to Vietnam to find out for myself. I didn't think to ask him if he was in bed when he found the snake.

I arrived in Bangkok at 9:00 p.m., met Emily, and we stayed at the Amarin Hotel. She gave me a sterling silver mug with a crest on it for my birthday.

June 4, 1969. Wednesday. Emily and I went to several places in Bangkok looking for a suitable top for the bar and finally found what we wanted. I bought two 4 x 8 ft. sheets of plastic laminate that I rolled up and tied into a cylinder held by two pieces of twine, one near either end of the cylinder. I also bought glue to apply it. It was a tight fit into a taxi, but we made it.

When I got to the airport, I had to carry the cylinder and my bag across the ramp to where the C-47 in which I was scheduled to ride back to NKP was parked. A breeze was blowing and as I walked across the ramp, a gust of wind caught the cylinder and blew it out of my hand. It started to roll as the wind blew harder. The material was brittle and already under stress due to the fact that it was rolled up. As it rolled along, it tore, almost completely coming apart. I dropped my bag and ran after it. As it developed its tear, it began to spread out, which caused it to stop rolling and I was able to catch up to it. It was a mess, and my first inclination was to just throw it away. But then what was the purpose of my trip to Bangkok? I couldn't just show up back at the squadron and say, "So sorry, but I didn't get the counter top material." I had to have *something* to show for my trip, so I left my bag on the ramp and used both hands to carry the ripped sheets over to the C-47 for the ride back to NKP. Then I went back for my bag. Boy, did I ever feel stupid, but I couldn't do much about it at that point.

The C-47 left Bangkok at 5:00 p.m. and made a stop at Korat. The airplane had an inoperative radio the pilots wanted to get fixed and left without telling the passengers where they were going. The airplane was parked on the edge of the ramp with a nice grassy area just behind it. With nothing to do, a couple of other guys and I lay down on the grass and relaxed. Before long an air policeman approached. He couldn't possibly be angry because we were lying in the grass. We weren't hurting anything. He said, "You'd better not lie there because there are snakes in this area." He didn't have to tell us twice.

After an hour and a half, another captain and I went looking for the crew and found them at the Officers' Club eating supper. Thanks for letting us know. So we ate, too. The Officers' Club at Korat was pretty nice compared to what I was used to at NKP. The USAF flew F-105s, F-4s, and C-121s from Korat. We remained at the Club for about three hours and arrived at NKP around 11:00 p.m. I had been in Bangkok less than 24 hours.

I didn't like the idea of having to tell about the shattered plastic top, but when I brought it to the Sandy Box I was told it wasn't needed after all as something else had been found to cover the counter tops. That was really good news to me as my stuff was in bad shape. I'm glad they didn't discover the other material until after I left on my mission. At least I provided the glue.

*

June 6, 1969. Friday. I flew two more of those useless missions over clouds in northern Laos. We were supposed to have a limit of two hours ground hold time for weather, but after a two hour and ten minute hold we finally took off at 3:40 a.m. and accomplished nothing. The second takeoff was at 6:55 p.m. and the weather was the same. I didn't understand why we kept getting launched on such useless missions. It must be to fill a square in some commander's record somewhere that, yes, we did get so many missions off and the fact they were good for nothing and put people needlessly at risk was not important. The missions each lasted three hours and twenty minutes.

*

June 7, 1969. Saturday. After twenty-five missions as a wingman, pilots checked out as flight leaders. The procedure was much the same as it was for the initial check out in the airplane and for the night check out: four missions as a leader with an instructor pilot on the wing and then a lead check ride.

Briefing was at 9:40 a.m. for an 11:40 takeoff for my first lead check out. The weather was better and we had a much better mission because of it. A flight of four F-105s was assigned to us to fac in on a storage area west of Ban Ban near the intersection of Routes 7 and 71. We struck the target before the F-105s arrived and then directed them to hit it. Even though we didn't get any secondary fires or explosions, the planners in Saigon can strike that target off their list. Nothing's left.

June 8, 1969. Sunday. I went to church in the morning then had my second lead check out flight today with a 2:35 p.m. takeoff. We went up to Ban Ban Valley, but clouds were too low to make a strike, so we found a Raven fac to help us find a target in the PDJ.

June 9, 1969. Monday. My third lead check out mission was today and it was my twenty-eighth mission overall. We struck a North Vietnamese base camp in far northern Laos, less than sixty miles from China.

*

Late this evening a Zorro pilot, First Lieutenant Lloyd Scott, crashed and was killed off the end of the runway just after takeoff. Lieutenant Scott, who was from Camdenton, Missouri, had just completed his night check out and was on his first solo night flight. All his previous flights had been in two-seat E models, but unfortunately he was scheduled for his first night solo flight in a single-seat H model. After eliminating all possible mechanical malfunctions, the accident investigation board, of which Harry Dunivant was a member, came to the conclusion that the probable cause was Lieutenant Scott's inexperience coupled with the change from a two-seater to a single-seater on his first night solo flight. The 602nd Firefly pilots knew the Zorros better than we knew the pilots of other squadrons on the base because we shared the Sandy Box (which was nearing completion) with them and because of the proximity of our living quarters. Even though I had only seen Lloyd Scott once just before he left to brief for his last flight, it still made me feel terrible that such a senseless tragedy could happen, especially when it so easily could have been prevented with a little care in scheduling.

Lloyd Scott was on his first assignment out of pilot training and might have become disoriented after takeoff. The base was brightly lit with a string of lights around the perimeter, but beyond that, there were only a few lights in an occasional isolated village on the Thai side of the Mekong and none at all in the jungle on the Laotian side. Moonlit nights were no problem for visual cues, and even starlight provided a dim horizon. The worst conditions for visual cues were moonless nights with a high overcast, which eliminated all natural light. Even the smallest sliver of moonlight helped immensely, both immediately after takeoff and while in the target area.

Once a pilot became familiar with the cockpits and characteristics of the single-seaters and two-seaters, switching from one to the other was routine.

Lloyd Scott most likely finished near the top of his class in pilot training in order to get a Skyraider assignment and so had a lot of talent for flying. But it was one of the first times he had flown an H model and he possibly didn't go to his instruments soon enough.

This accident reinforced my squadron's policy of checking pilots out in the H model on a noncombat flight, just for familiarization.

*

In the next few days I had routine missions with Ravens who were easy to work with because they found the target, marked it, and explained it, and all we had to do was hit it and go home—sort of like what F-4 and F-105 pilots did every day.

*

The political situation in the United States as well as the rest of the world at the time was such that the government made no acknowledgment officially or unofficially of our activities in Laos. We were not allowed to refer to Laos in letters home and awards earned for gallantry in action gave the location of the heroics as Southeast Asia; but the air force was deeply involved in the air war in Laos and forward air controllers were needed.

The Ravens were American military officers who wore civilian flight suits and had no insignia or identification of any kind to link them to United States military forces. They flew mostly out of Lima Site 98. The LS 98 airstrip was interesting because at the north end a mountain rose almost straight up from the terrain for several hundred feet, which meant takeoffs and landings were accomplished in opposite directions no matter what the wind.

June 10, 1969. Tuesday. I worked on disaster control in the morning and took off at 2:30 p.m. on my fourth lead check out ride with Colonel Stueck flying as IP on my wing. When we got to the bend in the river, I checked in with Cricket, the daytime Barrel Roll control ship who assigned us to a Raven who had a storage area for us to hit in the eastern portion of Ban Ban Valley. We got a couple of secondary explosions.

After working with the Raven, we went about six miles south of Xieng Khouang where I facced in a flight of F-105s on a target along Route 4. It was tough to even find the road because of overgrowth. My call sign was Firefly 28.

June 11, 1969. Wednesday. I flew my thirtieth mission and received my lead check. We worked with a Raven east of the Raven's Playground on an easy mission. I had good CBUs and rockets.

*

June 12, 1969. Thursday. The United States government installed electronic sensors along the Ho Chi Minh Trail in an attempt to find out how many North Vietnamese trucks were getting through to South Vietnam. Sensor airplanes were sent out to monitor the equipment and listen to the signals being generated. The engine on one of those planes failed this morning, and the pilot ejected and was picked up safely. But the airplane, which was loaded with sensitive equipment the air force didn't want the enemy to retrieve, was forty-four miles east of NKP and easily accessible to them. A couple of A-1s were dispatched to destroy it and its equipment before the enemy could get it, and I was assigned to do that. The downed airplane was in a permissive area, and it would have been a fun mission, but I was changed to a late afternoon flight with Lieutenant Colonel Tommy Tomlinson.

It was normal procedure to schedule a newly qualified leader with a more experienced pilot after his lead check to make sure he was doing things properly, to ease him into being a leader, and to keep him out of trouble, and tonight I had Colonel Tomlinson as my wingman with a 5:05 p.m. takeoff. My UHF transmitter didn't work, so he took over the lead. We worked below low clouds with a ground fac, Hunter, who was near high terrain on the southern edge of the PDJ. We attacked bad guys who had a 105mm howitzer. The air was hazy, and it was just at dusk and very unsafe because of the nearby high terrain. At one point, I started my pullout with a turn directly toward the mountain, then realized where I was going and turned the other way and flew up the valley. Poor weather, high terrain, and approaching darkness made for a very dangerous situation.

*

June 13, 1969. Friday. Clint Ward hit a mountain east of the M in the river along Route 7 near Ban Ban at 6:15 this morning. First Lieutenant Bob Moore was his wingman and reported no chute or beeper. (A beeper was a radio transmitter in the parachutes, which activated automatically to let anyone in the air know someone had ejected and there was a potential survivor.)

Clint was a top-notch pilot who was well respected by the rest of the guys. He had discovered twelve trucks bringing supplies in from North Vietnam and had stopped the first one with napalm when he hit the mountain. We last flew together on May 3.

*

June 14, 1969. Saturday. I took off at 1:00 a.m. after a two-hour delay because of weather and because my airplane needed a battery change. I was the flight leader with Colonel Tripp and Colonel Tomlinson on the wing. We flew around in the clouds for three hours and finally dumped our napes in the free strike zone north of Vientiane. Colonel Tripp was frustrated and unhappy about the crummy mission.

June 15, 1969. Sunday. Took off at 4:05 a.m. after a weather delay of an hour and five minutes and it was bad all the way to the target area. The PDJ weather wasn't too bad at first, but it soon socked in, so we went to the M in the river in the eastern part of Ban Ban Valley to finish striking.

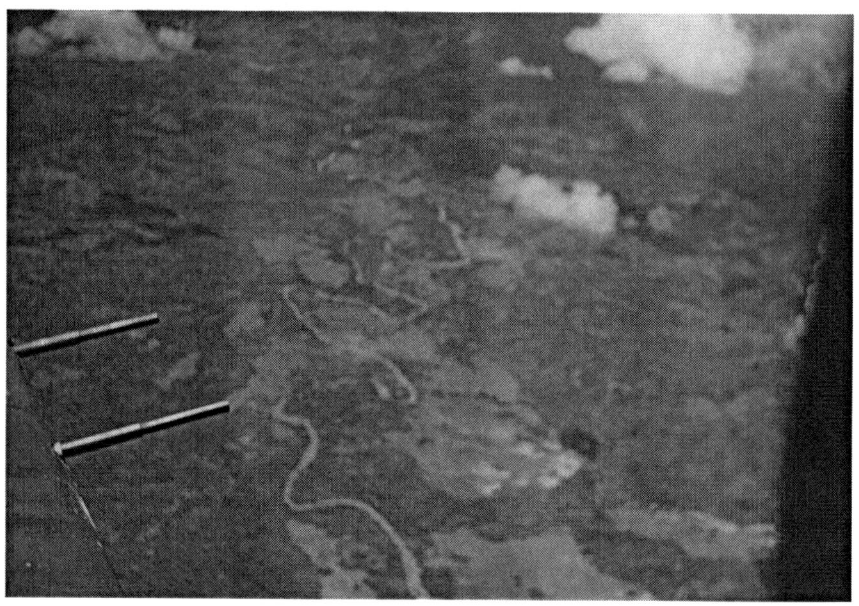

The M in the river in Ban Ban Valley

I also took off at 10:00 p.m. with Jack Hudson in the lead. We tried to work with the ground fac Poppy in the northwestern part of the PDJ, but he ran us around in circles. We used fifteen flares and still couldn't find the target. We finally ended up marking a target with napalm, but two of mine and four of Jack's were duds. We went through some bouncy thunderstorms on the way home. What a night!

Two airplanes, one of which was piloted by Jim Monk, were hit by ground fire today near the intersection of Routes 7 and 71 west of Ban Ban, but both made it back OK.

June 17, 1969. Tuesday. First Lieutenant Gene Smith, a classmate at Hurlburt, was my wingman and we took off at 12:25 a.m., an hour and twenty-five minutes late because of a maintenance problem on his airplane. We went all the way up to Sam Neua, but the weather was bad, so we went back to the PDJ where it was clear enough to make a strike. We worked with Pogo and hit troops on a mountain.

I went to bed about 6:30 a.m. and got up at 11:15 to go to the tower to be mobile control officer. A pilot meeting was scheduled for 7:00 p.m.

June 18, 1969. Wednesday. Briefed at 4:30 a.m. for a scheduled 6:30 takeoff, but we canceled because of weather.

June 19, 1969. Thursday. NKP has already logged eighteen inches of rain in June. Sixteen inches is normal for the entire month.

June 20, 1969. Friday. Takeoff was scheduled at 2:00 a.m., but we were cancelled at 12:55—which must be a new record for an early cancellation.

June 21, 1969. Saturday. I took off an hour and ten minutes late at 3:10 a.m. in aircraft #314, which was just back from overhaul. It had a new inverter switch that I didn't know about, so I aborted it and took the spare. My call sign was Firefly 34 and First Lieutenant Rich Croft was the wingman. We struck a storage area near Khan Kai.

June 22, 1969. Sunday. I was scheduled for a 1:00 a.m. takeoff but was forty minutes late because when I got to the end of the runway, it was closed temporarily because someone had blown a tire on landing. When the runway reopened, two flights of A-1s and two C-123s were ahead of me for takeoff. An A-1 in the first flight dropped a rocket pod on the runway. A pilot in the second flight saw and reported it, so the runway was closed again while it was picked up.

Tonight we went well north of the PDJ to 060/70 from Channel 113 to work with Kingpin at LS196. It was about twenty-two miles northeast of Ban Ban. Kingpin spoke very poor English, but he had a target for us on the top of a mountain. He was very hard to understand and I put out a lot of flares before he finally said, "OK, the target is right under the flare. You hit there." I felt like I was being trained to understand what he was saying.

Gene Smith was my wingman again and we each had six 610-pound napalm canisters. One of my napes hit the edge of a cliff, and I was fascinated watching it cascade off the side like a several-hundred-foot-high waterfall of fire.

Gene was partially through his strike with two napes and two CBUs remaining when we got a call from Tiger Mobile that he was under attack and needed help. The attackers broke it off when they heard us come. It was much easier for us when they continued the attack so we could see them, but when they weren't shooting, all we could see was darkness and we had to rely on the skill of the ground fac to tell us where the target was.

After Gene dropped his napes and CBUs, we both made several passes shooting our 20mm guns into the trees. We wouldn't normally do that in a high threat area because a gunner could pick up our muzzle flashes too easily, but we guessed the enemy had only small arms to return our fire and felt like they weren't much of a threat.

We couldn't tell how much damage we did, but we think we got quite a few bad guys. Tiger Mobile was pretty generous and gave us one hundred KBA (killed by air), but it might not have been as many as that. At any rate, it was a successful mission. We were airborne four hours and five minutes.

June 23, 1969. Monday. Took off at 2:00 a.m. with Gene Smith on the wing. My VHF receiver didn't work, so Gene worked with the fac who was Tiger Mobile again. It was quiet compared to last night.

*

Every few weeks pilots were allowed a four-day break, called crew time off or CTO, and allowed to go to Bangkok. The scheduling goal was for everyone to get a CTO every six weeks, but that didn't happen when the squadron was short of pilots. Transportation to Bangkok was by the twice-daily C-130s that made the rounds of the Thai bases, provided a seat was available. I was scheduled for a CTO to begin tomorrow, but since I wasn't on tonight's flying schedule, I looked around for a way to go to Bangkok as soon as possible. A regularly scheduled U-10 flight left every morning, and I managed to hitch a ride with him. The pilot was Ken Johnson and the first stop was Udorn.

Unknown to me when I left was that Seventh Air Force in Saigon had just raided us for four lieutenants to go to South Vietnam to be O-1 facs, and Gene Smith was one of them. We have been regular flying partners lately and I will miss him, as he was a good pilot and a congenial guy to fly with. The others were Rich Croft, Larry Howerton, and Larry Sarkozy. Another who left about the same time was a Zorro named Frederick "Flick" Guerrina. Croft, Howerton, Guerrina, Smith, and Jim George were classmates at the Air Force Academy. Since we would have fewer pilots, all leaves and CTOs were canceled until more arrived. When Colonel Stueck found out I had already left for my CTO he sent someone to the passenger terminal—known as the Aerial Port Squadron—to tell me my CTO was canceled and I couldn't go on the C-130 to Bangkok. But I had left on the U-10 just before the message arrived, so a call was made to Udorn to stop me. When I returned the call I was told to continue on. If I hadn't gone when I did I'd have been out of luck.

Major Dan Tauriello, whom I had known at Paine Field where he was the F-102 squadron safety officer before I entered pilot training, boarded the flight at Udorn. We stopped at Takli before arriving at Don Muang Airport in Bangkok about 12:30 p.m.

Ken was on a regularly scheduled rotation to Bangkok where he stayed overnight and picked up the same rotation the next day. A vehicle that was sort of like a panel truck was waiting to take him to the Chao Phya Hotel, and I hitched a ride into town with him.

*

Emily and I arrived at the Narai Hotel about 2:00 p.m. The Narai was the nicest Bangkok hotel we'd stayed in so far. The rate was 340 baht minus twenty percent for American military discount and plus ten percent for tips for the staff. At twenty baht to a dollar it came to a little over fifteen dollars per night, a real bargain in 1969. The price included fresh flowers each day that Emily identified as chrysanthemums.

Since I had flown a night mission, I was tired but made an effort to stay awake until 8:00 p.m. when I went to bed and slept for twelve hours.

June 24, 1969. Tuesday. The restaurant at the top of the Narai was called La Rotunde, and we ate lunch there. It was on the fifteenth floor, revolved every forty minutes, and offered a fine view of the city in all directions. For our evening meal, we ate in our room.

June 25, 1969. Wednesday. Emily and I went apartment hunting today. We ate lunch in the Narai's coffee shop, and I got fitted for a suit at an Indian tailor's shop near the hotel. He said the material was made in England. He was a very boring man who spoke in a monotone, but then what should we expect from a tailor?

We were so impressed with La Rotunde that we ate supper there. It was a very fancy French cuisine restaurant and we had escargot and onion soup for appetizers and peaches flambe and cherries jubilee for dessert, all the while enjoying the ever-changing view of the city at night. The whole meal cost about twenty-three dollars for both of us.

June 26, 1969. Thursday. We rented a beautiful, furnished, two-bedroom sixth-floor apartment with large rooms and windows in a complex named Embassy Place for about $241 per month including a telephone and air conditioning. All we needed was a rug for the hardwood floor and linen for the beds. The building was new, and we were the first tenants in that apartment. It was part of a complex that included two ten-story buildings and a pool. Our first choice of apartments was on the same floor on the other side of the building because it had a nice view of the grounds of the American ambassador's residence, but just as we were about to sign up for it, we were informed the Swiss Embassy had rented it for one of their people.

We went back to Mr. Personality, the tailor, for another fitting today.

Emily and I ate dinner with Chuck and Ethel Everett this evening.

June 27, 1969. Friday. Unfortunately, all CTOs had to come to an end and today I had to go back to NKP and war. We picked up my new suit, which fit well enough to meet Emily's approval, and checked out of the hotel. The hotel bill came to about $139 including the restaurant charges. I left my new suit with Emily as I had no need for it at NKP and caught the afternoon C-130 flight to the base.

*

Muong Sui, also known as Lima Site 108, on the western edge of the PDJ, fell to the Pathet Lao and North Vietnamese today. A lot of friendlies needed to be air evacuated by helicopters, and A-1s were assigned to escort them because of the danger of ground fire. A-1s were the hired guns needed to fire back if the helicopters were fired upon, since they didn't have the capability to do it. The fall of Muong Sui was big news in the English language newspapers in Bangkok.

While the air evacuation was underway, my roommate, Harry Dunivant, was making a strike about a mile and a half south. One of the escorting A-1s, who were from the Hobo squadron, began to run low on fuel and asked him to switch missions, which he did. Harry lucked out because the A-1 that switched with him took a hit in the engine. Two pilots were in the airplane because one of them, Major Bill Bagwell, was getting a mid-tour check ride. He was on his first mission after returning from leave and was about half-way through his tour of duty here. The other pilot was Lieutenant Colonel Bill Neal.

They turned south right away to try to get to a safer area and had to eject. When they tried to eject one found his canopy didn't go as it was supposed to and he ejected right through the plexiglass. He was better off than the other pilot whose ejection seat didn't work at all! When he pulled the ejection handle it came off in his hand and he was still sitting there, so he had to bail out over the side of the airplane. They were on the ground about twenty minutes before they were picked up safely.

Thirty-seven friendlies were left behind at 108 because darkness arrived before they could be evacuated. They will be picked up in the morning, but they might have a long night.

June 29, 1969. Sunday. I took off at 1:35 a.m. with Gene Smith on the wing. We orbited for an hour and a half before we were able to strike. We had received more air support in Barrel Roll in the form of more missions assigned, but it was too little too late.

June 30, 1969. Monday. Took off at 2:30 a.m., an hour late because of low air pressure in my canopy air bottle. Gene was on the wing again and the weather was terrible, so once again we brought everything back.

Chapter 8

Barrel Roll

Thunderstorm clouds in North America are extremely dangerous to airplanes and are to be avoided at all times. While the clouds along the Mekong River looked ferocious, they caused barely a ripple as the airplane passed through. They also produced static electricity known as St. Elmo's Fire. At night the arc of the prop became plainly visible in the bluish glow, as did the outline of the cockpit and the leading edges of the wings. Bomb fuses and the leading edges of napalm canisters lit up, causing anxiety the first few times I saw it. It was spooky enough to fly into those forbidding clouds. The glow around the prop wasn't too bad, but when the bomb fuses started to glow—now that wasn't pleasant! Would they go off? If they did I'd probably never know it. After what seemed like a long time I emerged from the cloud into clear air, the stars appeared above, St. Elmo's Fire disappeared, and I'd simply be on my way to the target area again.

During the monsoon, I had plenty of opportunity to watch St. Elmo's Fire, as I spent a lot of time looking out from the inside of clouds at night. It wasn't my favorite activity.

Static electricity occurred during the day, of course, but it wasn't visible. Think of what the daytime-only guys were missing! Think of what the ground-bound people back at the base were missing! Think of what the people back home were missing! Think of what I would like to be missing!

I was on the schedule almost every day for the next three months except for a trip to Bangkok for a CTO. It was not out of the ordinary to have malfunctions of parts of the airplanes we would either have to work around, or if they were serious enough, to RTB. Many takeoffs were delayed because of weather or mechanical malfunctions such as a weak battery, inoperative radios, low air pressure in the canopy jettison bottle, or inverter failure.

*

The O-2 facs, called Nails because of their call sign, lived across the street to the south from our building. Their airplanes were two-engine push/pull Cessna Skymasters and they were out over the Trail every night looking for trucks. I became friends with a Nail, Captain Jim Anderson, who wanted to go with me on night flights to see what it was like from the point of view of an A-1 pilot. I thought he was crazy for wanting to hang it out more than he had to, but he went along anyway. It was nice to have someone to talk to. I felt an affinity for him immediately because he had been a student at North Park College in Chicago, the school of the Covenant Church, my denomination, and he knew several of my high school friends who went to college there.

Jim Anderson (L) and me in front of a revetment

July 1, 1969. Monday. Took off at 1:55 a.m. with Gene Smith on the wing again. I was Firefly 36 in aircraft #063, an H model. We couldn't find our target south of the Birdshead because bad weather and lack of navaids prevented it, so we went west to help Pogo at 357/17 from Channel 113 on the western edge of the PDJ and hit what was left of a village. Pogo said he was three klicks (kilometers) east of the target. I facced in Shako, a flight of two F-4s, and one hit too long on a north-to-south pass—too far to the south—with his ordnance. Pogo said the bomb hit near the friendly position, so he must have been south instead of east like he said. This was a four hour mission.

It was Gene's last A-1 flight before leaving for his O-1 assignment. Ten pilots from the wing were taken—all lieutenants just out of pilot training who had between three and six months here in the A-1. They had to be at Bien Hoa, which was near Saigon, by July 5 to check out in-country. It will be a big change from A-1s to O-1s.

I also took off on another mission at 6:40 p.m. with Jim George on the wing. I facced for Sawyer flight north of Ban Ban then went over to 310/31 to hit with Peacock. The weather was bad, and we needed help from Spooky, an AC-47 who happened to be in the area.

The fuel flow of a reciprocating engine was determined by revolutions per minute (RPM) and fuel mixture. Takeoff RPM was 2800, METO (max except takeoff) RPM was 2600, and normal cruise RPM was 2200. The higher the RPM, the harder it was on the engine, and the more fuel it consumed, so I thought it was best to keep RPM as low as possible. When faccing, especially when fully loaded, and when making an attack, we used 2600 RPM with the mixture in rich. Because I had been working my engine pretty hard while working with Sawyer and trying to find Peacock's target, I ran low on fuel before Jim and had to RTB while he stayed to make his strike. This was a four hour and twenty minute mission.

*

July 2, 1969. Wednesday. Captain John Flynn, a Hobo, hit a tree while strafing near Lima Site 108 and was killed about 2:00 p.m. today. It's not known exactly what happened.

I took off at 9:45 p.m. after an hour and forty-five minute delay for weather. I was Firefly 35, with Rich Hall leading, and we struck with Quiet Man on the western edge of the PDJ. Several airstrips in that area date from the time Laos was a French colony, and we hit near one of them. Quiet Man was on the side of a runway with the bad guys just one klick away.

I could see Quiet Man's mark through scattered to broken clouds and made four passes. Quiet Man didn't like it at all that I was coming down through the clouds because he thought I would hit him, so after four passes I stayed below the clouds and could see his light much better. The moon was bright. I put two more napes on the bad guys from below the clouds, but the one on the right stub wouldn't release, and I had to manually pull it off using the cable. Then I made a couple of passes strafing with all four guns at once while also dropping CBUs. It was a fun mission because the moonlight provided good visibility even though the clouds were a factor, and we had a good target in a rather safe area.

July 3, 1969. Thursday. I was scheduled with Rich Hall again today, but after we were armed and ready at the end of the runway, a thunderstorm blew in and the supervisor of flying (SOF) in the command post canceled our takeoff. Rain poured down with lightning and thunder. We sat all ready to go with the canopies closed waiting for the rain to quit, but it just didn't stop. Rich called the SOF on the radio and tried to talk him into launching us but the answer was no, much to my relief. I had no desire to takeoff into that storm fully loaded.

After waiting for quite a while we dearmed, taxied back, and went inside. The rain finally let up after about an hour and a half, so we went out to try again. Right after I got strapped in the cockpit, the downpour resumed, so we called it a night. It was raining so hard I got soaked just opening the canopy and getting out of the cockpit to shelter beneath the wing. The second storm also featured lightning and thunder.

I went to the Officers' Club and played dice and drank beer with Jim George and Jim Anderson.

*

July 4, 1969. Friday. Mail service has been slow and erratic. Sometimes I received several letters one day and none for several days. I wondered why that happened.

The 56th Special Operations Wing's deputy wing commander, Colonel Patrick Fallon, was shot down today just south of the PDJ. Colonel Fallon was the second ranking officer on the base, was flying with the 602nd and getting a lead checkout with Jim Beggerly as his IP. He came up on his survival radio after landing in his parachute and said he was surrounded by the enemy. Then his radio went silent. He was seen being led away at gunpoint with his hands in the air. A lot of SAR missions were flown trying to rescue him, but to no avail. We heard the enemy had orders to take prisoners, and speculated he had been taken to Hanoi—at least we hoped so, because we felt conditions were better for POWs in Hanoi than they would have been with the Pathet Lao. Patrick Fallon was officially declared to be deceased on August 20, 1979—over ten years after he went down. We heard he had a wife and a two-year-old daughter. His location was 057/15 from Channel 113.

I didn't fly tonight because the airplanes had been flown in the SAR for Colonel Fallon.

*

July 5, 1969. Saturday. I got a package from home today with cookies and cinnamon balls. I liked the cinnamon balls and frequently took a couple along on missions and sucked on them on the way to the target area. Mom used the Sunday newspaper comic section to wrap things, which I liked because *Stars and Stripes* didn't carry the Sunday cartoons.

I felt sick today, so I went to see the flight surgeon. I had a slight fever of 99° F, but flew anyway.

Took off at 8:00 p.m. with Colonel Tomlinson and Rich Hall on the wing. I had an E model, aircraft #577, and we worked with Showboat at

112/28 from Channel 113. The weather was very poor and Mount Bia, which was about ten miles west of our target, rose abruptly from the surrounding terrain. The elevation of the target was about 5,000-6,000 feet, the moon wasn't up yet, layers of clouds had to be dealt with, and it was hard to see the ground. I was very careful.

I began to look forward to the end of the wet season because we weren't accomplishing very much and were wasting a lot of resources trying to dive bomb at night with the sky full of clouds.

July 6, 1969. Sunday. Took off at 10:25 p.m. in a Zorro E model, aircraft #878, with Jim Anderson in the right seat along for the ride, and Rex Huntsman on the wing. We were assigned to Hunter who was working with an AC-47 when we arrived, so we had to wait until Spooky completed his mission before we could go to work. The weather was bad again. After I pulled out of my last pass and turned toward home, Jim said we still had a nape on the stub station. I pulled the cable to manually release the two stub stations, which also jettisoned the centerline fuel tank, but Jim said it was still there. The right stub was not visible from the left seat of an E model because it was the closest-in station, and the view was blocked by the right side of the cockpit, so I couldn't see for myself. I declared an emergency for landing and touched down very carefully. When we arrived in the dearming area, the airman said the right stub didn't have a nape. Jim had seen the flare pod on the far outboard station and thought that was referred to as the stub. No harm was done except for an external fuel tank down in the jungle somewhere.

*

July 7, 1969. Monday. I worked on mobility at the squadron this afternoon. That kind of activity seemed suspiciously like a make-work project to me.

The restaurant at the Club had real butter again! Amazing! Dairy products weren't normally on the menu.

While I taxied out for takeoff tonight, my seat bottomed out and wouldn't come up, so I flew with it like that. Rex Huntsman led, and we worked first with Lulu and then with Hunter, but the weather was bad again, and we didn't do much good. This was a three hour and forty minute mission.

July 8, 1969. Tuesday. Took off at 9:55 p.m. with First Lieutenant Tony Wylie and Bob Bohan on the wing. We struck at a target the previous flight had found near Khan Kai and had a good mission in decent weather for a change.

An A-26 went in south of the PDJ tonight. They had been working under flares against the side of a mountain and apparently it came up to greet them faster than the pilot thought it would. The crew was pilot Major Jim Sizemore and navigator/bombardier Major Howard Andre, and both had become friends of many of us in the 602nd. The A-26 call sign was Nimrod, and they usually worked east of the base over the Trail but had diverted north tonight because of bad weather in Steel Tiger. Jim Sizemore was probably not familiar with the high terrain of Barrel Roll compared to Steel Tiger. Prior to NKP, he had been an ROTC instructor at Georgia Tech. A-26s were similar to the B-26 of WW II fame and were still doing the job in mid-1969. The losses seemed to go on and on. According to Chris Hobson's book *Vietnam Air Losses,* this was the last A-26 lost in the war.

*

The wing had had a lot of losses since I arrived, and they're all terrible to contemplate. All it took was one bad incident, one small error, and it was over. A man could do everything correctly—except for one small slip-up—or one unfortunate occurrance—such as an engine failure at the wrong time—and it was finished so quickly. It is probable that, except for one incident, each of the pilots who was killed might have led a long and productive life. A pilot could *never* let his guard down, especially while engaging with the enemy in such a hazardous endeavor as flying in combat because it could very quickly lead to a tragedy—permanently. We had to keep our wits about us and *always* be aware of high terrain, especially at night and in clouds. A pilot should never do anything foolish like pressing too low against big guns. Ultimately, we had to hope for the best, because something bad—over which we had no control—might happen at any time. It was a tough business. I tried not to think about it very much.

*

About this time a decision was made to send C-123s, call sign Candlestick, and sometimes C-130s with a call sign of Blind Bat, north to fac for us. They had a pilot and copilot up front with a navigator in the back of the airplane who would lie on the floor by an open door facing aft. He wore a parachute in case he fell out and had an unobstructed view of the ground below. He was equipped with a radio, an intercom, and a starlight scope, which was a new invention that magnified the available light to allow the observer to see much more clearly than he could with the naked eye. The Candles and Bats also carried logs with which to mark the target. They usually flew at 13,000 feet, above the Skyraiders. Their normal mission at night was against trucks on the Trail, but they began to be sent north because the weather over Steel Tiger had been unworkable.

Having Candles and Bats sent to Barrel Roll at night was an answer to my criticism of two months ago regarding the picture targets that had been assigned to Skyraiders. For that reason, they were a major improvement, as they could find picture targets much better than we could. While they did a good job and made things easier for us on the picture target and night reconnaissance missions, they took the fun out of working directly with the ground facs. I had come to take a proprietary interest in those people on the ground and I enjoyed talking with them and helping them out.

July 9, 1969. Wednesday. I was fragged (assigned) to a Candlestick tonight for the first time. Took off at 10:00 p.m. with Jim George on the wing. The weather was poor in the target area and Jim lost his #2 inverter, so we dumped our ordnance and came home.

We have more pilots now, so CTOs have been reinstated, but leaves are still not allowed.

A lot of rain fell today.

*

July 10, 1969. Thursday. I didn't fly and wasn't on the schedule for the first time since May 14 (except for my CTO). Jim George and I managed to get into a touch football game with some of the Nails. I pinched a nerve in my neck when I intercepted a pass and rolled over on the ground.

July 11, 1969. Friday. Took off at 7:25 p.m. with Jack Hudson leading, and he got into an argument with Alleycat over where we were to strike. We finally went to Pogo and had a good mission.

A typhoon off the coast of North Vietnam affected NKP today and the weather was very rough when we returned to the base. My landing was a controlled crash because it was raining too hard for me to see how high I was above the runway, and the windshield wiper wasn't much help. The airmen in the dearming area were soaked.

July 12, 1969. Saturday. We have a lot of pilots now, so I wasn't on the schedule again today.

July 13, 1969. Sunday. Took off at 6:35 p.m. with Major Jim Costin leading on my fiftieth mission. We tried to find a target in the PDJ, but couldn't because of the weather, so we found Candlestick 41 who facced us in on some trees. It was a useless mission. Jim Costin was another delta wing (F-102, F-106) ADC pilot.

July 14, 1969. Monday. Took off at 8:15 p.m. after a forty-five-minute delay because I had an engine sump light in the arming area and had to change airplanes. Rex Huntsman led and we struck with Tiger Mobile. The target area weather was poor but was good everywhere else with no thunderstorms for a change.

After Rex made his strike, it was my turn. As I was pulling off the target on my second pass I decided to drop some CBUs as I was bottoming out. I quickly switched the intervalometer and the rocket/bomb selector switch and pressed the pickle button. By then I had the nose pointed up and was climbing. I was quite surprised to see a rocket go shooting up into the sky. In my haste, I had selected the wrong station on the intervalometer, and instead of being on the station with CBUs, I got one with rockets and away it went. Rather embarrassing, but no harm was done. I won't do that again.

Then I heard on the radio, "Hey, who's shooting at me? Did you do that, Dick?" It was Rex, and the rocket had missed him by not very much as he was in his orbit watching my strike. I almost shot down my leader! How would I ever explain that back at the squadron? Rex never mentioned it again, for which I was glad.

July 15, 1969. Tuesday. Took off at 8:45 p.m., an hour and fifteen minutes late because of weather with Captain J. D. Hall on the wing. We were sent to Blue Moon, but he wasn't home when I called, so we went to Pogo. We hit a troop emplacement at 011/22 in the PDJ and got two secondary fires. The weather was good in the target area.

July 16, 1969. Wednesday. Went to an escape and evasion (E&E) review in the late morning, and played tennis with Jim Monk in the afternoon. Took off at 7:20 p.m. with J. D. Hall on the wing, and we struck at the M in the river in Ban Ban Valley with Candlestick 41. J. D. got a truck with his CBUs, which was unusual.

*

Apollo 11 was launched for the moon today, and I heard it live from Radio Saigon on 540 kilocycles while en route to the target.

A week ago we were fragged for sixteen sorties a day from 7th AF. They were cut to fourteen five days ago, and we'll be at twelve per day as of July 17. But the wing commander still wouldn't approve leaves nor more than two guys on CTO at a time from our squadron. We had six to ten pilots each day on stand by (not flying or duty officer).

July 17, 1969. Thursday. I didn't fly again. Went to a rules of engagement briefing then went into town.

July 18, 1969. Friday. I briefed at 1:00 a.m. but was canceled. I slept late and when I awoke, I was told six inches of rain had fallen in two hours. Wow! That's a lot. I'm sorry I missed it.

I attended a squadron pilot meeting this evening.

July 19, 1969. Saturday. Took off at 2:55 a.m. with Captain Don Combs on the wing. The weather was bad, but we found a hole in the clouds over the PDJ, so I put out a flare. Incredibly, someone shot at it. Don saw where it came from, marked it, and we had our target for the night. It must have been a new guy, because it was a dead giveaway of his position. I bet that's the last flare he ever shot at. My CBUs went right through the area and Don's napes started some secondary fires. Why would anyone shoot at a flare?

left to right, A1C David Chisholm, Captain Don Combs, A1C "Andy" Anderson with their airplane "The Proud American"

I played tennis in the afternoon and then ate at the Thai restaurant.

July 20, 1969. Sunday. Took off at 5:55 p.m. with Jim Monk in the lead. Candlestick 41 helped us hit at Lima Site 108, but the weather was so bad that Jim dropped two napes on each of three passes, and I dropped all my napes on one pass, because I could barely see where the target was. I dropped all my CBUs on the next pass.

July 21, 1969. Monday. Early this morning, I listened in my room to the lunar landing on Radio Saigon. The touchdown was at 3:16 a.m. in Thailand. I waited to listen to the broadcast of Neil Armstrong actually setting foot on the moon, but it was delayed twice and I finally gave up. It was broadcast just after I went to bed. It was very exciting and I was disappointed I missed seeing it live. I saw it a few days later on a delayed broadcast.

I was duty officer in the afternoon.

*

The situation was deteriorating in northern Laos, because the North Vietnamese were pouring troops in. The good guys, with our help, had pretty well beaten the Pathet Lao, but the North Vietnamese sent in 12,000 troops according to the intelligence estimate.

The 602nd was cut back to ten regular missions and two Sandies per day. July 22, 1969. Tuesday. Took off at 10:40 a.m. with Don Combs leading. I was in a G model, #546. A-1Gs didn't have autopilots and parking brakes like A-1Es. I had an engine sump light as I crossed the Mekong, so I declared an emergency, dumped the ordnance, and came back and landed. Since I crossed the river I got credit for a combat mission even though it lasted only thirty-five minutes. That airplane had previously been written up for a sump light—I continued to take them very seriously.

They gave me *another* G and this one worked OK. I took off at 11:40 a.m. and we struck near the caves at Ban Ban. I had my camera along and took pictures. The second flight lasted two and a half hours.

Don Combs en route to Barrel Roll. Don was shot down in this same airplane a few months later.

Night loads were mostly napalm, bombs, CBUs, and rockets, and the day load for a strike mission was mostly 500-pound hard bombs, CBUs, and rockets. The guys had been teasing me that when I'd get back to days I would be off target with hard bombs, but I hit right on the target.

In the last three weeks, four or five airplanes and three pilots haven't returned because they were strafing too low. One guy who was lost had been warned about it. His response was, "Yeah, but it's fun." It may have been fun, but it was also very dangerous. It was easy to get caught up in the heat of the battle and to press in and forget about minimum altitudes. It was also easy to sit in a briefing room and say, "don't go so low," but it was hard to back off in the cockpit while in a battle. The target would be visible and it was easy to keep pressing because there it was, and the pilot would feel safe and invincible. But he *had* to fight off that feeling. Because of the recent losses, the wing commander issued a new restriction—a minimun altitude of 3,000 feet above the terrain on any pass.

*

July 24, 1969. Thursday. Took off at 1:40 a.m. in aircraft #070 with Don Combs on the wing. We struck with a C-130 Blind Bat near the Birdshead where the eastbound road turns south east of Ban Ban. The weather wasn't very good, but it was an easy mission and we were back in less than three hours.

More rain. The roof of my room had a leak, so we called a repairman.

The NVA are continuing to pour into Laos and will probably win the war. General Vang Pao's troops beat the Pathet Lao, but they won't beat the North Vietnamese Army.

*

I had another takeoff scheduled for 11:30 p.m., but it was canceled after a two-hour delay because of weather in Barrel Roll. I was the flight lead with First Lieutenant Noel Frisbie getting his night check ride on the wing with Jack Hudson in the right seat. While we were waiting in the airplanes for the weather to improve, Someone decided it would be a good idea to send us to Steel Tiger because the weather was better. As the flight leader I objected because I hadn't been to Steel Tiger and over the Ho Chi Minh Trail at night, because we had briefed for a Barrel Roll mission, because we had a Barrel Roll weapons load that was different from a Steel Tiger load, and because the tactics and hazards were different. The command post duty officer ultimately agreed with me and canceled the mission. It was the reverse of what might have happened to Jim Sizemore on July 8 and a good way to get Trouble to rear its ugly head.

As of today we've already had forty-two inches of rain in July. The all-time record for any month was fifty inches in August. Normal for July was eighteen inches and twenty inches was the August average. Ten inches fell on one day this month and nine inches on another.

July 25, 1969. Friday. I attended a commander's call this afternoon and was scheduled for an 11:30 p.m. takeoff but was canceled again because of target weather.

July 26, 1969. Saturday. I awoke about noon to the sound of someone pounding on my door. I struggled out of bed to find Bob Bohan, who wanted to play tennis. So he and I went over to the courts and played for two hours in the midday sun.

I ate kobe steak at the Thai Restaurant on the base this evening with Jim George, then briefed and took off at 11:30 p.m. with Jim in the lead. We struck at some nape fires from an earlier mission along Route 4 east of the PDJ in poor weather and got a secondary fire. We were glad to get rid of the ordnance and go home because the weather was so bad.

July 27, 1969. Sunday. I went to church with three other guys from the squadron this afternoon.

Took off at 11:30 again. I was in the lead with Noel Frisbie still trying to get his night check ride with Jack Hudson. The weather was bad again with an overcast of about 7,500 feet MSL in the PDJ. I went down to 7,000 feet, where I could see the ground, pipped out a flare, and saw a road I recognized as Route 71. Anything in the area was fair game to hit, but we were too low to dive bomb—especially at night. Since not much was going on in Barrel Roll and we needed to get rid of our ordnance, we just dropped it by level bombing and went home. We weren't very accurate. This was my sixtieth mission.

I received a letter from home today postmarked July 20. That was pretty slow service. My mother included a newspaper clipping from *The Chicago Tribune* about the North Vietnamese invasion of Laos, which said they had brought sixty tanks into Laos. Our intelligence said it was more likely twenty. They were suspected to have been stored in the northern PDJ, which has a lot of hills and valleys in which to hide things.

*

NKP A-1 pilots felt we had a severe lack of publicity on the home front for what we were doing in Laos compared to the jet guys. The Seventh Air Force newspaper very seldom mentioned anything about A-1s or our work, but it seemed like each issue had at least one article about F-100s at Tuy Hua or Phan Rang "killing one hundred enemy and damaging one hundred meters of trench," while we got no recognition. The reason, of course, was the political situation didn't allow our activities in Laos to be acknowledged. It was a constant source of irritation to A-1 pilots, because it was like we didn't count.

The newspaper article from home told of an F-105 going down in northern Laos—which I remembered—when the pilot just rode it in north of Ban Ban along Route 61. An F-4 crash was also written about—which I didn't remember—but in that time period we lost at least four A-1s, and nothing was said about them.

*

I found out Jim Beggerly and I were recommended for a Silver Star for the May 21 mission. I thought it was a cinch because a letter accompanying the recommendation was written by a major general who stated that we had saved the outpost.

*

Ubon was attacked this evening. An American security man and his dog were both shot and injured and two airplanes were damaged. At NKP we wondered why the bad guys didn't target us, as it seemed we were quite vulnerable and not very far from the enemy.

*

Rest and relaxation assignments were decided by the length of time a GI had been in the combat zone. Locations included Hawaii, Hong Kong, Japan, the Philippines, Malaysia, Australia, Taiwan, and Bangkok. Everyone leaving for R&R at a particular time bid for destinations, and the guys with the most time got to pick first, so it was advantageous to take R&R later in one's tour of duty. We were guaranteed a certain number of days at the R&R spot plus travel time. The farther away the R&R location (like Hawaii), the more travel time was allowed.

*

Emily left Bangkok about 6:30 p.m. on a train for an overnight trip to Nong Khai, which is a few miles north of Udorn and about 300 miles north of Bangkok. She had a first class sleeper coach. At one point in the night, she was awakened by the car swaying back and forth on a rough road bed. The train slowed nearly to a stop. The car was not air-conditioned, but it did have shutters. She could hear crickets chirping just outside her window and branches of trees scraping along both sides of her rail car.

On the train she met some Americans. One was a USAID employee stationed in Vientiane who had his family with him, and another was stationed in Luang Prabang. Yet another was the public relations director for Air America who lived in Taiwan and who traveled around this part of the world quite a bit as part of his job. The Air America man asked about me, recruiting for a job when I got out of the air force, as they liked ex-military pilots. Emily suggested we use that as a last resort if I can't get a job anywhere else. The pay was good, but the risks were high. An Air America job would mean coming right back to Laos, which wasn't very high on my career list of things to do.

*

Took off at 11:30 p.m. with Noel Frisbie on the wing. We struck at the junction of Routes 4 and 5 in the PDJ. The weather was good at first, but it deteriorated as we were working. My call sign was Firefly 42 and I was in aircraft #713. The mission lasted three hours and twenty minutes.

I've had twenty-one missions in the month of July, more than anyone else in the squadron, which was an advantage for me to get off the schedule for Emily's visit.

July 29, 1969. Tuesday. Emily arrived in Nong Khai a little after dawn on July 29 and took a taxi to the Mekong. Since there were no bridges, she took a river taxi—similar to a dugout canoe with a motor on the back—to Laos. The USAID guy rode with her and had a car waiting for him across the river, so he gave her a ride into Vientiane and showed her around town. She discovered Vientiane was a good place to buy jewelry and found an 18-carat gold bracelet for $137 that she really liked. It had excellent workmanship, and the price was determined solely by the weight.

The city looked run down, but the French architectural influence was very apparent. It was easy to see it had been quite an attractive city in its day.

She spent the rest of the day in Vientiane and rented a hotel room for the night. The building was not very modern but was well kept, and the food was good. The Lao currency was kip, worth about 500 to a dollar. The Laotian people she met were as anxious to get Thai baht as the Thais were to get dollars, because baht were much more valuable to the Laotians than kip.

While in Vientiane, Emily met a family of four Americans—a husband and wife and two children—who lived some miles north of the city and whose house had been attacked by the Pathet Lao. They hid in the basement for six hours while the enemy made themselves at home, rummaging through their belongings, eating their food, and stealing things.

Emily took a cab back to the river taxi terminal. She was very concerned the border police would not allow her to reenter Thailand, but she had no problem, and went directly to Nong Khai airport for the flight to NKP.

Nong Khai was a large town with no paved streets, no hotels, no restaurants, and no sidewalks. It had very little of what we westerners have come to expect in a city.

The entire trip, first class overnight sleeper on the train from Bangkok to Nong Khai, Thai Airways from Nong Khai to NKP, and the flight back to Bangkok cost forty-five dollars.

For Emily's visit to NKP, I planned for her to stay at a hotel in town. In order for me to stay overnight, I had to have a pass signed by the base commander, and I didn't find out until the day before that the request needed to be submitted a week in advance. I decided to try to get it signed that day and personally walked it to the base commander for his signature.

I didn't fly today because of bad weather. Jim George, Rex Huntsman, and I went to a movie on base this evening.

July 30, 1969. Wednesday. Emily's flight from Udorn arrived about 12:25 p.m. The airplane was an ancient DC-3, and the airport runway was a grass strip in the town of Nakhon Phanom. We got a room at the Nakhon Phanom Hotel, which had opened only two weeks earlier. It was quite nice, especially for NKP.

We bought some clothes from an Indian tailor, who gave us a guided tour of the town in his BMW. The city was bigger than I thought. It was the location of the provincial jail and had a slaughterhouse, among other things.

I didn't fly today because of Emily's visit and because I've already flown so many missions in July.

July 31, 1969. Thursday. Emily and I went to the base and I took her to my hooch room. A lot of the guys were around, so I introduced her to everyone. A lot more people than usual were in my room today. We ate supper at the Thai Restaurant on base and again spent the night in town.

August 1, 1969. Friday. At least three restaurants in town were suitable for Americans. We walked in a little park on a bluff above the river and saw a guard supervising convicts who were working on something in the water. We could see a rainstorm coming, so we looked for shelter and found the lobby of a hotel. While waiting out the rain shower, we met an American woman from Alabama with her six-year-old child. The husband and father was a civilian engineer for a company doing contract work on the base. She was in the midst of a year of living in the hotel.

I had had two nights off the schedule, and it was time to go back to work. I took off at 11:35 p.m. The weather was the best I've seen in quite a while in the PDJ. First Lieutenant Jim Herrick and J. D. Hall were on the wing. We had to wait for a flight ahead of us to get off the target, then we struck with a Blind Bat at 050/33 from 113. This mission lasted three hours and forty-five minutes.

August 2, 1969. Saturday. I went into town about noon to get Emily and we ate at the Nakorn Room Restaurant.

Took off at 11:40 p.m. with First Lieutenant Jim Matthews and Rich Hall on the wing. We flew around Barrel Roll for a long time and finally dumped our ordnance in the PDJ because the weather was bad and we didn't have much of a target. I was Firefly 42 and flew aircraft #593.

August 3, 1969. Sunday. I slept for about an hour, then got up to go to town early, but I had to wait until 8:00 a.m. to leave the base. On Sunday the Thai Airways flight to Bangkok left from the base, so after breakfast Emily and I went to the airline office in town for a ride. The van was too crowded to include me, so I took a taxi. After Emily's flight left, I went back to bed.

*

Took off at 11:20 p.m. with Jim Matthews and Jon Ewing on the wing. The Blind Bat wasn't available tonight, so after holding for quite a while, I got to do my own faccing with Pogo. We got ten secondary fires including three big ones that were burning vigorously when we left. I don't know what it was that could have burned like that, but it wasn't brush.

August 4, 1969. Monday. I worked on disaster control and mobility in the afternoon and watched the film of the moon landing on TV. I was scheduled for an 11:30 p.m. takeoff again, but we canceled after engine start because of local weather.

I was also canceled on August 5, 6, and 7 due to weather. This has been a dull week, because of not much flying. I played tennis the afternoon of August 7. I went to the map room to make up my own personal chart of the target area.

Cancellations typically occurred around 11:00 p.m. to midnight, and I was ready to fly a four-hour mission when the flight was scrubbed, so I wasn't ready for bed. My wingman and I weren't the only ones whose flights were canceled on these evenings, so frequently we had a crowd of pilots late at night with nothing much to do. The Officers' Club had a basement room called The Hole, which was a natural gathering spot for socializing. It was a good opportunity to talk to pilots from other squadrons, drink beer, roll dice, and throw glasses against the concrete wall to watch them shatter. Officers who weren't flying combat missions were not well accepted in The Hole at times like that.

Jim George managed to get into a few poker games and did quite well. He lived on his poker winnings and sent his paycheck home to his wife. He said, "Those guys are so easy." I knew better than to try to play poker, as I had had some expensive lessons while on alert at Dover.

Chapter 9

IP

Northeastern Laos is a pretty big place, and most of our targets were pinpoint locations that had to be found either as coordinates or from a ground fac whose location was given when we checked in with Alleycat. If we knew where we were going at the time of briefing, we could locate the target on a map and get a heading from a prominent landmark such as the bend in the river.

Once in the area of a prebriefed picture target on a moonless night, we needed to drop a flare to find a landmark. Ethan, the EC-121 radar picket ship, could orient a pilot if all else failed. Ethan also monitored our location to let us know if we strayed over North Vietnam. The 1969 rules of engagement forbade that.

If I was assigned to a ground fac, I'd fly to approximately where I thought he should be and call him on the assigned VHF radio frequency. If it was Pogo, for example, the conversation might go like this:

"Pogo, do you hear my airplane?"

If he did, he'd say, "Charlie charlie, I hear your airplane." We usually had our lights out, so the only way he could determine if we were near was by hearing our engines. For some reason, charlie charlie meant yes.

"Turn on your light so I can see your location." If I could see the light I'd acknowledge it and ask, "Where is the target?"

"Three klicks east." So I would go over there and put out a flare. Pogo might say, "Target 500 meters north of your flare." I'd go 500 meters north and pop out another.

"OK, Pogo, is the target under the flare?"

"Charlie charlie, you hit under the flare." I would put a nape down and he might say, "Target is one hundred meters northwest."

If I were out of flares, I'd have the wingman come over and pop one out. Then I'd say, "Where is the target from this flare?"

"Target under the flare." I would drop another nape.

Pogo might say, "Very good! You number one pilot, that's where the target is!" I was cleared to deliver the rest of my ordnance.

*

August 8, 1969. Friday. I took off at 6:15 p.m. and was about forty miles up the river when my wingman had runaway nose down trim, so we aborted the mission and RTBd. I held for an hour west of the base to burn off fuel and then landed a very heavy airplane.

August 9, 1969. Saturday. I took off at 11:55 p.m., twenty-five minutes late because my airplane had low air pressure in the canopy bottle. The weather was bad in the target area again, so we dumped some of the ordnance in the PDJ at 042/23. We started up Route 61 to Sam Neua but came back because we were getting too low on fuel to go so far. This was a worthless mission. I don't understand why we were sent out in such crummy weather.

An F-4 Tiger fac went down late this afternoon along Route 13, which runs from Vientiane to Luang Prabang. Both guys were talking on their survival radios and were doing OK. Sandies and Jollies went out to get them first thing in the morning loaded for a fight because they didn't know what to expect in that area.

*

Five Zorros had their last missions tonight, including Major John Williams, who was in my class at Hurlburt and who was going to a desk job in Saigon. Lieutenant Colonel Brink was going to Udorn to be a detachment commander in T-28s. The other three were going home including Bob Keith, whom I knew when he flew F-101s at Suffolk County, New York, when I was at Dover.

August 10, 1969. Sunday. The F-4 guys who went down yesterday were picked up this morning and taken to Udorn, their home base. They weren't too far from home, but were in an unfriendly place.

Took off at 11:35 p.m. with Captain Russ Keeling leading. We drove around for a while and finally struck with Blind Bat 02 near the Birdshead. The wind was easterly, and I was striking from west to east, so I was short with my napes until the last one, which I put it right where I wanted and started a big fire. I don't know what it was, but it was a nice blaze. We didn't see any ground fire.

August 12, 1969. Tuesday. My missions of last night and again tonight were canceled because of target weather.

The air force continually instilled safe practices in pilots and crews. Part of that effort was training to exit the airplane as quickly as possible—called emergency egress. Today I went to the flight line with my parachute, helmet, and survival vest and practiced emergency egress. I completely strapped in to the airplane wearing all my gear as if I were going on a mission, and at a signal, I unstrapped my seat belt and parachute harness, removed my helmet and oxygen mask, and got out of the airplane as quickly as I could. I did it in nine seconds.

*

Ban Ban is at the junction of Route 61, which runs north to Sam Neua, and Route 7, which starts a little north of Vinh, on the coast of North Vietnam, to

Khan Kai, in the northeast part of the PDJ. Khan Kai is in the area of the Roadrunner and Arrowhead Lakes, and the Arrowhead Lake points right to Khan Kai from the south. Roadrunner Lake is just north of Arrowhead Lake. It was a hot area with 37mm guns that we had to avoid in the daytime. The enemy also had big guns near the Birdshead.

Roadrunner Lake in the northeast PDJ

Arrowhead Lake

August 13, 1969. Wednesday. I played tennis for two hours this afternoon then took off at 11:35 p.m. with Jim George on the wing and flew around quite awhile before we finally got assigned to Red Hat. We had a good mission even though Red Hat wasn't too sure where the target was. The weather was better than it had been lately.
August 14, 1969. Thursday. The base disaster control people visited the squadron for an inspection this afternoon and went away happy. I went into town with Jim Herrick. Played a set of tennis with Colonel Stueck, who won 8-7. Then Jim George and Russ Keeling joined us for doubles.
August 15, 1969. Friday. I was squadron duty officer at 7:00 a.m. today. The job involved answering the phone and taking care of whatever problems might come up.

I went to the base control tower this afternoon to be mobile control officer.

The flying schedule was still slow because of the cutback last month, but we were scheduled to soon be back to sixteen sorties plus two Sandies.
August 16, 1969. Saturday. Took off at 6:30 p.m., fifteen minutes late because the internal fuel tank wasn't full when I arrived at the airplane. Captain Stu Bischoff led and we struck a fragged target with Candlestick 41.

*

The dates of the Woodstock music festival in upstate New York were August 15-18, 1969. I didn't know of it until many years later and I doubt if any of my contemporaries were aware of it because we were in an isolated environment regarding certain news stories and I don't think *Stars and Stripes* covered it. From what I've heard, it was an important event in the anti-war movement with a lot of protest songs and illegal drugs. "Meanwhile," quoting Richard K. Kolb in the September, 2009, issue of *VFW Magazine*, "8,429 miles around the other side of the world, 514,000 mostly young Americans were authentically serving the country that had raised them to place society over self." According to the VFW, 109 Americans died in Vietnam during those four days.

*

Ordnance and fuel were trucked in to the base. The rail line stopped fifty miles away, so everything that wasn't airlifted was brought in by truck from Bangkok, which helped the Thai economy by keeping the truckers and associated industries in business.
August 18, 1969. Monday. Took off at 6:05 p.m. with Lieutenant Colonel Tomlinson leading. We armed reccied Routes 4 and 7 west of Lima Site 108

with no luck and then went to about a half mile east of Khan Kai (just east of Roadrunner Lake) for a strike. Colonel Tomlinson's UHF receiver didn't work, so I facced in Ketchup—a flight of two F-4s. We had a good mission and left some secondary fires burning. This was my seventieth mission, and it lasted four hours and fifteen minutes.

Raven 46, a pilot named Dan Davis, went down in Barrel Roll today.

I heard the Johnny Cash song "A Boy Named Sue" over the ADF radio while taxiing out for takeoff a couple of nights ago and had a good laugh.

The air force had a buffer zone ten miles from the North Vietnamese border. Ethan called three times on this mission to tell me I was in the buffer zone and I'd better go west. It would be nice if someone put a row of bright lights along the border.

August 19, 1969. Tuesday. I've been on the schedule every day so far this month, but have only flown eight missions because of weather cancellations.

*

My third CTO began today, and I left on the afternoon C-130 flight, which was late, to Bangkok. I arrived at the apartment at 11:20 p.m.

August 20, 1969. Wednesday. The apartment, on the sixth floor of Embassy Place, was new to me because, even though I was present when Emily rented it, construction wasn't complete. So I really enjoyed settling in. It had big windows looking east and north with a small walkout balcony on the east side. It was fully furnished, had two bedrooms, hardwood floors, and a small kitchen. We frequently had the windows open wide to take advantage of the beautiful weather.

The Two Vikings Restaurant featured smorgasbord on Wednesday nights, so we went there for supper.

August 21, 1969. Thursday. The United States military had a large enough presence in Bangkok for the army to have a base exchange, so Emily and I went there today.

August 22, 1969. Friday. We went to Ploenchit Shopping Center and then to a store called Star of Siam to look at dinnerware. For supper, Emily prepared a local fish called pla krapong, which resembles red snapper. She bought the fish and fresh vegetables at a supermarket across the street from the entrance to Embassy Place.

August 23, 1969. Saturday. Whenever we went to Bangkok on CTOs, we were responsible for making sure we got back on time. If the afternoon C-130 flight was full, as it frequently was, we had to go on the morning flight even though it was a CTO day we were supposed to enjoy.

The air force had recently instituted a new check in location for the flights in downtown Bangkok, which was very convenient. I had to be there at 5:20 a.m. for the 7:00 a.m. departure from Don Muang, and the bus took us right to the door of the airplane. The report time for the flight was so early that I decided to stay up all night and sleep when I got back to NKP.

*

August 24, 1969. Sunday. The weather had been hot. I took off at 10:00 a.m. with Noel Frisbie leading, and we hit a troop concentration with Raven 41 faccing. My plane was an E model and I was pretty accurate with my bombs. This mission was short, lasting only two hours and thirty minutes.
August 25, 1969. Monday. An F-105 was lost in Barrel Roll today thirty miles east of the PDJ, and the pilot was killed.

*

Normally, my physical activity consisted of playing tennis and walking. Only the commanders had Jeeps and the rest of us had to ride the bus, which made a regular circuit on the base, or walk. Toward the end of summer, Someone decided it would be a good idea to see what kind of shape we were in by having us run a mile and a half in twelve minutes. I wasn't fat and I wasn't out of shape, but I wasn't in condition to run a mile and a half in twelve minutes, either.

Late in the afternoon today we all dutifully lined up and at the signal, took off. I thought I was going to die. I made it, thanks to Russ Keeling's watch running slowly at the end. Those who failed to run fast enough had to eat at the fat table and do extra conditioning even if they weren't overweight and were in reasonably good condition. Curiously, I didn't see any one above the rank of captain out running, even though some of our majors could have used some time at the fat table.

*

I was scheduled to get my instructor pilot check out this afternoon, but no airplane was available.

I looked forward to the night's mission because the weather was clear and the moon was full. The airplane I was assigned this evening didn't have a brake lock, so I had to hold my feet on the brake pedals while the armers were doing their job at the end of the runway. Because of the run, my leg muscles were so unsteady I could barely control them. My feet were dancing on the brakes like a person's chin chatters out of control when he is so cold he gets the chills. It wasn't very safe.

Took off at 10:55 p.m. with Captain Dick Walter on the wing. We followed Candlestick 45 around for a while, then held, and eventually struck a ford at the M in the river to make it unusable. The problem was we had the wrong ordnance to try to knock it out. We had napalm, when 500-pound bombs were needed for that kind of job, because napalm doesn't make a crater like a bomb does. We each had two 500-pounders, but we needed more than that to knock out a ford. Why wasn't that mission assigned to fast movers in the daytime? This was another wasted effort.

My UHF receiver was intermittent. The weather was good in the target area and it was really nice working at night under a full moon—it was almost as bright as day. The base had a storm while we were gone, but the weather was nice where we were.

August 26, 1969. Tuesday. Took off at 10:55 p.m. with Noel Frisbie on his first mission as a night leader. We struck with Blind Bat 01 northeast of the PDJ in marginal weather. Noel struck first, which was normal, but he did it with his lights on, which wasn't. I didn't say anything to him because I thought we were in a relatively safe area and nothing much was happening. I planned to talk to him quietly in the TUOC bus about it after landing.

When it was my turn, I made four passes with my lights out and had a good mission, putting my napes right on the target. As I pulled up from my fourth pass, Fris asked me to turn on my lights so he could see where I was, so I did. As I climbed through 9,000 feet, a gomer shot at me with a 12.7mm gun! If I had had any ordnance left, I'd have gone after it. He must have been counting airplanes and passes and had been waiting until I was on my last pass. When I turned on my lights, it was a chance to shoot safely, so he did. I turned out of the way and no harm was done, but it demonstrated bad guys are all over the place. I was surprised at the brazenness of daring to shoot at a Skyraider with a little 12.7. Maybe he just wanted to make a point.

*

August 27, 1969. Wednesday. Ordnance had pins to prevent it from being inadvertently fired or dropped while on the ground, and one of the last stops before takeoff was the arming area next to the end of the runway to have the pins pulled. The first stop after landing was in the dearming area, so pins could be placed in any left-over ordnance. It was a dangerous job because something might fall off the airplane or a gun might fire at just the wrong time, and the armers and dearmers had to be careful to not walk into the whirling propeller. They were out in all weather, from the burning sun of the hot season, to the torrential rains of the monsoon, to the middle of the night when visibility was poor.

In order to make sure the pilot was not doing something to injure the armers, we were required to keep our hands in full view of those on the ground at all times when they were doing their thing. We had to keep our hands on the glare shield or on the canopy rail until they signaled their job was complete. Once the airplane was armed, we were required to maneuver in such a way as to keep the nose pointed away from the area of the base where people were, just in case a gun should fire or a rocket go off at the wrong time. It was similar to the most basic rule of handling a gun: Never point it at anything you don't plan to shoot.

My friend Doug Scroggs's job on the base was weapons loader and armer/dearmer. His wife, Bonnie, had come to Bangkok to live for several months just like Emily was doing. Embassy Place had two towers, and she rented an apartment in the one opposite Emily's. When I called Emily just before briefing this morning, Bonnie was visiting, and she answered the phone.

I received my instructor pilot check out this afternoon with Rich Hall in the left seat. Since we were going on a local training flight, the airplane had no ordnance. As we passed the arming area at the end of the runway I spotted Doug and motioned him over to talk. He was wearing an intercom earphone that he plugged into a communications receptacle, and I told him I had just talked to Bonnie. Doug was a quiet guy who seemed to be intimidated by the officer/enlisted man gulf. He thanked me for telling him.

Rich and I were scheduled to fly awhile and it was a good excuse to have some fun, since we had an airplane full of fuel and no ordnance, and maybe I could practice some right seat landings. But the carburetor temperature went up immediately after takeoff, so we went to a right downwind pattern and landed. We were airborne less than five minutes, but it was called a successful IP check because I was just required to demonstrate I could takeoff and land safely from the right seat. Some check out!

*

One day Rich was flying in his A-1 and decided to take on the enemy with his .38 caliber pistol. He shot out of the cockpit, aiming forward of the wing at whatever target suited him. He failed to account for the 150-knot wind caused by the speed of the airplane and how it would affect the trajectory of the bullets, and he shot holes in the top of the wing. I'm not sure how he explained that when he got back, but I'm glad I didn't have to.

*

Instructor pilot was not the most desired of duties for several reasons, most of them hazardous. The right seat didn't have a sight for ordnance delivery, so the IP had no control over accuracy. It was so much easier to do it yourself.

The IP flew with pilots with varying degrees of experience, so he had to be alert for the unexpected, which was not a comforting thought over enemy territory. He was along to answer questions and to prevent the new pilot from doing anything stupid until he had a chance to get thoroughly acquainted with the job.

Two-seat A-1Es and A-1Gs, sometimes called fat faces, presented a unique hazard for those, such as an IP, who found it necessary to get in and out of the right side. The engine constantly leaked oil that streamed back in the airflow over the fuselage and the top of the right wing, causing it to become slippery, and the handholds were oil covered and slick. It made the trip from the ground to the cockpit and back with a full load of parachute, helmet, vest, and personal survival gear in the night lights a bit of an adventure in itself. A right seat rider had to climb up and walk about three steps uphill on the wing to get into his seat. The oil was dirty and if the pilot was careless and rubbed any part of his personal equipment or clothes against the side of the airplane, he was going to end up with dirty oil on whatever he touched.

A slip could be dangerous and painful, as Don Combs found out when he fell off an oily wing and landed on his tailbone one night. The distance from the trailing edge of the wing to the ground was about thirty-three inches, enough for a nasty fall while carrying a lot of extra gear.

A more appropriate term than instructor pilot would have been safety observer. Passes were made whenever the left seater was ready, not when the IP was ready. Accuracy was the left seater's responsibility, not the IP's. He didn't even have a way to gauge how accurately the ordnance had been delivered, because he was not in position to see while pulling out. The only controls on the right side of the cockpit were a stick, rudder pedals, and a throttle.

So while on the attack, the IP was not much more than a captive passenger who could do little more than pull back on the stick if the left seater was beginning to press the attack too much.

It wasn't fun, whether over mountainous terrain or guns, to ride along on a 40° dive bombing pass at night. At least if I were in the left seat or a single-seater, I had the intensity of the business at hand to keep my mind off the hazards. It was like being on a gigantic roller coaster with someone shooting at you, never knowing if the wheels were going to fall off or if it was going to blow up at any moment.

I was not given a choice of being an IP. Having flown another airplane before coming to the A-1, I was a comparatively experienced pilot and was expected to assist in checking out new guys. It would have been a little easier to swallow if the air force paid me more to do it, but the only reward was a minimum of prestige and a maximum of exposure.

*

A standing joke about the R3350 engine was when an airplane returned from a long mission, the pilot would say to the crew chief, "Fill the oil and check the gas." With extra fuel in a stub tank, the airplane was capable of flying for seven hours, and several pilots flew specialized operations missions that long.

*

August 28, 1969. Thursday. Took off at 6:35 p.m. in aircraft #593, call sign Firefly 41, with Jim Herrick who had recently checked out as a flight leader. We struck with Candlestick 41 at 010/24 in good weather. This mission lasted only three hours and five minutes. When we got back to the hooch, Jim and I played ping pong until we were thoroughly hot and sweaty.

August 29, 1969. Friday. Took off at 6:35 p.m. with Jim Anderson along for another ride in the right seat and Jim Herrick leading. A Candlestick fac had found a target for us on Route 61 halfway between Ban Ban and Sam Neua, but by the time Jim had finished his strike, I had only about three minutes to make four passes at the target because a deck of clouds was moving in, a flight of F-4s was ready to go, and we had to get out of their way. On the last pass, I didn't even see the target when I rolled in, but I knew where it was supposed to be. I picked it up as I got below a cloud deck, made a quick right turn and put some CBUs on it. I don't think we did much good, but a secondary fire was blazing when we left. A big moon provided good illumination.

The Officers' Club had an enjoyable show after we landed.

*

August 30, 1969. Saturday. In northern Laos, the good guys were pushing the bad guys back and we had a couple of theories as to why: First, floods in North Vietnam were causing transportation problems, and second, the roads in North Vietnam were muddy and the troops were hungry.

The good guys owned the southern third of the PDJ for the first time since 1964, which was a big change from a couple of weeks ago.

I took off at 6:30 p.m. with Tony Wylie on the wing. I was Firefly 40 in aircraft #713. We were sent north of Ban Ban and then rerouted back to 035/24 in the PDJ where Poppy had some trucks spotted. Unfortunately, he had north and south confused and I expended all my flares before we had that matter cleared up. I could see lights on the ground, and when I mentioned it on the radio, an American spoke up and said he had good guys "all over the place" and not to hit their flashlights. He said, "If you see a lot of lights on the ground, that's us. Don't hit us." I was surprised at how well I could see flashlights from the air.

Yesterday, one flight had killed three friendlies and another flight killed five, and they were pretty upset. I wasn't about to hit something unless I knew exactly what it was. Meanwhile, Poppy had trucks spotted—and his directions confused. We had a full load of ordnance ready to go near where Routes 4 and 7 junction.

Just before the moon came up, I ran out of flares, but I could see the road and an east-west runway just south of it and another road just south of that. Tony said he could see a couple of trucks. Finally I saw the lights of one, so I armed up a 500-pound bomb, rolled in, and put it in the middle of the road, cratering it. The truck had been traveling east and I put the bomb right in front of him so he couldn't go anywhere. He stopped, turned his lights out and I lost track of him.

Poppy said, "He's stopped," and tried to tell me where he was, and I went in on another pass. He said, "Very good bomb, but you didn't hit him." AHHHH!

I saw marks on the ground to use as reference points, but I was still having a hard time seeing the target and difficulty communicating with Poppy. I was bombing blindly from the marks. Poppy said, "He's going back the other way!" So I dropped a couple of bombs and rockets to the west and still didn't get anything.

By now I was out of ordnance, and it was Tony's turn. Unfortunately, he didn't have flares, and couldn't see much either. While he was striking, I called Alleycat and told him we had a target, but were out of flares, almost out of ordnance, and needed some more airplanes. Another flight of A-1s was on its way with flares, so Alleycat sent them to us. I briefed the leader about the situation and they took over as we left to RTB. They got two of the trucks and facced in a flight of F-4s who got two more. Eventually, five of the ten trucks were destroyed. I did the groundwork locating the target, and the other guys got the trucks. That's teamwork. We did it all in three hours and thirty minutes.

Part of the problem on this mission was that we had hard bombs instead of napalm that would have burned and given me a reference.

August 31, 1969. Sunday. Russ Keeling and I played tennis in the afternoon and then went to church before briefing for my mission.

Took off at 10:55 p.m. with Jim Matthews leading. We followed Blind Bat 05 around the PDJ while he tried to get a target from Poppy. We were near last night's strike, and finally Poppy found a truck for us, but we were too low on gas to stick around and get it. This mission lasted four hours and forty minutes.

September 1, 1969. Monday. Took off at 10:45 p.m. with First Lieutenant Daryl Heusinkveld on the wing. (Daryl was frequently called Hoisy.) We flew around with Candlestick 45 for quite a while until we got a call that Red Tiger had a gun shooting at him, so we turned south toward his position. On the way, I saw the flash of a gun that Hoisy and the Candle also saw, but due to the limitations of dead reckoning navigation at night, none of us thought we were in Red Tiger's area yet, so we let it go. It turned out to be the gun we were looking for, but by the time we were aware of that, we lost its location. I requested from the Candle permission to fac for myself and he said yes. I asked him for flare support, which worked well. We hunted and hunted with Red Tiger for the target and were really frustrated by our inability to find it.

The ground facs were handicapped by language differences and by their different perception of location and terrain features compared to what we could see from above.

Today was Labor Day at home.

September 2, 1969. Tuesday. Jon Ewing and Rich Hall had their last flights and party tonight, which I had to miss because I had a 6:35 p.m. takeoff with Hoisy leading. We struck with Hilltop near where we were last night with Candlestick 41 flaring. The weather was poor because a monsoon off the coast of North Vietnam was affecting NKP. It brought almost constant rain the last couple of days.

At this time, the good guys owned almost all the PDJ.

We had a hard time determining how much damage we were inflicting on the bad guys, but we probably zapped a lot of them. Every once in a while, we would get an intelligence report from different sources, including Raven facs, telling us we were doing serious damage to the gomers with our night attacks.

*

The local NKP radio was Armed Forces Thailand Network (AFTN). The signal was strong enough to be received only within about five miles of the base, so often I'd listen to it on the ADF while taxiing out. Then I'd switch to Radio Saigon while en route to the target area and back to the local station after landing.

Ho Chi Minh died today.

*

I was assigned to Sandy duty September 4, so I turned my schedule around from nights to be ready to go at 4:30 a.m. Pilots on the first day of Sandy duty were Sandy Five and Six and were on a forty-five minute ready schedule. The second day was a fifteen minute day, with call signs Sandy Three and Four, and pilots on the third day were Sandy One and Two. We pulled alert with the Jolly Green Giant helicopter crews and the staging area was known as Jolly Ops. The building had bunks, but there was normally too much activity for sleep.

September 4, 1969. Thursday. Jim Monk was Sandy Five today and I was Sandy Six. We were scrambled off at 3:50 p.m. for a SAR in Barrel Roll. The downed pilot was a Laotian who was picked up before we arrived in the area. We went into an orbit over the PDJ where I saw cattle. They belonged to the good guys now, but if they were bad cattle we could have shot them because the bad guys kept their food on the hoof. They must have left in a big hurry to leave their cattle behind.

A little before dark, we were sent to work with a Raven, but my ordnance wouldn't release. I went to an ordnance dump area and got it off by pulling the jettison cables. I was finally released from duty at 8:30 p.m. This was my eightieth mission.

September 5, 1969. Friday. Sandy alert again today. Jim Monk was Sandy Three and I was Sandy Four. We took off at 3:15 p.m. for our orbit over northern Laos. We flew cover for an exfiltration, or exfil, near the junction of Routes 7 and 71 and then struck with Blue Moon just before dark. The weather was good over the PDJ, and I got to see territory I hadn't seen much of because I flew so many nights. This mission lasted five hours and twenty minutes, so it was about 10:00 p.m. before I got back to the hooch.

September 6, 1969. Saturday. I was Sandy Two all day, but we didn't fly.

September 7, 1969. Sunday. I went to church in the morning then took off at 6:35 p.m. in aircraft #546 with the call sign Firefly 41 for my first ride in the right seat as an IP. Stu Bischoff led, and we struck with Lobo southeast of the PDJ. Lobo said we had twenty KBA.

Senator Everett Dirksen died today.

September 8, 1969. Monday. Took off at 6:40 p.m. in a real dog of an E model in the right seat again with First Lieutenant Larry Dannelly in the left seat and Dick Walter leading. We tried to strike with Black Lion, but the weather deteriorated, so we brought everything back.

September 9, 1969. Tuesday. I took off at 10:35 p.m., twenty-five minutes late because an F-4 arrived with battle damage, took the barrier, and closed the runway. I was the leader tonight and Frank Monroe and Don Combs were on the wing. We had a flight of F-4s to fac in on a picture target storage area south of the Birdshead. I had only two flares, and the target was in a remote area far from obvious landmarks for dead reckon navigation with no moonlight, so I had a hard time finding it. Fortunately, the F-4s had inertial navigation system (INS); they could also receive the tacan signal at their higher altitude and had flares of their own, so they could almost do their own faccing. I tried to get Alleycat to give us a decent target with a ground fac because I knew the assigned target would be difficult to find and its value was marginal, but he didn't have anything.

Each of the three A-1 squadrons at NKP have had their mission assignments cut back by two yesterday and two more tomorrow. We had just received some new pilots and were overmanned again.

Chapter 10

Strike Mission

September 9, 1969. Tuesday. Transcript of mission tape.

Briefing is scheduled at 8:10 p.m. at the TUOC building for a 10:10 takeoff. I will be the flight leader in aircraft #665, a single-seat A-1H. On the wing will be Captain Frank Monroe getting one of his night check out rides with Don Combs in the right seat as his instructor pilot. My call sign for the mission will be Firefly 42 and Frank and Don will be 43.

A briefing room in the TUOC building is assigned to each flight, and various briefers stop by to tell us what's going on this evening. First we get our assignment for the mission—what the target is, pictures of it, and its location. Then we get the information on what aircraft we are to fly and what ordnance load we'll have. The intelligence briefer, First Lieutenant John Wilkinson, brings us up to date on the military situation in Laos and tells us whatever of significance has occurred since last night. He also tells us what the base altitude is for the night. All mentions of aircraft altitude over Laos will be made in reference to base plus or minus a few thousand feet. Tonight's base altitude is 8,000 feet. It's used so we don't broadcast our altitudes to the radar controllers or to each other, in case the enemy is listening.

Soon a weather forecaster drops by with a report on the conditions in the target area and locally.

After those briefings are finished, we talk to each other about what we will be doing tonight. Because I'm the leader, it's my responsibility to brief the mission, and, since Frank is new to nights, I cover things more thoroughly than I would with a pilot with whom I've flown often and I know he knows night procedures.

When we leave TUOC, the first stop is the personal equipment building to get our parachutes, helmets and oxygen masks, survival vests, and .38 revolvers. We leave behind wallets, rings or any other personal things in case we are captured by the enemy. We take along whatever amount of money we think might be useful to bribe our way out of any unpleasant situation in which we might find ourselves.

The PE building is clean and the colors of the flight suit, vest, and helmet are green and brown camouflage. My helmet has a slight smell of sweat, sort of like a football player's helmet. A faint smell of engine oil is on my equipment. The room is well lighted, and the floor is shiny clean like it has a fresh coat of light gray paint. I have the option of stepping into a metal cage to test my survival radios. The cage is wired to prevent a radio signal from inadvertently escaping, which would create a false alarm that someone is down. The last thing I get before going out the door is my .38 revolver that I slip into the holster.

We get a ride to the flight line and our airplanes in the TUOC bus, a plain panel truck painted dark air force blue with no windows in the back and metal bench seats facing inward along either side. The airplanes are not parked together, so we establish a time to come up on the radio before starting engines.

The flight line at night has a lot of activity. The van delivers me right to my airplane and I step into the glare of the floodlights onto the pierced steel plank. PSP is used to cover the ground on the flight line area and taxiways, but not the runway itself, which is asphalt. PSP presents no problems except it tends to be slippery when wet. It's a constant reminder, if we need one, that Nakhon Phanom is, at least for USAF operations, an outpost near the frontier—sort of a modern-day fort with walls of barbed wire and high intensity lights guarding the perimeter. Within those walls we are safe from external forces, and, since we're in Thailand instead of Vietnam, we are relatively safe beyond those walls as well, but there's always the chance of infiltration by unfriendlies. After all, it's a war base in wartime. Hence the perimeter protection.

The ramp area is well lit, and of course lights at night in the tropics bring swarms of insects. After the sun goes down a typical temperature is somewhere in the upper seventies, with humidity to match.

If a person is lucky and enterprising, he might find a rice bug or two lying on the PSP. The huge beetles gorge themselves on rice and fly toward the lights until they can't fly anymore and fall. The local people buy rice bugs for a baht—five cents—and a smile, open it up and eat the rice inside.

The crew chief meets me at the airplane. First I check the log book, then take my parachute and helmet up to the cockpit by climbing up the left wing where I place my parachute in the cockpit and my helmet so it straddles the canopy rail. I climb down and do the walk-around preflight inspection of the airplane and the ordnance. I check to be sure the weapons load I was assigned is in fact the load I have and to be sure everything is in order.

Then it's up the left wing, onto the nonskid track next to the fuselage, using the handholds for safety, and settle into the cockpit. The crew chief helps me get into my parachute, fasten the seat belt and shoulder harness, buckle and tighten parachute straps, and plug the hose into the oxygen line and the headset into the communication line. An external power cart is providing electricity. The crew chief goes back to the ground and stands in my view so I can signal when I'm ready to start the engine or if I find something that needs to be fixed.

I do the cockpit check of all switches and gauges and at the designated time call Firefly 43 on the radio. They're all set, so I give the crew chief a circular sign with my right index finger to let him know I'm ready to start the engine. He signals all clear, so I engage the starter. When starting a big reciprocating engine like the R3350, all cylinders must be fully lubricated before start, so I count sixteen prop blades—four complete rotations—before moving the fuel lever to the on position. It fires right up with a big cloud of white smoke and an instant breeze, and I check the engine gauges and switch to aircraft electrical power. When I'm satisfied it's running OK, I signal to the crew chief to disconnect external power. The breeze from the propeller cools the tropical night air.

I check in with Frank and Don again and their engine is running smoothly, so I call, "Ground, Firefly Four Two Flight taxi," and we receive instructions to runway 15. I salute the crew chief and turn right out of the flight line parking area. On the way, I observe 43 is behind me. The Skyraider has a tail wheel directional lock that I engage whenever I'm taxiing straight and on takeoff and landing and disengage whenever I turn. It is something an A-1 pilot gets used to and does without thinking, although it was new to me when I was first introduced to the airplane.

We taxi into the arming area and turn to face northwest with the base to our right rear, so when the pins are pulled by the armers, if something inadvertently goes off, it won't go into an inhabited area.

After we're armed, I taxi away and hold short of the runway to do a mag check, which consists of running the engine up to 1700 RPM and moving the magneto switch from both to left, back to both, to right, and back to both to check for excessive RPM drop. I pull the prop lever full back and right back up to see via the pitch change that the prop regulator is working. It doesn't take long and is part of the preflight ritual all pilots flying recips do before every takeoff. Jet engines are comparatively simple and have no similar procedures. I also do a flight control check.

I call the tower to tell him we're ready to go, but an F-4 is on final approach diverting in with an emergency, so we have to wait.

Tower: "Roger, sir, the first aircraft to land will be the emergency, and we're trying to find out what his buddy is going to do."

Firefly 42: "OK." After a pause, I request to takeoff before the airplane with the emergency lands.

Tower: "You'll be holding for the emergency that is coming up on six miles, and he'll be taking the approach end of the barrier."

Firefly 42: "Rog, you can't clear us for an immediate (takeoff)?"

Tower: "I can't let you go. Radar is holding you."

So we wait and are twenty-five minutes late for our scheduled takeoff. We have a front row seat to watch the F-4 take the barrier without incident.

"Firefly Four Two, are you on the radio?"

"Firefly Four Two, affirmative."

"Firefly Four Two Flight, taxi into position and hold."

"Firefly Four Two, on and hold."

Another airplane's on final approach, and someone says, "That's a pretty close final."

Before taking the runway, I ask, "How close is that guy, Tower?"

"Firefly Four Two, hold short of the runway, traffic's on final."

"Roger, hold short." So we wait for a C-123 to land.

"Firefly Four Two Flight, taxi into position and hold."

"Firefly Four Two, on and hold."

It's time for the before takeoff checklist. The most important things are mixture full rich, cowl flaps open, prop RPM max, wing flaps set for takeoff, fuel pump on, ejection seat pin removed, and rudder trim five units to the right. Firefly 43 will release his brakes thirty seconds after I release mine. I taxi to a stop slightly left of the runway centerline, and Frank taxis slightly right and just behind me.

After waiting for the C-123 to clear at the end of the runway, the tower says, "Firefly Four Two, C-123 clearing at the end, winds 120° at 2, change to departure control frequency, monitor guard, cleared for takeoff."

"Firefly Four Two Flight cleared to go," I respond and order Four Three to check in on departure's frequency.

"Four Three," he responds.

I will soon be about 200 miles away from the safety of the base and many miles over enemy territory, diving to the ground at a 40° angle with the possibility of someone shooting big guns at me. If anything should go wrong with the airplane then, I might have a very difficult time surviving. But perhaps the most risky part of the whole endeavor is the takeoff. The margin for error is very small due to the heavy weight, the explosiveness of what I'm carrying, and the unreliability of the engine. The ejection seat is *supposed* to be a zero-zero system (zero speed, zero altitude), but I know malfunctions occur about as often as safe ejections, and therefore the risk is high in the event of a problem. If an engine failure happens at a critical time in the takeoff and a seat failure occurs when an ejection is attempted, I probably won't survive. That sequence of events is a real possibility.

*

In my mind, I can see hundreds of moving parts in that big engine going first one way and then another, pistons and valves going up and down, the cams rotating, the sparks in the plugs—all producing the rotation of the shaft that drives the propeller. At idle, the rotation is gentle, like a sweet song, a lullaby, perhaps—producing a soft breeze. If at idle for a long time, the spark plugs can load up, causing misfiring, popping, and a loss of power, so a runup of engine RPM is in order every few minutes to keep the plugs clean.

At takeoff power, the gentle breeze becomes a hurricane and the sweet song becomes a deep-throated rumble as pieces of the engine seem to want to pull themselves apart in their haste to go first this way and then that way. Each cylinder produces 150 horsepower. Every part in a cylinder has a counterpart in seventeen other cylinders. Any failure can start a chain reaction that will cause the engine to fail within seconds. Twenty-eight hundred RPM puts a lot of stress on those parts, which is why we don't use takeoff power any longer than necessary.

An interesting limitation to the engine is the bearings are not constructed for back winding—that is, pointing the nose down with a low RPM and forcing RPM to wind up through the force of the air. It'd be similar to putting a car transmission in low gear at the top of a hill and using the engine as a brake on speed. Don't do that.

The critical period of the takeoff will not be over until I've got enough speed and altitude to bail out over the side in the event of a double failure of engine and ejection seat. Prior to such a bailout, a few seconds would be required to pull the cables to release the external ordnance. At every takeoff on every mission, that thought goes through my mind, but I just take a deep breath and push the throttle forward. I won't begin to relax until I pass through 1,000 feet above the ground.

I turn on the rotating beacon, landing lights, and transponder, push the throttle part way open, and release the brakes. It begins to roll down the runway, slowly at first, then accelerates as I push the throttle all the way forward. The environment is pitch black except for the small white runway edge lights on both sides, my landing lights, instrument lights, and the lights of the flight line on the left. I do a quick check of the engine instruments—2800 RPM, 56 inches of manifold pressure, oil and fuel pressures good. The airplane wants to pull left with all that engine torque out front, but five units of right rudder trim and a lot of pushing on the right rudder pedal keep it straight. In addition to a visual check of the instruments, I listen carefully for any strange noises that might indicate a problem.

As I approach 95 knots, the tail comes up. Gradually the left torque decreases, and I can relax the pressure on the right rudder as the speed increases. Aircraft 665 is loaded to max takeoff weight, and in the warm air it isn't anxious to fly. I have to coax it into the air by very gently pulling back on the stick as the speed increases past 100 knots. Once I'm airborne, I raise the landing gear handle and monitor the gear indicator lights to assure they go out. The time from main gear liftoff to runway end is surprisingly short. Then in a moment, not much more, I pass the base perimeter lights and fly just above the trees. It is dark, and I transition to instrument flying as I cross the lights. The engine sounds good. I retract the flaps on schedule and accelerate to 140 knots, the speed I need to climb. I can relax a little now, and when I reach 1,600 feet, I begin a 180° right turn to a heading of 330° to parallel the runway in the opposite direction from which I took off. I can see the base down to my right. When I reach the 300° radial of the NKP tacan, Channel 89, I begin another right turn to a heading of 060°, a direct line to the Mekong River and Laos. I can see the lights of the base and NKP town and take care not to get disoriented. Before long, I've got enough altitude, I'm well oriented as to up and down, and I can relax a bit before we begin our combat for the evening.

"Firefly Four Two, this is departure, radar contact."

"Firefly Four Two."

I pull the throttle back to 52 inches manifold pressure and the RPM back to 2600, mixture still full rich, METO power and turn off the landing lights.

After about nine miles on the 060° heading, I cross the Mekong, which I can just make out in the night light, and turn left to 330° to parallel the river and level off at 6,500 feet, as briefed. I pull the power back to cruise, RPM to 2200 and lean the mixture. I call departure control and say, "Firefly Four Two Flight level at base minus one point five." All trips north to Barrel Roll are done on the Laotian side of the big river.

"Four Two, thank you," is the reply. After a couple of minutes, he says, "Firefly Four Two Flight, go to local channel six. Good night."

"Roger," I reply. "Firefly Four Three, channel six."

"Four Three," is Frank's response.

"Firefly Four Three check in."

"Four Three," says Frank. He's letting me know he is with me on the frequency and everything is going normally in his airplane.

I check in with the controller on the new frequency. "Firefly Four Two Flight outbound level at base minus one point five."

"Roger, Firefly Four Two, understand base minus one point five. I have you now on a 320 (degree radial from the NKP tacan) for 22 (miles) off (Channel) 89. (He is receiving both transponders.) Barrel Roll altimeter is 29.70."

Frank and I both reply, "29.70."

By now my vision has become totally acclimated to the illumination available in the night, which isn't much. I have become very familiar with the cycles of the moon because of the help it can give in finding the target or even just in maintaining orientation.

Tonight we have no moon at all and a clear sky, so I have only starlight to provide illumination. I can see the stars and all the way to the horizon and can maintain spatial orientation while in straight and level flight. But I would be foolish to depend upon that as a reference when pulling off a target after a roll in and a 40° dive, especially in an area of high terrain. I have to depend upon instruments then. I can barely see the Mekong in the darkness, swollen near the end of the monsoon season, and I can navigate from it as a visual reference. But after the Mekong and I part courses at the big bend, I will have very little to guide me. I will be able to see Phou Bia and a few lesser peaks because their profiles form part of the horizon as I pass near them, but all terrain features directly below will be obscured. It will not be easy to find the target tonight.

We're sent to Ethan's frequency. We don't normally hear much from them unless we go too far east, but it's necessary to check in as we approach the bend in the river. I push the mixture, RPM, and throttle to climb power and begin the ascent to 10,500 feet. Frank will go to 11,000 feet. Shortly after passing the fence, we douse our external lights, requiring us to be at different altitudes in order to have positive separation.

"Ethan, this is Firefly Four Two, Four Three and we're 38 miles out of 89 (on) about the 328° radial." He replies and will keep track of us.

Soon I check in with the night control ship, Alleycat, who is a C-130 orbiting somewhere in the area. "Hello Alleycat, Firefly Four Two Flight."

"Firefly Four Two, Alleycat," a very deep voice replies.

"Roger, we're out of Channel 89, requesting information."

I am asking him if he still wants us to go to our assigned picture target or if he has a ground fac who has a target. Our assigned targets are storage areas south of the Birdshead—a remote section of Barrel Roll. I have no way to navigate visually because of the lack of light, our altitude is too low to receive the tacan signal from Channel 113, and I have only two flares—certainly not enough. Frank has four, which I might have to use before the night is over. Instead of a flare pod, tonight they're attached to the wing station just as bombs are, so we must drop them using the bomb switch position instead of rocket.

The targets for our flight were selected by intelligence people from pictures taken by a reconnaissance airplane, probably an RF-4 or an RF-101 that flew over them at high speed, hence the name picture target. Someone spotted something he considered suspicious, deemed it worthy of a strike, and assigned it to our flight tonight. I've been given a copy of the picture and the coordinates, as if either will do any good. So we have a target we can't find because we have no precise way to navigate to it, not enough flares to find it in a familiar area let alone someplace this remote, with few outstanding landmarks nearby and a flight of F-4s I'm supposed to fac. We're also twenty-five minutes late because of the emergency back at the base and F-4s are notoriously short on fuel even when we're on time. I wish the idiot who dreamed this one up was sitting right here with me, so he could see the improbability first hand. But he's probably sound asleep in his bed in Saigon dreaming up some other stupid idea. Why can't these targets be hit in the daytime, when the pilots might be able to find them?

If a ground fac has requested help we'll go find him and maybe have a target worth hitting. Sometimes when we check in with Alleycat he has one for us, but not tonight.

"Roger, Firefly Four Two, I'm going to take you up on Route 7 about ten klicks east of Beta 22 all the way east. Are you familiar with targets number one four and one five?"

"I think I have them listed in my folder here."

"Roger, I'd like to check out these two targets," says Deep Voice. "Looks like you're gonna fac for target one five and one four is your secondary for tonight."

"OK." Here comes my sales talk. "If you have a ground fac, we'd sure like to work with him because we don't have enough flares. I have negative 225 (flare) pods tonight. I have on my aircraft a total of two arc 24s and I believe my wingman has four, so we're very restricted on flares." After a pause in which I can hear a call to Spooky, a C-47 in the area, I ask, "Alleycat, Firefly Four Two, do you copy?"

"Firefly Four Two, stand by one." At least they're considering my request. All this time, we're still headed north toward Barrel Roll.

"Alleycat, this is Firefly Four Two. We're also approximately twenty-five minutes late because the runway closed for an emergency. We've got Olds flight assigned to us at 1650 zulu, and we'd like a little more time for him if we could, please, to get something set up here." I am pleading for relief.

"Firefly Four Two, Alleycat. We'll try to hold him on a tanker, but we're not too sure we can do it."

"OK. We'll do what we can."

"Firefly Four Two, Alleycat."

"Alleycat, this is Four Two, go ahead."

"OK, we'll hold him up as long as we can. And go on up to the one I told you, that's ten miles east of Beta 22 and start there and work east and check out target number 15 first."

"Roger, we'll do what we can." I am not very happy with this assignment. I had been hoping I could talk him out of this foolishness, but now we're stuck with it.

"Altimeter for tonight is 29.72. Contact Ethan on (frequency) two five four decimal eight for flight following up to that point."

"Firefly Four Two, copy." After a pause I say, "And Alleycat, if anything comes up for us in the meantime, we'd sure appreciate any help we can get on this."

"I'll do as much as I can."

"Firefly Four Two." We switch frequencies.

"Ethan, Firefly Four Two would like to begin climb to base plus two point five, please."

Ethan: "Cleared to two point five."

"Understand we're cleared. Firefly Four Three, do you copy?"

"Four Three, roger."

In a few minutes, I call, "Ethan, Firefly Four Two Flight level base plus two point five." I pull the engine controls back to cruise power.

"Roger, copy," Ethan replies.

Alleycat calls me back, "Four Two, can you come up on my primary victor?" He's asking me to contact him on his VHF frequency.

I go to his frequency and say, "Alleycat, Firefly Four Two on your primary victor, I'm on uniform (UHF) now."

"Do you have a rendezvous with Olds flight yet?" He wants to know where he can tell Olds flight to meet me.

"We can give you a rendezvous for them. Let's see. Why don't we make it about zero seven zero for fifty-seven as a preliminary. And have they checked in with you yet?"

"They have checked in. What time do you want for TOT?" TOT is time over target.

"OK, we're not even going to be in the target area for another twenty or twenty-five minutes and when we get there it's going to take some time to scout out the area and check the weather and see if we can even find the place. I'd like at least thirty minutes. I can call you in a few minutes and advise you if I need a little more."

After a pause, I say, "Alleycat, Firefly Four Two, do you copy?"

"Roger Four Two, stand by one (minute)."

Then another aircraft comes on the frequency. "Alleycat, (this is) Bat One." Blind Bat One is a nighttime C-130 forward air controller.

"Bat One, Alleycat. Go (ahead)."

After a pause in which Bat One does not respond, Alleycat calls me back. "Firefly Four Two, Alleycat."

"Alleycat, (this is) Four Two. Go ahead," I reply.

"Can we make an on-the-hour TOT?" he asks.

"I'll give you that as a preliminary and let you know in about twenty minutes or so if I can handle them then or if I'll have to push it back a bit," I reply.

"Roger," says Alleycat.

After a few minutes Alleycat calls back and says, "Do you think you can stay clear of the line?"

"Say again about the line."

"Can you stay clear of it?" he repeats. He is referring to the border between Laos and North Vietnam. It is quite sensitive politically, and our target is not very far from it. We don't want to cross it, but I have no obvious reference to tell me where it is.

"We can give it a try. The only way we have the means to stay clear will be through Ethan (guiding us)."

Alleycat responds, "Rog, use Ethan and go to target one five and see if you can find it OK."

"OK, we will," I respond. Alleycat is apparently searching for something else for us to do that would be more productive. I had clearly stated our limitations and he is aware of the problem, but he's a victim of the system, too. No other targets are available, and he has to do *something* with us, even if it's useless.

Another voice comes through the radio. "Firefly Four Two." It's Ethan. "You have traffic bearing 360 (degrees) for ten miles. He's at base plus nine."

"Firefly Four Two, copy. No joy." I tell Ethan I hear and understand his message, but I don't see the other airplane.

Soon I call Alleycat. "Alleycat, Firefly Four Two."

"Firefly Four Two, Alleycat. Go."

"Roger. Out of the two targets, one four and one five, one four will be the easier to find, if we can find it at all, because of the fact that it's right next to ground references. The other target is out in the middle of nowhere and I'll—and I don't see any possibility of being able to find that one. But one four we'll be able to find if we can get into the general area. There are some pretty good references near it."

"Roger, if you can find—locate it—you can begin working on that," comes the reply from Alleycat.

"OK, we'll give it a try and see what we can come up with." After a pause, I ask, "And Alleycat, Four Two, do you still want us to armed recce the road from ten miles east of Beta 22 over to the target or do you want us to go directly to the target?"

"Negative, go directly to the target." I am glad to hear that because I have enough on my mind without trying to armed recce the road, too.

"Rog, understand."

It's time to check in with Ethan again to find out where we are. "Hello Ethan, Firefly Four Two."

"Four Two, Ethan. Go."

"Roger, Four Two would like vectors to 069 at 57 off Channel 113, please."

"Copy 069 at 57 from 113?" Ethan asks for confirmation. I know I am headed in the right general direction, but I need to know precisely where the target is. "Firefly Four Two, your pigeons 146 range one one." This is direction and distance to the target.

"Understand 146 range one one."

"That's affirmative."

"OK, and we'd like to have you keep track of us, please, because that's the only reference we have, and I don't know if we'll be able to find it from that."

"Roger. Copy, will do."

A few minutes later I call, "Hello, Alleycat, do you have a frequency for us, please?"

"Firefly Four Two, Alleycat. Roger, use Bravo frequency."

"Understand, Bravo frequency," I confirm. Then I call Frank and say, "Four Three, set in Bravo frequency manual and leave it on Channel Eight."

Shortly, Ethan says to me, "123 range of 8."

I reply, "123 range 8." A couple of minutes later, I ask again, "Ethan, Firefly Four Two, can you give us another hack on our target, please?"

"132 range 6," says Ethan.

"Understand 132 range 6."

"Affirmative." Then, "You're about a half mile north of it."

"Roger, thank you." That's about as close a vector as I'm going to get, so I drop a flare. At this point, anyone within a hundred miles in the air knows where we are, as does anyone in the vicinity on the ground, because we have a lot of light all of a sudden. "Firefly Four Two, I just put out a flare," I say to let anyone on the frequency know who is responsible for it. "Firefly Four Two Flight, let's go manual." I direct 43 to change radio frequencies.

"Firefly Four Three, check in," I direct.

"Firefly Four Three."

With all that light, if a terrain feature of significance is under the flare, I will be able to see it. A flare is suspended in the air under its own small parachute and from a distance looks like a bright fireball just hanging above the ground. After dropping it, I get in position above it and circle to the left. Since 43 and I have our aircraft lights out and are above the flare, we consider ourselves invisible from the ground. We are still maintaining altitude separation from each other. A wide area is exposed to the light, and the intensity of the illumination of ground features varies with the distance they are from the flare, the height of the flare, and haze or clouds in the air. In certain seasons, wind currents will blow flares away from the intended area quickly, but in September, winds are light, so I can count on it remaining in the area until it burns out, which is several minutes.

"OK," I say to Frank, "do you see anything that looks like a road?" Even though we are in the vicinity of the target, I have to spot it visually and then put a mark down before the flare goes out. Close is not good enough. If I can find a road, I might be able to orient myself in relation to the target and proceed from there.

"Negative," he says. All we can see are a lot of trees, which are no help at all. The jungle here looks just like the jungle over there if we have no recognizable landmarks. We expand our area of search to the fringes of the illuminated area, but we still see nothing to help.

"I can't either." Now is when I wish the idiot who assigned these targets to A-1s at night was here with me to see how difficult this is. But I surely wouldn't want him in the left seat flying with me in the right seat. He's too dumb.

Don says, "It looks like your flare is too high to be effective."

"Yeah, I know it," I say. "I still can't see anything." The flare burns out and the area goes dark again. I say, "Crown King, you said earlier that I was just half a mile north of it, so I'll put my last flare out just a bit south here." I select the station where my last flare is mounted, fly a little to the south and drop it. Once again the darkness is broken by the brilliant light of a million candlepower, and we resume our search in a left hand orbit for any recognizable landmark. After a minute or two, I say, "I still don't see anything that looks like a road." The target is near a road, and if we can't see a road, we can't see the target.

All the while, I know Olds flight is going to be checking in soon, and I need to have a target for him. I'm out of flares, but Frank and Don still have four left. Frank says, "I can flare further south yet."

"OK, why don't you go on down there and put out your flares? I'm all out," I say.

"I'll try."

"OK, and I'll stay out of your way. Just tell me which way to go." With 43 flaring, we will be crossing altitudes, and we need to keep positive separation.

"All right."

I say, "I don't think that this is the right area." I turn out of the way and climb to 43's altitude, and he descends to drop his flare. We resume our search.

Frank says, "There's a stream. If we knew where the road is to the stream..."

"Yeah, I saw the stream," I reply, "but if you look off to the east, there's nowhere for the road to get into the mountains. I'm sure it must be farther south or north, I don't know which."

So I call Ethan back to ask where we might go to resume our search for the target. "The target is nine miles east of your position," says Ethan.

NINE MILES? What do you mean nine miles? You tell us the target is here, and then you don't volunteer this is not the right area until I ask again?

Why didn't you *tell* me we're not in the right area without being prompted and before I had expended my flares?

After that, of course, I lose all confidence in Ethan's ability to help us find the target. Then Olds flight checks in on our frequency ready to hit the target I can't find. I am quite exasperated when I respond to Olds. "We've got four flares left for the whole cotton pickin' flight here, and we got vectored into this area by Ethan, and now he says it is nine miles farther east yet."

Olds says, "I've got some flares aboard if it'll help you any."

"Yeah, hey, it just might." It's the first good news I've had in a while. "We could sure use them. We're going to head nine miles on a 090 heading and see if we can find this thing. How much flight time do you guys have?"

"About twenty minutes." How did I know he was going to say that?

"It may take us all of that to find this thing." Then I tell Olds, "This is Four Two, I'm going to be switching back and forth to Ethan's frequency to have him give us vectors now and then to the target.

"Hello Ethan, Firefly Four Two."

"Firefly Four Two, go."

"I'm heading 090 at this time. Do you have range to the target now, please?"

After a pause Ethan says, "Your bearing is 036 range seven now."

"OK, 036 range seven." Do we have any reason to believe this one is any better than the last vector? "I left the other target heading 090, and I'm just wondering why the target is now northeast of me instead of straight east as you told me before."

"Well, that's a good question," Ethan says. "However, other aircraft are in your area, and I'm not getting a really good stretch on you, but I did get a good stretch that time, and it looks like 036 at seven, depending upon which way you turned last time."

"OK, I'm steady on 036 heading now," I say. I switch back to UHF tactical frequency. "Olds, Firefly Four Two."

Don says, "Four Two, this is Four Three, they've got tacan. They can spot the place for us." The F-4s are higher and have line-of-sight capability to receive Channel 113 over the top of the mountains and can help us find the target.

"Oh, beautiful. OK. We still need 036 at seven now. Olds, this is Four Two."

"Go ahead."

"The target is 069 at 57. I understand you have tacan."

Olds says, "I'm showing 53 miles now."

"When you show yourself over the target, have at it."

Olds then says, "The tacan broke on me." He has lost his lock on the navaid, and without it, we're back to dead reckoning. At least we think we're in the correct area now. However, I'm out of flares, and it's tough to be an effective leader at night without flares.

Olds comes over to where he thinks the target is and drops a flare. In the light I see what appears to be a road and possibly the picture target near the road. Since this area is all enemy territory, it's close enough for me. I push the mixture lever to rich, select internal fuel, RPM to 2600, and the throttle to 52 inches, level at 10,000 feet, adjust the mil setting on the sight, and, with the intervalometer, select a station with a log. I also have to make sure the function selector switch is in bomb and not in rocket, otherwise the log won't leave the airplane.

We use a 40° dive angle, even at night, for napalm and 500-pound bombs. In order to get into position above the target, the pilot needs to line it up with the stub station on the left wing. The left and right stub stations are usually the ones carrying the heaviest ordnance since they are closest inboard.

The first time I lined up the stub with the target it seemed as if I was directly on top of it and I would be going straight down in the dive. Accurate ordnance delivery provides very little room for error. Anybody can simply throw something down, but in order to be accurate it has to be done just right. The dive angle, the mil setting, the altitude of release, the rudder trimmed to neutral, and the wind all have to be taken into account. Then maybe, if I'm lucky, I might hit the target. Sometimes the target is moving, like a truck.

Once everything is set up, I roll in. Control stick hard left into a sharp left turn and let the nose drop quickly, but smoothly to 40° down. DOWN. My heart is pumping hard. I'm in a steep dive. I have to do it right and fast. Line up the target in the sight. It's getting bigger as I get closer to the ground. Airspeed is increasing! Quick! Right there! Pickle at 8,000 feet, only 2,000 feet from roll-in altitude. Not much time. NOW! Pull out! Pull hard, but don't over G! All the remaining ordnance is trying to pull the airplane toward the ground. Smoothly pull to four Gs. Watch the artificial horizon. It's the only visual reference I can count on. Pull! Get the nose up! Don't go below 7,000 feet because rocks can be anywhere below seven. There's level. Bring it on up. Twenty-five degrees nose high. I have plenty of speed, so keep the nose up. Here comes 8,000 feet. Then 9,000. I can let the nose down a little now and look around to see if anyone is shooting. No ground fire? OK then, where did my mark land?

"Olds, this is Firefly Four Two."

"Go ahead Four Two."

"The target is about fifty meters north of my mark. Go ahead and hit it. We'll be out of your way to the west."

"OK."

So we go a few miles to the west and try to keep our eyes on the target as he strikes it. I can see his bombs going off on each pass and his ordnance is somewhere in the vicinity of my mark. Everything is dark around me except for the lights of my instrument panel, the very faint starlight, and the occasional flash of Olds's bombs. I don't see much in the way of secondary fires, but we have a secondary explosion or two.

"Olds flight, we're off target and going to RTB. Do you have any BDA for us?"

"Roger, Olds, you worked it over pretty well, but I only saw two secondary explosions. Good job," I say. "And thanks for helping us locate the target."

"OK. Good night," he says as he leaves the frequency.

I call 43, "How's your fuel?"

"We've got 2300 pounds." It is time to start being concerned about that.

"How much is external?" I ask.

"About 250 pounds."

"You have 2300 total, right?"

"Right."

"I have 2150 internal fuel and I don't know what I have external. I'll go ahead and hit this target, and I'll let you come on in. Then we'll RTB." I know I have no chance of finding target 15 and we have this one pretty well marked, so we go after it.

"Four Three, did you get a good look at the target while we were flaring it and looking for it?"

"No, not real good. I was staying out of the way of you and the fast movers."

"OK, I just went texaco (minimum fuel to begin a strike) with 2150. The target is just north of the northern-most log (marker)—if you take the distance between the two of them as one unit, it is just about half a unit north of the northern-most one. It's right across the road." After a pause to get myself into position, I say, "I'm going to be at roll-in altitude here in a minute and I'll be in hot." Then, "I'm going to have to get over to the other side of these things here before I can see them."

Frank then says, "Now where do you want it in relation to the northern-most log?"

"I want it about fifty meters, or a hundred meters north of the northern-most log. Put it in the area." Soon I say, "OK, I've got both of them (the logs) in sight now, and I'll be in hot here in a minute." Frank acknowledges my transmission.

"Four Two is in hot. I'll put down a couple napes here and get a good mark." After the pass, I ask 43, "Do you see the two napes?"

He doesn't respond at first and I call him again. Still no response. Then Don says, "Four Two, we have somebody calling us."

"OK," I say, "can you hear him? I can't."

43 says, "Calling Firefly Four Two, Four Three, say again."

A voice says, "This is Spike. I'd like to go through your area at base altitude. I'm at base minus two."

I hear him that time. "How far out are you, Spike?" Who is Spike and what could he possibly be doing up here needing to traverse our area in the middle of the night? Why should he get priority to pass through our area when we're in the midst of a strike?

"We're about thirteen minutes out," he says.

"OK, let me know when you're coming in, and I'll pull off target then." I'm getting low on fuel and need to finish the attack, so I continue to direct Frank. "Four Three, this is Four Two. Do you see two napes burning?"

"Yes," says Frank.

"That should be right in the area—string your ordnance just a bit to the north. I believe those are right on the road, just about. The target is just north of the road."

"Firefly Four Three, roger."

It is still my turn to strike. "Four Two is in hot. I'm going to drop all four of my bombs on this pass." I'm getting low on fuel and can't stay over the target much longer. After the pass, I say, "Off target, I only dropped two." After seeing where they land and explode, I say, "And they were a bit long. I was afraid of that. That's why I only dropped the two."

Frank asks, "Are we going to take our CBU home?"

"That's affirmative," I reply. "I'm going to make one more pass with bombs, and then I'll stand off and let you come in. Spike, (this is) Four Two, where are you now?"

"We're about thirty miles south, and we'll be there in about ten minutes."

"OK, let me know when you're within about ten miles."

"Wilco," says Spike.

I say to 43, "That one nape sure is burning bright isn't it?" He agrees. "Four Two is in hot." After I come off target, I say to 43, "Do you see where those two hit? That's right in the area of the target."

"I didn't see those last two. Where were they in relation to the napalm?"

"They were just north thirty meters, and that should be just in the center of the target area. I'm going to pull off here to the south, and you're cleared in whenever you're ready. I'm through base plus two right now. I'm back Christmas tree (I've turned my lights back on). I'm going to save my CBUs and my Luu 59s and RTB with them."

"Four Three, roger."

"Spike, where are you now?"

"I'm about twenty-five miles south, and I'll be there in about seven minutes."

"What speed are you guys making?"

"180."

"Four Three, this is Four Two. I'll be holding at base plus three and above here."

"Roger." The airplane is lighter now and is much easier to handle and more willing to climb. I go to eleven thousand feet and pull the power back as I continue to circle the target area, ever alert to the possibility of ground fire. I am out of napes and bombs, but if someone decides to start shooting at Frank and Don, I am still able to roll in with my lights out to keep the bad guys' heads down with CBUs and rockets.

I watch 43 make his strike, and as he comes off the target on his last pass, it's time to RTB. "Four Three, this is Four Two. Say your armament status, aircraft status, check all switches off or safe and lights on."

"Armament status is code one (he dropped it all except for his flares), aircraft status is code two for a cockpit light out, and the right side communications panel is broken. All switches safe and lights on," comes the reply.

*

We are on our way home, and I can relax a little. I don't think we've done too much good, but I didn't have very high expectations going into this mission.

As we approach the Mekong River southbound, it's time to check out with Ethan. "Hello, Ethan, Firefly Four Two Flight. We're crossing the fence now and we'll be going off your frequency."

Ethan replies that he wants me to stand by for a minute, then tells me of another flight headed northbound in our area and their altitude.

"We're at base plus three point five and base plus four," which gives us altitude separation from the other flight.

I still can't see very much in the moonless night, but I'm receiving the NKP tacan, so I know my approximate position and that I am about to cross the river into Thailand. The stars are still very clearly visible, and I can see a faint horizon. Little by little I begin to see the lights of NKP. On the Thai side of the river, it's still dark below except for an occasional light. "Firefly Four Three, go to channel six and stand by," I command. I hear no response, so I repeat it twice more with still no response. I try to get him to hear me on FM, "Firefly Four Three, this is Four Two on fox, go to channel six and stand by." This time he hears me.

Next I try to call maintenance on our UHF frequency to tell them the status of our airplanes and ordnance, but he doesn't hear me. After three attempts on UHF, I call on FM. "Hello Sundial, Firefly Four Two Flight on fox."

"Firefly Four Two, Sundial."

"This is Four Two on fox, we tried to call you on uniform and had no answer. I'm seventy-six miles out at this time. Firefly Four Two is code one aircraft and code two armament for willy pete luu 59 pod on station six. I only shot one rocket and the other six did not dispense. Firefly Four Three is code one armament and code two aircraft for a light writeup and the communications panel on the right side of the cockpit is bad."

"Roger, Four Two," says Sundial. Now he knows what to expect when we get on the ground and can maybe decrease the turnaround time for the airplanes.

Next I check in with the ground based traffic controllers at NKP. "This is Firefly Four Two Flight inbound to Channel 89 about 315 at 72 heading 170 at base plus three point five and base plus four."

"Firefly Four Two Flight, roger, stand by for radar contact. The field is VFR, altimeter 29.75, landing (runway) one five."

"29.75," I respond.

"Four Three copy, 29.75."

"Four Two Flight, I have radar contact at this time, you're cleared to four point five and five point five at your discretion." We are over friendly territory and we have no further need to use base altitude as a reference.

"Four Two Flight copy, and we'll stay at this altitude for another twenty miles or so," I say.

"Roger, I copy that," says the controller. "Call when you'd like to descend, and I'll clear you."

In a few minutes I call out of our altitudes for three point five and four point five. Shortly I call level at four point five and begin to receive instructions for a GCA.

The weather is good at the base and I could land visually, but I elect to make the instrument approach to the runway for practice. I push the RPM up to 2600 again, mixture rich and adjust the power to slow to 140 knots with the landing gear and flaps down. Landing lights on. Over the end of the runway. Throttle idle. Pull back gently on the stick. Make a nice three point landing and let her roll out. Keep it straight on the runway. Plenty of runway. Braking not needed until the end.

I turn into the dearming area that is brightly lit like a high school football field. Except for the turn off the runway, do not face the airplane toward any populated area on the base until the dearmers are done. Slide the canopy back. Hands on the canopy rail to keep them in sight of the dearmers at all times while they are safetying the remaining ordnance. Hope none of the dearmers mistakenly walk into the arc of the prop. That big prop could really give a guy a headache. Frank and Don pull in beside me in the dearming area.

In a couple of minutes the ordnance is safetied and the dearmers motion for me to taxi to parking. I have already received my parking location so I call ground control to taxi in. I maneuver into the parking spot designated for this airplane and the crew chief directs me in with his flashlight wands and motions when to stop. I turn off electrical switches and then shut down the engine by moving the fuel lever to off. The engine dies of fuel starvation. I insert the ejection seat safety pin, continue to turn off switches, and begin to unstrap from the seat belt and shoulder harness.

The crew chief helps me out of the cockpit and down the slippery wing. We speak briefly about the airplane, and I sign the logbook. My legs are stiff from sitting in one position for four hours. I board the TUOC crew bus that also picks up Frank and Don. We turn in our parachutes, helmets, vests, and .38 revolvers at the personal equipment building, then walk to TUOC for debriefing. Since Frank is the trainee, he fills out the flight report for both airplanes. I tell him how many passes I made, what I dropped on each pass, our BDA (which wasn't much), and what ordnance we brought back to the base. The form is rather detailed and Don and I review it before turning it in.

In the TUOC bus and building we talk about the flight what was wrong and right. I comment on the report form that this type mission is very difficult at night with no navaids and not enough flares. My statement is only a brief expression of my frustration.

The flight took three hours and thirty minutes, rather short for Barrel Roll at night, especially considering the difficulty of finding the target. It was my eighty-fourth mission. We are finally released from duty after 3:00 a.m.

Chapter 11

Lulu

September 10, 1969. Wednesday. Took off at 9:45 p.m. with Larry Dannelly and Bob Bohan on the wing. After flying around for quite a while, we ended up dumping our ordnance because of no targets. There might have been something good in that, but I don't know what it could have been.

September 11, 1969. Thursday. Took off at 9:45 p.m. in aircraft #779, an A-1H, with Frank Monroe and Don Combs on the wing. I had my tape recorder along. The only place to put a tape recorder in H or J models was on the fuel selector lever on the left side of the cockpit behind the pilot's seat, and when the external tank ran dry and the engine quit, I banged the recorder around a bit reaching for the fuel tank selector.

My call sign was Firefly 42, and Frank and Don were Firefly 43. We were directed by Alleycat to work with Lulu, whose position was a little southwest of the 7,247 foot mountain northeast of the PDJ. Lulu had a target for us along Route 7. Base altitude this night was 7,000 feet. Alleycat let us know Candlestick 41 was nearby flaring. As we approached the area I established radio contact with the Candle. Lulu was also on the frequency.

Candlestick 41: We've got movers (trucks) down here along the road and we've got enemy positions along the road. We're in the process of attempting to mark his (Lulu's) position and to find out where the enemy are—they're evidently right close to his position.

Firefly 42: OK, we'll just wait nearby. We're at base plus three and base plus three point five and we'll just wait until we hear from you.

Candlestick 41: Lulu, turn on your strobe light now, please.

Lulu: Charlie charlie.

Candlestick 41: Do you see my mark on the ground?

Lulu: Charlie charlie.

Candlestick 41: Is it red?

Lulu: Charlie charlie. Ground marker red. My position is 800 meters southwest of your ground marker. There are friendlies about sixty meters south of your ground marker.

Alleycat: Candlestick Four One, can you use some fast movers in there?

Candlestick 41: We've got a slight deck (a thin layer of clouds) right at about 9,000 feet. At this time I think it will be workable for fast movers, but I can't guarantee anything for when they get here.

Alleycat: They'll be there in about forty-five minutes. I'll call you later.

Candlestick 41: Lulu, is the red marker almost on the road?

Lulu: Charlie charlie. There are friendlies about fifty meters from the red marker on the road—to the south—about fifty meters south of your ground marker. You can strike about 800 meters southeast of your ground marker.

Candlestick 41: We will drop a marker on the enemy's position. You take a look and see if it is OK. (Pause.) Firefly Four Two, we are below your altitude and you will be running through our altitude both on your roll in and on your pull out. Is that OK with you?

Firefly 42: That's fine with us.

Candlestick 41: We'd like to stay at this altitude and we can make sure we get together—in contact before we clear you in. It'll be a little bit rougher, but we can work it that way.

Firefly 42: You can just let us know where you are and what heading you're on and we'll do it that way.

Candlestick 41: Lulu, we've got a flare out now. Is it over the enemy position?

Lulu: Negative, about three klicks to the southwest. (Lulu seemed to be very capable.)

Candlestick 41: Three klicks southwest.

Lulu: Charlie charlie. You cannot see your ground marker? I cannot see your ground marker at the present time. About three klicks southwest from your present flare.

Firefly 42: I can see your marker. Your flare is right over a ground marker.

Candlestick 41: That's the friendly position.

Lulu: Your target is about five to six hundred meters southwest of your flare.

Candlestick 41: Lulu, I'm going to drop another flare. You tell me if it is over the enemy position.

Lulu: The target is about 400 meters south of your present flare.

Candlestick 41: OK, south 400 meters to the enemy position.

Lulu: Charlie charlie. Do you see the road? Do you see the main road? Southeast of the last two flares. About two hundred meters southeast of the last two flares. The wind is blowing your flares. The target is about three hundred meters southeast of your two flares.

Candlestick 41: Firefly, this is Candle. Are you following all this?

Firefly 42: Roger, I've got it all.

Candlestick 41: OK, it's getting a little confusing here. We're not going to be able to pinpoint these guys here unless you work them over.

Firefly 42: He said it was the wind that was blowing the flares away. It looks like the weather is going to be moving in pretty fast.

Lulu: You see the flare—the mark south side of the road? Bad guys about 600 meters southwest—about 600 meters.

Candlestick 41: Firefly, we've got some marks strung out in a wide area—basically on a heading of about 240. To the southeast, we've got a group of three of them that are fairly close together, and then further on to the southwest, there are two of them that are pretty far apart. We're going to give you instructions off the group of three.

Firefly 42: OK, I've got them in sight.

Candlestick 41: Out of the furthest one of that group of three, to the west, you come off of it (on a heading of) two four zero the distance between the first one in the group and the third one.

Firefly 42: OK. And that's where you want it, is that right?

Candlestick 41: That is affirmative. We're going to hold to the south.

Firefly 42: OK, I'll drop one bomb. And I understand that you want it in line with those other marks, is that right?

Candlestick 41: I want it on a heading of two four zero off the third one the distance between the first one and the third one.

Firefly 42: OK, and I'll be rolling in here in a second.

Candlestick 41: Lulu, this is Candle. We'll drop a nape now, so you watch for enemy position.

Firefly 42: Four Two is in hot. (Pause.) It looks like I might've got a dud.

The night was very dark with no moon and a deck of clouds moving into the area. I knew the 7,247 foot mountain was off to the northeast of our position about seven miles and I knew that as long as I stayed clear of it I would be in no danger of high terrain in this area provided I didn't go below 7,000 feet. So I rolled in at ten, pickled at eight, and pulled out at seven, just like I always did at night in Barrel Roll. It was a guarantee of terrain clearance.

I knew where the Candle wanted me to hit, but I wasn't fully sure of where the friendlies were or even of what the target was. But the Candle took responsibility for the location of the strike, so I just rolled in where he said to hit. My first nape failed to ignite on impact, so we couldn't see where it hit. As I made my pass, the Candle went to the south and climbed to 11,000 feet to be above the strike. As I pulled off the target, he asked me to flash my landing light so he could see where I was, which I did.

Firefly 42: What's the terrain elevation here?

Candlestick 41: The terrain elevation is 4,000 feet. Lulu, Candlestick Four One. Did you hear the noise from the airplane when he dropped his bomb?

Lulu: Yeah. I heard him very, very loud.

Firefly 42: I'm in hot again. I've got my lights on this time.

I was sure I was in a safe area and considered the danger from other airplanes to be greater than the danger from ground fire. I used the rotating beacon, not landing lights.

Firefly 42: That one's a bit short of where I aimed it.

Lulu: Candlestick Four One, that was in the bad guy area. We have friendlies about six hundred meters to the east.

Firefly 42: I'm out of napes, but I have four Mark 82s and CBUs. Lulu, I'll be coming in with two bombs this time—you be ready to spot them, OK?

Lulu: Roger roger.

Candlestick 41: I understand napalm was good. You want one more same place?

Lulu: Charlie charlie. One more same place. And we've got friendlies six hundred meters to the east.

I told the Candle what I had left for ordnance and what Firefly 43 had for his ordnance load.

Candlestick 41: Firefly, this is Candle. If it's all right with you, we've got one too many people here. If you'd like to coordinate with Lulu here, we'll get out of your hair.

I didn't need to be asked twice for that offer.

Firefly 42: Lulu, this is Firefly Four Two. I'll be coming in to drop two bombs this time. You be ready to spot them, OK? I'll put them in the area of that fire on the ground.

Lulu: Charlie charlie. Friendlies are to the east. You're cleared to come north to south.

Firefly 42: I understand you want me to come in north to south. I'll be around in a second. Firefly Four Two in hot. (Pause.) Did you see the two bombs, Lulu?

Lulu: Yeah, very good.

Firefly 42: OK, I've got two more.

Lulu: Firefly, you put your next bomb about 200 meters south-southwest of your last bomb.

Firefly 42: OK, 200 meters south-southwest of the last bomb.

Lulu: I've got friendlies about 600 meters to the east.

He wasn't going to let me forget about his friendlies.

Firefly 42: OK, friendlies 600 meters to the east. I've got two more bombs and some CBUs. (Pause.) Firefly Four Two in hot from the south. (Pause.) I'm off to the west. Did you see those go off, Lulu?

Lulu: Roger, roger. Very good. Very good. And you have CBU?

Firefly 42: Yes, I have CBU and rockets left.

Lulu: You put CBUs in a hundred meters south of your bomb.

Firefly 42: I'll put rockets in first one hundred meters south, and I'll put CBUs in next.

Candlestick 41: Firefly, we're just holding overhead, if you need any help, just holler.

Firefly 42: I think we've got things in hand for now, thank you.

Candlestick 41: Roger.

Lulu: Firefly Four Two, Lulu.

Firefly 42: Go ahead.

Lulu: From your ground marker, twenty (meters) to the east is the friendly position.

Firefly 42: I have them in sight. That's the friendly position.

Lulu: From the ground marker, twenty to the east is the friendly position, and you'll see us about 400 meters to the southeast from the friendly position.

Firefly 42: OK, I have your position in sight, Lulu.

Lulu: Roger roger.

Firefly 42: I'll be coming in here very shortly with rockets. (Pause.) Firefly Four Two in hot with rockets and I'll hit a hundred meters southwest. (Pause.) I'm coming off.

Lulu: Very good.

Firefly 42: And the CBUs are off.

I dropped a few CBUs at the bottom of the pass as I was pulling off after I had shot the rockets.

Lulu: I think next time come in north to south.

Firefly 42: You want me in north to south next time?

Lulu: Charlie charlie. Next time I need you come in north to south when you drop your CBU.

Firefly 42: OK, CBUs will be hitting the ground in just a minute. (Pause.) Do you see the CBUs?

Lulu: (More excited) OK, very good.

Firefly 42: It'll take me about a minute to get around to the north to come in from that direction, Lulu.

Lulu: On the next pass I want them about one hundred meters south of the CBU on the last one.

Firefly 42: Understand, you want them one hundred meters south of the CBUs. And I'll be coming in here shortly.

Lulu: Roger roger.

Firefly 42: Lulu, I'm off here to the north, and I can't tell which mark is which, so I think it will be—OK, there it is, I've got it in sight now. I'm coming in hot.

Lulu: Very good.

Firefly 42: I'm off, and I'm winchester (out of ordnance). Firefly Four Three, you'll be cleared in. Do you have the position in sight?

Firefly 43: Roger, I'm not in position right now to strike yet.

Firefly 42: The CBUs should be going off—there, do you see the CBU, Lulu?

Lulu: Oh, number one! (One was good, ten was bad.)

Firefly 42: OK, Four Three, take your time to get into position, and I might be able to help you out on the position of the—where he wants it.

Lulu: The target for Firefly Four Three is about three hundred meters south of the rockets. There is another target.

Firefly 42: Four Three, did you copy that?

Firefly 43: Yeah, he wants me to hit three hundred meters south of yours.

Firefly 42: Yeah, he says there's another target. If you take the distance from the nape fire and the lights right next to it, I'd say that's pretty close to three hundred meters, and if you go straight south about that distance instead of west like that one is. Do you see what I'm talking about there? (Pause.) Firefly Four Three, I'm going to let you go ahead and talk to Lulu, and if you need any help, Candlestick can probably help you locate the target.

Candlestick 41: Firefly Four Two.

Firefly 42: Go ahead Candle, this is Four Two here.

Candlestick 41: Do you think we can put some fast movers in on the targets? Are they lucrative enough?

Firefly 42: Weather wise, there is no problem at all right now. He says there are troops. I don't know how many, but I'd say there's probably something pretty lucrative for them to shoot at.

Candlestick 41: About how long will it be before you'll be done?

Firefly 42: It depends upon how long it takes Four Three to locate the target and get in there. I'm off winchester now. Four Three, this is Four Two, do you have me in sight?

Firefly 43: Roger, I've got you in sight. You want me about 300 meters south of the nape fire?

Firefly 42: That's affirmative. That's where Lulu wants it. You go ahead and talk to Lulu.

Firefly 43 made his strike, talking to Lulu as Candlestick 41 got ready to fac in a flight of F-4s. When Four Three was finished, we turned south, and I talked to Lulu for BDA.

Firefly 42: Lulu, do you have any KBA for us?

Lulu: Roger, are you ready to copy?

Lulu was pretty sharp.

Firefly 42: Ready to copy.

Lulu: UG274617. (The coordinates of the location of the target on our maps.) One hundred over one hundred (we each put all of our ordnance in the target area) and killed many bad guys.

Firefly 42: UG274617. One hundred over one hundred and killed many bad guys. We enjoyed working with you and we'll see you tomorrow night maybe, OK? Candlestick Four One, we're going to RTB, and we'll leave it in your hands.

Candlestick 41: OK. Do you need any information from us?

Firefly 42: No sir. I think we've got it all.

I checked out with Alleycat as we headed south for NKP. This mission lasted three hours and five minutes. We landed about 12:45 a.m. on Friday, September 12. I'm not sure Lulu had a good target for us, but he probably put us in on the best he had. It was a fairly safe mission as no one was shooting at us that we could see. The biggest danger was the mountainous terrain.

*

September 12, 1969. Friday. Took off at 10:40 p.m. with Frank Monroe in the left seat and Jim George leading. We were holding in the weather when the DC generator failed. It reset OK, but I decided I didn't want to take a chance on it, and, with the weather being what it was, it seemed like a good idea to abort the mission. We flew two hours and twenty minutes.

*

Harry Dunivant received notification today that he had been promoted to lieutenant colonel, so he had a big smile. Harry kept regular office hours at the wing, and even though our schedules didn't mesh very well, he was very considerate of the fact that I had often just returned from a mission when he was getting up to go to work, and we got along well. Many times I arrived at the room after he had left for the day, so we often didn't even see each other.

Harry Dunivant

I played tennis today.

My missions on September 14 and 15 were canceled because of target weather. About this time, I became certified as an FCF (functional check flight) pilot and on the fifteenth flew an FCF in aircraft #713 because it had an engine change. FCFs were required for an airplane when it had undergone an engine change, flight control adjustments, or similar work by maintenance before it was sent out fully loaded on a combat mission. I also attended a squadron pilot meeting in the evening of the fifteenth.

*

A hobby of some of the pilots of the 602nd was stereo tape decks, a turntable, and associated equipment. I recently bought a tuner-amplifier, which is the centerpiece of it all, and Harry wired it. I also bought ear phones so I could listen when he was asleep. When he finished, several guys came to hear for themselves what the latest equipment sounded like. Even though I had high quality speakers, part of the demonstration included listening to the earphones. Usually whoever was wearing the earphones would say something about how nice it sounded. He would, of course, be listening to music and have the volume turned up a bit, but he would be the only one in the room able to hear it. Whenever the listener made a comment, someone would say, "Huh?" and soon he would be shouting at the rest of us, and we'd have a good laugh. Sometimes it didn't take much to amuse us.

September 16, 1969. Tuesday. Took off at 1:40 a.m. as the flight leader, call sign Firefly 36 in aircraft #665, an H model. The mission lasted three hours and thirty minutes. We worked with Lulu at 050/40 from Channel 113.

I got to bed about 6:15 a.m.

*

I took off again at 8:45 p.m. with Lieutenant Colonel Lucky Lowman on the wing, and we struck with Blue Moon. We had a pretty good mission, and Blue Moon said we had ninety KBA, but I have to wonder about his figures. He reported it, so I repeated it on my flight report, and it was turned in to 7th Air Force HQ in Saigon as ninety KBA. Is it possible this was the way inflated enemy kill reports were passed all the way to American TV screens during the war? Maybe we did hit the target pretty well, but ninety KBA? If figures like that were multiplied for all of Southeast Asian operations for every day of the war, we probably would have had enough KBA to kill everyone in North Vietnam at least one and a half times. Maybe twice.

When we got back to NKP we had to hold for forty minutes because someone was having an emergency and the runway was tied up.

September 17, 1969. Wednesday. Took off at 3:50 p.m. in aircraft #076 with Jim Beggerly leading. We struck with Poppy and had a very good mission, but Jim had low engine oil pressure and had to RTB before I was finished striking, so I finished alone. This was my ninetieth mission.

Colonel Stueck had his last mission today and will be going home soon. I hate to see him go, as he was a good squadron commander, and I liked him. His next assignment was to an aircraft carrier as air force liaison officer for six weeks. He thought that was a pretty cool assignment, and so did I.

September 18, 1969. Thursday. I didn't fly today because I had to get plague and cholera shots and I'm grounded for twenty-four hours. I got one in each arm, so I'm sore on both sides. I will begin a Sandy tour of duty tomorrow, so I've been getting my body turned around again from very late nights to very early mornings.

September 19, 1969. Friday. I set up early for Sandy alert then went back to bed and slept until about 1:00 p.m. Took off at 2:55 for the November Orbit over Steel Tiger, but the weather was not good for any action, so we just bored holes in the sky. Rex Huntsman was the leader.

September 20, 1969. Saturday. I was Sandy Four today and we took off at 3:00 p.m. for orbit over Barrel Roll.

*

Our new squadron commander took command today. He was from the Hobo squadron.

September 21, 1969. Sunday. I was Sandy Two today, but we didn't even take-off because of bad weather due to a big storm off the coast to the east.

September 22, 1969. Monday. Back on nights. Took off at 8:50 p.m. with Noel Frisbie leading. The weather was very good, and Lulu gave us one hundred KBA. We had a good mission.

September 23, 1969. Tuesday. Took off at 7:35 p.m. in the right seat of a G model with Frank Monroe in the left and Bob Bohan leading. About the time we got to the bend in the river, we were turned around to go to Steel Tiger for a hot target that needed some Skyraiders ASAP. The target was 135/150 from NKP, which was a long way in the other direction from where we were, and by the time we arrived, the hot project was over. We struck with Blind Bat 02. The weather was good and we had a bright moon.

Since May 27, I've had eighteen weather cancellations.

September 24, 1969. Wednesday. I had an FCF with takeoff at 11:35 a.m., then boarded the afternoon C-130 flight to Bangkok for my two-week mid-tour leave.

*

September 26, 1969. Friday. Emily and I mailed Christmas gifts home from the House of Siam store that was directly across the street from JUSMAG. In the evening, we took Bonnie Scroggs to dinner at La Rotunde at the Narai.
September 28, 1969. Sunday. This morning we went to a Baptist church not far from the apartment. We ate lunch at a pancake house nearby and spent the afternoon swimming and sunning in the apartment's pool.
September 29, 1969. Monday. We ate dinner at the Two Vikings, which was not as expensive as La Rotunde, and it had larger servings.
September 30, 1969. Tuesday. We went to the United States military base exchange where I bought a camera for Dad then to the commissary for groceries. The BX was a long way across town, so we hired a taxi and driver for much of the day. The commissary had fresh apples from the United States. Apple trees need cold weather, so they are a delicacy in Thailand and are expensive and of poor quality if they are ever available in the local markets. Apples sold for fifty cents each in a Bangkok supermarket, but at the BX they were sixty nine cents a dozen. When we came out of the commissary grounds, several youngsters appeared with big smiles and their hands held out for us to give them the treat of an apple.

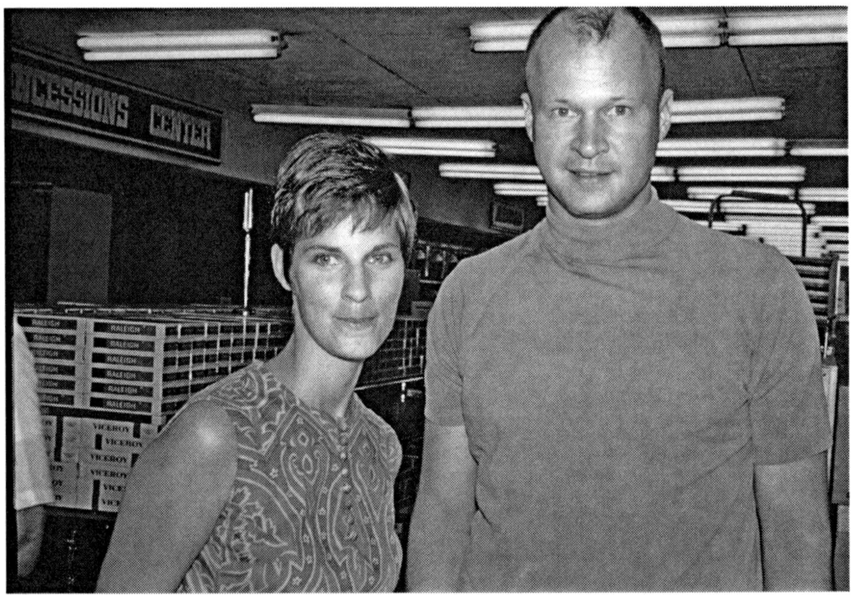

Emily and Dick at the Bangkok commissary

Bangkok traffic was congested and the air polluted from the exhaust of cars, trucks, and buses on the streets. Buses were always crowded as they moved from stop to stop, with people frequently hanging out the doors. Most difficult of all for Americans was that they drove on the wrong side of the road—the left. Unless one knew the city pretty well, the layout of the streets seemed to be haphazard, and it wasn't hard to get lost, so renting a taxi was sensible.

Students on a bus in Bangkok

October 1, 1969. Wednesday. We went on the Grand Palace Tour in the morning and the Temple Tour in the afternoon. We were required to be suitably dressed for the Grand Palace Tour, which started at 9:00 a.m., and that meant a suit and tie for me, and a dress for Emily. The weather was sunny and warm.

October 2, 1969. Thursday. We were up at 5:30 for the 7:00 a.m. Floating Market Tour, which was mostly on the west side of the Chao Phraya River. Our conveyance was a small barge, and the trip included a look at the King's Royal Barge and the Temple of Dawn. We were back at the apartment by noon and went swimming again in the afternoon.

In the evening we were invited to Linnea Bolin's apartment for dinner. Linnea was a U. S. State Department employee who worked at the American Embassy in Bangkok, and was the sister of a friend of my parents in Princeton who suggested we get together. She was delightful and we had a very pleasant time.

*

October 3, 1969. Friday. Johny's Gems was a favorite store in which to shop for bargains. Its location was far off the beaten path and difficult to find, so we called Johny and he sent a car to take us there. The driver also took us home when we were done shopping. Johny provided complimentary coffee, tea, or soft drinks. He was customer friendly, his prices were reasonable, and he had a very good business. Emily and I went to Johny's for more Christmas shopping and we bought a bronze dinnerware set for ourselves.

Doug Scroggs was in town for three days on a CTO, so he and Bonnie came over this evening to look at my slide pictures of Laos.

October 4, 1969. Saturday. We had a quiet day at the apartment and swam in the pool. Doug and Bonnie joined us for dinner at the Imperial Hotel's restaurant.

October 6, 1969. Monday. We rented a taxi at the Manhattan Hotel to do errands around the city.

*

Back at the war, Jack Hudson earned an Air Force Cross on this date for leading the exfiltration of friendlies from a bad area in southern Laos.

*

October 7, 1969. Tuesday. We ate dinner at the Erawan Hotel where the chef put on quite a show. He brought a portable grill to each table, and as he was cooking, he sang out loudly and clearly each ingredient he was using. When his creation was properly cooked he served it with great flourish. Everyone in the restaurant knew just what everyone else had ordered.

We went from the Erawan to the Lido Theater to see the Clint Eastwood movie *McKenna's Gold*. The Lido was large and beautiful, nicer than any theater I had been in in America, with roomy reclining seats and an excellent sound system. The film was presented in English with Thai language subtitles and was a fine experience.

October 9, 1969. Wednesday. We stayed at the apartment all day. I started to get organized to go back to NKP.

*

The C-130 flights were booked full, so I found a ride on a C-47 in the evening. The flight back took two and a half hours.

October 10, 1969. Friday. Upon my return to NKP, I learned sad news about Bob Moore. He was on takeoff at dawn October 3 when he aborted. He had the airplane pretty well slowed down when his landing gear collapsed and his external fuel tanks ignited, a fire broke out, his ordnance exploded, and Bob was killed. He was loaded for a long mission, with fuel in the stub tank as well as the usual 1800 pounds in the centerline. It was not determined whether he raised his gear handle for some reason or if the airplane swerved because of a malfunction of the gear or a brake. Either way, Bob didn't make it. He was in aircraft #030.

Bob was a graduate of the Air Force Academy and was one of the bright young guys in the squadron. He was well respected and well liked and I'll miss him. I really hate the losses we're experiencing—and for what?

*

Even in a wartime operation mundane things such as an annual instrument check were required and I had mine today with Major Tom Hipps as my IP. It took forty minutes. I also received my DFC today for the May 21 mis-

Receiving DFC from wing commander Colonel Sam Crosby (USAF photo)

sion in a nice ceremony in the TUOC auditorium, which was in no danger of being confused with the Lido in Bangkok.

A few days ago, three helicopters went down, all in the same area. All the crewmen were picked up and two of them had been shot, one in the leg and the other in the back, but neither was wounded seriously. A flying crane was brought in to try to recover them. One was lifted to 6,000 feet at which time it began to oscillate on the cable. The crew had no choice but to cut it loose and the chopper scattered over a large area when it hit. Fortunately, no one was injured or killed.

A navy F-4 went down and when the back seater came down in the trees, one of his feet caught in the crook of a tree and broke his leg. He hung by his broken leg upside down unable to move for an hour and ten minutes until the rescuers were able to find him. He had no flares or smoke to signal and only a radio to tell the Sandies and Jollies when they were overhead.

He'd say, "You're coming, you're getting closer. You're over me. You're going away!" until they could pinpoint his location.

An exfil was under way with friendly troops east of NKP and when the chopper landed the pilot told them he couldn't carry them all out. They told the pilot if he didn't they were going to shoot him down. So they all got on and when they got back to NKP, fifty-four got off the helicopter. Two Americans were left on the ground and another helicopter was called in to pick them up. All the while ground fire came from around the area.

In another incident, two people were on the ground and were picked up by a helicopter. After they were away, a third called on his radio, "Hey! You missed me!" So they had to go back to get him.

Every day seems to bring something eventful. It's a wonder anyone can survive all this action.

Chapter 12

Udorn

The monsoon was still a factor in October, but the season was beginning to wear itself out. I continued to fly nights most of the time and had many missions in the right seat as a night IP. I was on the schedule almost every day.

Airplane parts were at times unreliable, including inoperative heading indicator, fuel boost pump, trim, radios, and console lights. It may sound like we had sloppy maintenance, but that wasn't the case. Maintenance was very good, and the crew chiefs worked hard to keep their airplanes in top shape and were proud of the work they did, but we were operating old airplanes that had seen a lot of service before they arrived at NKP.

A-1s were originally designed for the navy by Douglas Aircraft Company in 1947 and for many years were flown off aircraft carriers. They had the navy features of foldable wings and retractable tailhooks, which air force pilots weren't accustomed to. The navy deployed Skyraiders, which they called Spads, from 1964 to 1968. Then the air force discovered they were almost ideally suited for search and rescue operations.

We were told they were shipped by sea to Cam Ran Bay where they were overhauled, modified for our use, and then flown to NKP.

Throughout their use with the navy, they didn't have ejection seats and part of the modification at Cam Ran Bay was to install what was called the yankee system. It was designed for the canopy to be jettisoned first and then a rocket behind the pilot's head fired to pull him out of the airplane via a strap connected to a harness. Parachute deployment completed the process. It was a good design when it worked, which was not one hundred percent of the time.

If a pilot had to make a premature departure from an A-1 before the yankee system was installed, he had two choices: He could bail out over the side and use his parachute as had been done before ejection seats were invented, or he could ride it in. The Skyraider was an ideal plane to crash land (if any airplane is ideal to crash land) because of the armor around the cockpit and the resulting structural strength, and it had been successfully done several times.

Many pilots flying A-1s had learned to fly in jets with their much more reliable engines. They also had flown only airplanes with modern, reliable ejection seats that were an integral part of the airplane design. When I began A-1 training at Hurlburt, I was unfamiliar with reciprocating engines, cowl flaps, tail wheels, constant speed propellers, and the attack mission itself. I had been out of pilot training for almost three years when I arrived at NKP, and my experience had been in trainers and F-106s, which had a very different mission from A-1s. Small wonder Lloyd Scott, who crashed in June and who was fresh out of pilot training, was overloaded at a critical time!

If a pilot should find that his yankee system didn't work, he was unlikely to find a piece of ground in all of Laos level enough to belly it in. And if there *was* a level strip of ground, odds were the enemy controlled it, and his chance of survival would be pretty bleak. We were told that, as a general rule, the good guys held the high ground and the bad guys held the low ground and valleys. Since Laos looked like a tree-covered washboard from the air, the prospects for a belly landing were poor. Add the fact that I was doing most of my flying at night when a belly landing was out of the question, and it became clear I was going to have to be more thoroughly prepared for the unexpected than I had been in the past.

These matters had been discussed as separate items in safety meetings, but it had not been put together into the form of, "What if it happens at night, fully loaded over the mountains and *then* the seat doesn't work?" What then?

The only alternative was to go over the side. Some guys tried and didn't have time to completely separate from the airplane before impact. External stores had to be jettisoned to lighten the load as much as possible in order to increase the glide ratio, and *then* bail out. A-1s glided much better when they were clean and didn't have 8,000 to 10,000 pounds hanging under the wings.

This was hardly an earthshaking discovery, but it was another lesson experience taught me. The failure to accomplish that very basic procedure of jettisoning ordnance had probably contributed to the deaths of several pilots who were lulled into complacency about the reliability of the engines and ejection systems.

*

Inspections revealed cracked wing spars—some worse than others. The ones that weren't cracked too badly were restricted to four Gs, and a writeup was required for more than six Gs. A G is one times the force of gravity, so four Gs is four times the normal force of gravity that we all feel on the surface of the earth. Pulling Gs was unavoidable when pulling out of a dive bomb pass and four Gs was the standard, even using our normal 40° dive angle. All the airplanes had G meters.

The airplanes whose wing spars were more seriously cracked were restricted to three Gs, and we were required to write them up if we exceeded three and a half, which was a much more serious limitation because it meant 40° dive angle attacks were not possible. In those airplanes, we used a 30° dive angle, which completely skewed the reference point used to determine when we were in position to make a pass, and we had to use different mil settings on the gun sight. The three-G limitation problem wasn't taught at Hurlburt, and we were not issued guidelines on how to set up a 30° attack and what mil settings to use. We had a wide variety of weapons to deliver and each required a different mil setting on the gun sight. We didn't have the opportunity to experiment to see what worked and what didn't, so the result was erratic accuracy in the three-G airplanes.

Whenever a plane was written up for being over-G'd, maintenance had a detailed procedure to inspect and recertify it for flight. To their credit, as far as I know, no one ever complained about an over-G write-up, so there was never any pressure on pilots to cover it up. It was simply a fact of life with our old airplanes.

Some of our planes came from the South Vietnamese Air Force, of all places, which might make one feel like he was flying for a banana republic instead of the United States Air Force. The Vietnamese were reported to be very good pilots because they had flown Skyraiders for many years and hundreds of missions. But they didn't fly in clouds or at night.

*

October 11, 1969. Saturday. My first mission after leave was in the right seat and I took off at 9:00 p.m. as IP for Dave Friestad with Daryl Heusinkveld leading. A C-130 fac with the call sign Pintail had found some trucks south of the Birdshead. I listened to the Mets-Orioles World Series game on Radio Saigon when we weren't striking. Orioles won 4-1.

October 12, 1969. Sunday. I went to church in the morning, then flipped a coin with Russ Keeling to see who would fly an FCF. Russ flew it. Took off on my mission at 9:00 p.m. with Frank Monroe leading. The weather was bad, and we ended up hitting where an earlier flight had struck, but it wasn't much of a mission. We flew four hours and five minutes and should have stayed home.

A decision had recently been made to demobilize the A-1 squadron at Pleiku, and some of their airplanes and pilots, as many as twenty, were to be transferred to NKP.

October 13, 1969. Monday. I had two FCFs this afternoon, both in G models—one for an engine change and the other for a prop change. The FCF call sign was Clown.

Took off at 8:55 p.m. in aircraft #455 with Friestad in the left seat and Hoisy leading. We struck with White Rose who told us we had thirty KBA.

October 14, 1969. Tuesday. A survival equipment refresher course was required after six months of a combat tour. Part of the course was practice egress, which I did again today. This time I was out in seven seconds—two seconds faster than on August 12.

The wing had received two pilots from Pleiku, both of whom were in my class at Hurlburt—Don Travis and Bob Karre. Seven more were due to come in the next few weeks. Two missions have been cut from the schedule starting tomorrow—to twelve per day, counting Sandies.

Our loads had lately become a little lighter, which made takeoffs easier.

*

Took off at 8:20 p.m. as Firefly 36 with Frank Monroe on the wing. We were assigned to armed recce the road east of the Birdshead. We had no moonlight and no easy landmarks in that area from which to navigate. After a few minutes of searching, I saw lights on the ground, so I popped a flare to try to figure out where I was and saw a road I hadn't seen before with trucks stopped on it. I was a little uneasy about it, though, so I called Alleycat for permission to strike. Permission was denied because we were over North Vietnam, so we had to leave a nice fat target and find something else to go after. One of the realities of the war was the rules of engagement we had to live by.

On November 1, 1968, President Johnson stopped the bombing of North Vietnam, and in return, there was an unwritten agreement the North Vietnamese would not bring surface to air missiles (SAMs) or radar guided guns into Laos. That was OK as far as I was concerned.

We headed west and found trucks in the eastern part of Ban Ban Valley. The weather was moving in, and we had to hurry, but I hurried too much and armed my centerline fuel tank by mistake. No fuel remained, but the tank had a charge about the size of a shotgun shell at the attachment point to the bottom of the airplane. When I hit the pipper, it popped off with a jolt. I thought at first I had been hit by ground fire, especially when I smelled the gunpowder smoke drifting into the cockpit. I immediately turned south to get away from the road. Then it dawned on me what had happened. We were striking lights-out in a remote area and had not seen groundfire, so it was unlikely I had been hit, which left only one explanation. I was embarrassed about bombing off an empty fuel tank, but no harm was done. Unfortunately, the clouds prevented us from getting the trucks we had seen. In addition, I over-G'd the three-G airplane. It was my first lead mission in three weeks and it just wasn't my night.

*

<u>October 15, 1969.</u> Wednesday. United States involvement in Vietnam was controversial almost from the beginning. As the years passed, protests became more and more frequent and intense. The pilots who were my peers in the air force almost universally supported our efforts to defeat the Vietcong and

North Vietnamese, so we could leave that country in peace and with honor. Many Americans didn't see it that way and we who were serving looked upon them with disapproval (to put it nicely). We felt they were undermining our efforts and encouraging the enemy while we and hundreds of thousands of American soldiers in Vietnam were putting our lives on the line daily.

A major anti-war protest rally was held across the United States today. It was estimated that two million protesters demonstrated nationwide including 250,000 who marched on the capitol in Washington, D.C. It didn't affect us directly, but those of us who were actually fighting the war could only shake our heads in dismay at those who were making our efforts more difficult and giving comfort and encouragement to the enemy.

*

October 16, 1969. Thursday. During briefing for tonight's mission Jim George and I talked about the fact that neither of us had had a real emergency situation lately. I should have known that would be the catalyst to have one. We took off at 8:20 p.m. with me in the lead. We struck with Pogo, and on my fourth pass, the canopy started to slide back. I knew immediately what the problem was because the canopy slide was hydraulically powered. Sure enough, when I checked the hydraulic pressure gauge, it read zero.

So I turned south for the base with a detour to the jettison area to get rid of my remaining ordnance. If the gear collapsed on landing or if it wouldn't come down at all I didn't want to slide along the runway atop napalm and bombs.

1. The ailerons were boosted by hydraulic pressure, but I didn't notice the loss of it.

2. The landing gear had an emergency system that worked the way it was supposed to.

3. The flaps were hydraulic, so I made a no-flap landing. I came in about 10 knots faster and flatter than normal, which was not a problem.

4. The brakes had a separate hydraulic system that worked. Airspeed was slow to decrease, but with plenty of runway the landing went smoothly. No sweat.

This was my one-hundredth mission.

*

Jim Monk, who had been my flight commander, had a new assignment as wing frag officer to replace Harry. The job required checking the wing's mission assignments on each day's flying order from Seventh Air Force and then specifying which munitions were to be loaded on the airplanes.

My new flight commander was to be Major Ron Marzano, who had just arrived. Officer efficiency reports (OERs) were written for each pilot in a flight by the flight commander.

The New York Mets won the World Series today.

October 17, 1969. Friday. Took off at 8:20 p.m. with Jim George on the wing. I was Firefly 36 in aircraft #206, an E model. We armed reccied Route 7 near the Birdshead and didn't find anything, so we went over to Blue Moon who said he had two companies of bad guys and a tank along a river. I put down a log marker and Blue Moon said to hit it, so I put a nape right on it. Jim and I worked the target over pretty good, but Blue Moon didn't get too excited and we didn't get any secondary fires, so I don't think he had a very good target.

October 18, 1969. Saturday. Took off at 9:05 p.m., forty-five minutes late because of hydraulic problems in Jim Matthews's airplane, #314, the same one I lost hydraulic pressure in two nights ago. Jim was the leader and we armed reccied Route 7 east of the Birdshead. We saw a truck moving west on the road and Jim asked me if he should pop out a flare or go after the truck. I said, "Go after it." So he circled to get into position, rolled in and scored a direct hit with a nape. We watched awhile, then Ethan called to tell us we were one mile inside North Vietnam and to go west. Ethan's accuracy isn't always the best—I've seen them as much as ten miles off—but he could have been right tonight because the truck was moving with his lights on in what he must have thought was a safe area. So we turned west. Soon we saw a large explosion back to the east. We figured it might have been whatever was in that truck cooking off. It was a big explosion and provided quite a sight. We flew west to work with Hilltop in the northern PDJ, but he had a language problem and couldn't tell east from west. It was frustrating for us as I'm sure it must have been for Hilltop. We flew around some more, but couldn't find anything else to do, so we dumped our ordnance and came home. This was a long mission—four hours and twenty minutes.

October 19, 1969. Sunday. I went to church in the afternoon. Jim George and I ate in the Thai Restaurant on the base. He was to be my wingman tonight and I liked flying with him because he was a good pilot and we knew what to expect from each other.

We took off at 8:50 p.m., thirty minutes late because Jim discovered an H model load on his airplane that was an E. The loads had to be different because the fat faces had heavier empty weights than the single seaters, but the same max gross takeoff weight limit. We worked with Peacock first and then with Lulu. Both reported DK82 mortars shooting at them, which we could see as we neared the area. As soon as the bad guys knew we were nearby, they stopped firing and we had our usual difficulty pinning down their exact locations. It has been said that in a duel between an airplane and a big gun, the gun will win. But at night, when we had lights out and they couldn't see us we had a big advantage if we knew where they were.

The heading indicator was inaccurate on my airplane, but I managed to work around it.

*

I was on stand by for FCFs on October 20 and 21.

October 20, 1969. Monday. I had an FCF in the afternoon with a 2:30 takeoff, but sent it back to maintenance because the airplane had UHF and VHF radio failure and bad trim. I went directly from the FCF to briefing for my combat mission and took off at 5:10 p.m., twenty minutes late because my first plane had a fuel boost pump failure. Jim George led and we armed recced Route 7 and then went to work with Red Tiger in the PDJ. Red Tiger seemed to really like the show and was very easy to please. I had a three-G limit E model and over-G'd it when I pulled 3.7 Gs on one of my passes.

October 21, 1969. Tuesday. I had two FCFs this afternoon; the first was the airplane I rejected yesterday. They both passed.

I was assigned as the wingman with a new leader for my combat mission tonight in aircraft #314, the same one in which I had hydraulic failure in five nights ago. When I arrived at the airplane, smoke was coming out of it, so I requested the spare. After I got strapped in, I found the circuit breaker for the console lights kept popping, which grounded it. By then maintenance had 314 ready to go, so I took it. Then, after a one hour and fifteen minute delay for maintenance problems, we had to wait another thirty minutes for weather.

We were assigned to Hornet in the northern part of the PDJ who was under attack by a 37mm gun being used as ground-to-ground artillery. We could see the tracers about twenty miles ahead of us and I really got excited because it was a fat target. With our lights out and the sound of his shell fire ringing in his ears, the gunner couldn't see or hear us, and we had a good chance of getting a direct spot on his location from a roll in position. Even if the lead's first nape missed, I could be in position to find that gun, and we'd get it!

With the autopilot engaged, I turned on a map light to double check that the coordinates Alleycat had assigned were in fact where we saw the gunfire.

The A-1 was not an electric jet with fancy onboard computers that would take us to a given location just by pressing a few buttons. We didn't even have a weapons delivery computer to help us line up a bomb drop. It was purely seat-of-the-pants flying that took effort, skill, and concentration to get right. Everything had to go right for a bomb or nape to hit exactly on target, and nailing a small target such as a truck or gun emplacement from 4,000 feet above the ground was difficult at best. The job was made immeasurably easier if we could get a target location eyeballed as we rolled in instead of working through a third party such as a Laotian ground fac with limited English skills or with an airborne American who had his marks scattered all over the place.

A sighting of muzzle flashes at roll-in was even better. I was really excited tonight because maybe we had a chance to have a target just begging to get clobbered. All we had to do was sneak up on it.

When I turned out my map light and looked out I couldn't believe my eyes. The leader was over the target and had put out a flare! It was hard to sneak up on the gun when a flare was popped right over his position! Now neither of us knew where the target was and the gunner surely wasn't going to volunteer now that he knew Skyraiders were anxious to take a pop at him. We were back to working with Hornet: "...the target is 200 meters from my position."

Maybe he had east mixed up with west. Maybe the target was 200 meters northeast of his position, maybe 300 meters east. It was a poor substitute for a direct observation at roll in. Hornet directed us to the target, but we knew we didn't get it because as we left with all our ordnance expended, the shooting started again and we couldn't do anything about it. I made several passes, and even shot my guns without success.

I was in a rather delicate position because the wingman was supposed to follow what the leader did. Since I was with an inexperienced leader, maybe I should have spoken up—which I'll do next time. I had assumed he would know to not announce our arrival, and I felt like a fisherman who had let a big one get away.

As I pulled off the target the last time, I pulled the propeller RPM lever back and the engine started to run rough. Then the sump light came on. It was on for only a few seconds, but it got my attention, and I immediately turned southwest toward Lima Site 98. The area between LS 98 and Vientiane was controlled by the enemy and I kept climbing so I could glide as far as possible if the engine quit. But it smoothed out and the sump light was out, so I relaxed a little. The landing strip at LS 98 was 4,000 x 75 ft. with a mountain at the north end and no lights. It was no place to land a Skyraider at night, but was a friendly place if I had to bail out.

A twenty-five nautical mile no-fly zone existed around Vientiane, which was on an almost direct line between LS 98 and Udorn, the closest American base. Because I had declared an emergency, I was allowed to violate the twenty-five-mile radius and flew about five miles east of the center of the city. The lights of Vientiane were shining brightly in the darkness and looked peaceful and inviting from 15,000 feet. I hadn't been that close to a large city at night in many months, and looking at the serenity of the lights was like a tranquilizer. The war suddenly seemed far away, even though I was in a warplane and had been deeply engaged in combat just minutes ago.

As I approached Udorn and the lights of the base came nearer, the engine was running smoothly and I glanced to the east. NKP was 106 miles away. Should I overfly Udorn and try to make it to NKP? It would be a lot easier for the maintenance people if I could get it back to our base. I thought of stories I'd heard of pilots who had overflown a perfectly good runway in order to get home only to discover to their dismay that the airplane couldn't make it, so I decided to land at Udorn and sort out the engine problem in the daylight tomorrow. The instruments were normal and the light didn't come on again.

At NKP, when an airplane diverted from another base because of a maintenance problem or if it had been shot up, the crew were referred to as visiting firemen, and an officer was assigned to meet the pilot to make sure he was comfortable and had food and a bed. At Udorn, the duty was rotated among the squadrons and the host was called Peter the Greeter.

When Peter the Greeter came to meet me he said, "I know you," and I said, "I know you, too." It took two hours of searching our memories to recall that we had been in the same small group of trainees at the survival school training compound at Fairchild AFB, Washington, almost a year earlier. His name was Dave Kumler and he had an empty upper bunk in his room that I used. The guy in the lower bunk had been a radar observer in F-101 Voodoos at Suffolk County, New York, and I knew him from diversion flights when I had been flying F-106s at Dover. It was a pleasant surprise to run into guys I knew, however slightly.

<u>October 22, 1969.</u> Wednesday. I got to bed after 3:00 a.m. and was up at 10:00. When I got to the flight line, I discovered no one had been working on my airplane. When a pilot diverts to another base maintenance was *supposed* to work on the airplane for him, but nothing had been done. I waited around awhile and finally remembered someone had told me I had to take care of my problem. I searched for a mechanic and finally found a young airman who would take a look at it. He reported all external areas of the engine appeared to be intact—no blown gaskets or cylinders—and he decided to change spark plugs. He didn't know what type of spark plugs an R-3350 needed. I didn't either, but he said he would find out. I waited about three hours while the spark plug hunt was on. It was very difficult to find out who was in charge because everyone I talked to passed the buck by saying someone else was looking for spark plugs. Finally I went to the sergeant in charge and said, "OK, who is looking for spark plugs?" The answer was NO one.

I found the first airman and suggested we go to the airplane together and I would start the engine so he could see if there were any visible external problems. When we got to the airplane, I asked, "By the way, how much experience do you have on recips?"

"I really don't know much about them, sir," he answered, which raised a red flag. Before I started the engine I asked if he had found anything that would cause the sump light to illuminate. He said he had found three pieces of fuzz around the chip detector and indicated with his fingers they were a quarter to a half inch. Now we're getting somewhere. I called the maintenance desk at NKP and the mechanic said, "Don't even start it. We'll come over and look at it, and we'll send an airplane to pick you up."

Dave Friestad, who was on his second tour of duty in southeast Asia, came for me, and we made arrangements to meet at one of the squadrons. While there, I met two pilots, Terry Stine and Steve Rogers, who had been T-38 instructors in my element at Laughlin AFB when I was in pilot training. Two others who had been in the class behind mine at Laughlin were there, too. I also saw a pilot I knew from Perrin AFB in F-102 training and yet another who had been a T-37 instructor at Laughlin with whom I had flown.

Dave and I got back to NKP about 7:00 p.m.

*

Four pilots were scheduled for CTOs to start today, but three guys got sick, so only one got to go. Everyone else was pushed back for a month and a half. We were not overmanned like we were a month ago.

October 23, 1969. Thursday. Took off at 4:50 p.m. with Tony Wylie (AKA Wyliecat) leading. We armed reccied Route 61 from Ban Ban to Sam Neua with no results, then went to Rocket Mobile who facced us in on troops 300 meters south of his position. I had a good mission and put my bombs right on the target. Rocket Mobile said the bad guys were headed south when we left.

October 24, 1969. Friday. An F-100 Misty fac went down 133 miles southeast of NKP today and a SAR effort was begun, so I didn't fly tonight because of no available airplanes. The survivors were in a bad area, and a Jolly Green helicopter was shot down. Eventually both crew members were pulled out of the woods after a very difficult fight. Technical Sergeant Donald G. Smith, the parajumper on the helicopter that was shot down, received an Air Force Cross for his actions in rescuing the Misty pilots and the helicopter crew.

October 25, 1969. Saturday. I flew tonight as an IP in the right seat with Dave Friestad in the left and Jim Herrick leading. We took off at 4:40, while it was still daylight. I took along my camera and got several pictures of Jim in the other airplane, the Mekong, karst, and the full moon just above the horizon. By the time we arrived in the target area in Barrel Roll, sunlight was fully gone, so this could be counted as a night check out mission for Dave.

*

Jim Herrick northbound toward Barrel Roll in an A-1H. Note the karst.

October 26, 1969. Sunday. An F-4 fac, Wolf 05, crashed against a mountain in southern Laos at 6:40 this morning. No chute or beeper. Two months later, I found out the pilot was Captain Gray Warren who had been in the 95th at Dover when I was there. Gray was an Air Force Academy graduate from Des Moines, Iowa, and was one of the truly outstanding people I have had the pleasure to know.

Fourteen months earlier, in late August, 1968, Gray, Captain R. D. Watkins, and I flew F-106s from Dover to Loring AFB in northern Maine in order to fly target missions the next night. R. D. had flown one hundred missions in F-105s over North Vietnam in 1966 when F-105s had a very high casualty rate, and he showed Gray and me a few things about tactical fighter tactics on the trip to Loring. The weather was good all the way and we had a fine time, the three of us. After we passed Bangor, we canceled our IFR clearance, descended to tree top level and zoomed along just above the contour of the land at high speed—up and down the hills. When we arrived in the Loring area, we passed low over fishermen in their boats on nearby lakes. We lit the (after) burners and engaged in mock dog fights. The best part of any trip to Loring was when I opened the canopy after landing, took off my oxygen mask, and smelled the fresh pine-scented air.

When we arrived at our visiting officers' quarters (VOQ) rooms, we got a six-pack of beer and savored the fun we had just had. The Loring Officers'

Club had Maine lobster on the menu that night, and I learned how to eat it. We had a great time together and life was good.

Just over two weeks later, September 13, 1968, R. D. was killed in a T-33 right after takeoff at Barksdale AFB, Louisiana. In a T-bird! After surviving one hundred missions in a Thud over the North. His engine lost a compressor blade on takeoff and he tried to come around for an immediate landing, but the airplane was heavy with fuel and just wouldn't fly because the engine was coming apart. He stayed with it a little too long. His ejection seat was found to be about half-way up the track, indicating he tried to eject an instant too late and the sequence was stopped when the airplane impacted the ground. The engine blade was found at about the 6,000 foot mark of the runway.

And now Gray was dead, too. What a terrible tragedy!

*

October 27, 1969. Monday. Jim Herrick disappeared near the Birdshead this afternoon. He had gone through a hole in the clouds to check Route 7 and never came back up. Jim George was his flight leader. Going through a cloud hole in mountainous terrain is a very dangerous proposition. I had flown with Jim several times, and he was a good pilot and a fine young guy who had a great future. We played ping pong and went to town together. Once again, I was saddened by the loss of a friend. Unfortunately, this war is killing our best and brightest, and Jim Herrick and Gray Warren fit at the top of those categories. What a waste! They were really good guys with a lot of potential and were my friends. Jim was from Panora, Iowa, and had graduated from Iowa State University. His goal in life was to be a veterinarian. He would have celebrated his twenty-fifth birthday tomorrow.

Jim Herrick (USAF photo courtesy of the Herrick family)

*

The following is Jim George's account of his last mission with Jim Herrick as written to the Herrick family.

The call sign of our flight of two A-1s was Firefly 32, which was also my individual call sign, with Jim flying as number two, with a call sign of Firefly 33. Our mission was road reconnaissance and traffic denial along Route 7, from Ban Ban Valley in northern Laos to where it entered North Vietnam in the area called the Fish's Mouth. The purpose of this type of mission is to prevent the enemy from moving supplies along the roads, making it difficult for them to resupply their combat troops. We were basically looking for any targets, primarily trucks, along the route. (There were some antiaircraft gun emplacements along this route structure as well, but as a general rule, we did not attack guns unless fired upon, and then only if the conditions were in our favor.) Jim and I would start our work that day in the Ban Ban Valley, pick up the route, and follow it in an easterly direction to the North Vietnamese border. Our briefing was about midday with an early afternoon takeoff.

En route to the target area, we checked in with the Airborne Command and Control Center (ABCCC—whose radio call sign was Cricket) and we were told that our mission was as scheduled, and we were informed that the weather was not the best. They also asked us for a PIREP (a pilot report on the weather).

Jim was a flight lead himself and had told me during our pre-mission briefing that he had been flying and leading this particular road reconnaissance mission for, as I recall him saying, the past few days. [NOTE: That would not have been exactly correct, since I had flown with Jim on another type of mission on the 25th, but was, I'm sure, essentially correct.]

Jim said that he had been watching one or two bombed out truck hulks located right at a 90- to 100-degree bend in Route 7, where the road turns into the Fish's Mouth and runs into

North Vietnam. Jim stated to me in our briefing his desire to check out the truck hulks to see if they were moving them—salvaging parts, or anything. I had agreed to Jim's request to try and have a look at these as we accomplished our road reconnaissance mission.

When we arrived over the Ban Ban Valley, flying at about 10-12,000 feet, the weather was solid undercast with smooth tops at about 7,000 feet. Thus we were able to set up in the clear that particular day over the center of the Ban Ban Valley with a few of the mountain peaks protruding slightly from the cloud deck below around the perimeter of the very large valley. We did what was our usual check to see if the weather was workable underneath the clouds: Jim, as wingman, held in a high orbit while I, as the flight lead, did a spiraling descent on instruments through the clouds down to about 2,000-3,000 feet above the valley floor. I don't recall, after all this time, the elevation of the valley floor—I think it was either 1,000 or 2,000 feet. (Note here that as flight leads, Jim and I had an incredible storehouse of such facts and particulars in our heads. There were very few aids to navigation to determine our precise location over Laos, so we generally used time, distance, and heading from a known point to navigate, and our knowledge of the terrain was essential to successful combat missions, especially in a single-pilot aircraft such as the A-1.)

When I broke out of the clouds, the weather was quite clear, with good visibility, and I told Jim to begin his letdown. Jim then made the same instrument descent, and we rejoined underneath. We then turned south to locate the road, which crossed the southern portion of the valley, and started our road reconnaissance, with Jim flying about a half mile back and off to the side in a trail/cover position.

As we worked east towards the Bird's Head, the weather was slowly deteriorating, and the terrain rose gently, squeezing us a bit between the clouds and the ground. It didn't look good. As the road turned back south over the Bird's

Head, the terrain again became gradually lower, which was a plus, but at the same time just a few klicks (kilometers) further south, the ceiling was also lowering, and the clouds looked more ragged below the undercast. I think I made a 360 in that area to evaluate continuing, all the while with Jim following me visually. My decision, after looking to the south again, was that it was too bad for us to work under the clouds, and I felt it was getting dangerous for us, so I said something like, "This is too bad to work and I'm turning north and climbing up." Jim acknowledged that transmission, and, expecting that Jim was still following me visually, I began a climbing right turn into the clouds, which would take us away from the very high terrain that was to our left to the north and east of the Bird's Head. (This type of instrument climb, in trail, was again a fairly standard procedure for us, somewhat like the letdown in reverse.)

Not too long after starting the climb, I broke out into clear visual conditions on top of the clouds, and looked back over my shoulder for Jim. When I didn't see him, I radioed "Position, two?" to which he replied something like "I'm in the clear over the Bird's Head." Thinking he was on top with me, but I just had not seen him yet, I asked his altitude, and his reply was "4500 feet." Since this would have put him only about 1,000 feet or so above the terrain in the area, it was obvious that he had not followed me up for whatever reason. I asked him to climb on up, and I said that I would be switching frequencies to give Cricket a PIREP on the weather.

What happened to Jim from then on is unknown. When I finished my PIREP, I returned to our UHF radio frequency and again asked Jim his position. He didn't respond. I called a few more times, trying all three types of radios that we were equipped with, without success. I then contacted Ethan to see if they were showing his aircraft on their radar display, hoping that he had just lost his radios. No luck. I circled the area in the clear on top, looking for Jim's plane in the event he had had a complete electrical failure or something, again to no avail.

By now, fearing that Jim had been shot down or crashed and that he may need help, I decided that I needed to retrace our flight path looking for him. I did so by going back to the Ban Ban Valley, doing the same spiraling letdown we had both done initially, on instruments through the clouds, flew the same path back down Route 7, past the Bird's Head, same deteriorating weather.

Since Jim had expressed a strong interest in the damaged truck hulks, which were just a few kilometers further south from where I had called off our road recce, I felt that he may have decided to go on down there to have a look before climbing up. Thus when I reached that point where we had previously stopped, I decided to continue on, despite the poor weather. The weather was so much lower down by the big, sharp left turn into the Fish's Mouth that I didn't think I could make the turn, so I did a wide right 270 degree turn to the west, where the terrain was lower and I could stay visual, and then headed back straight east to fly over the road. Rolling out of my 270 and starting back over the road to the east, which had high terrain immediately on both sides of it, I found myself trapped over the road bed, but I was now committed. I was under a solid one hundred foot overcast, in between the rocks that formed a narrow valley that was only a couple of wingspans wide and one hundred feet tall at best (road on the bottom—mountains on both sides—solid overcast above). I resisted the urge to pull up into the clouds and stayed in the clear hoping my wingtips would fit down the walls of the valley, and by luck, skill, or the Grace of God, I was able to think clearly.

I remembered that the road, with one little jog, ran very straight into NVN, and after passing that jog, I just did an instrument climb on that easterly heading to a safe altitude.

I again tried contacting Jim on the radio, tried Ethan, etc., with no results. Knowing where I had just been, I thought it was possible that Jim may have ended up where I had just been, trapped in that little valley between the clouds and the mountains, and that he may have been shot down or crashed in there somewhere. So, after doing some more map and terrain study, I decided to retrace our steps yet again: same letdown on instruments over the Ban Ban, same flight along Route 7, same poor weather. This time, as I entered the confines of that little valley under the clouds, I flew the entire valley looking for Jim's plane—in case he had stayed under the weather like I did the first time. I knew the odds were that, in making the decision to do this, I may end up going into NVN, so I had also studied the terrain further east prior to this letdown, and I had turned off my transponder. I flew Route 7 below the clouds at fifty to one hundred feet, seeing nothing, and I finally turned north in better weather inside North Vietnam, beyond the big high ridge line that had been off to my left, or north, as I flew east over the road.

Finally, feeling that I had done all that I could, with a great sense of sadness that Jim had been shot down or crashed, I headed back to NKP by myself, arriving just as it got dark. All the while, I was hoping against hope that Jim had just lost his radios and was returning home on his own, being unable to contact me, but it was not to be.

Over the next few days, pilots from our squadron tried to find signs of Jim's aircraft, but the weather stayed poor with clouds obscuring the area. Finally, several days later, Jim's crash site was located somewhere in the high terrain to the north and east of the Bird's Head. We will never know with any certainty what happened to Jim after those last radio calls. He may have been fired upon, since that was known to be a very hostile area and he was down there on his own. He may have taken hits, which could have crippled his plane or his ability to communicate, and, along with or in combination with these possibilities, he may have gotten disoriented in the weather or he might have had some instrument malfunction, which might have put him in an untenable situation. I can tell you that, even without any outside problems, it was not an easy situation that day.

You expressed in one of your early emails that your family had not been aware that the war was going on in Laos. That was true for all the families at that time. Our government's official position was that it was not. Let there be no doubt in any of your minds…it was a shooting war in Laos. The 56th Special Operations Wing at NKP had two other squadrons of A-1s, in addition to the 602nd-our squadron—for a total of about ninety to one hundred aircraft and pilots. In just the year that I was there, the wing lost twenty-one aircraft and seventeen pilots. Also, let there be no doubt in your minds that Jim was a good young pilot. This was true in order to be high enough in his pilot training class to win an assignment to the A-1, and further, to be checked out as a flight lead in combat. He was, like all of us, dedicated to what he was doing and determined to do it to the utmost of his ability.

While it was a very painful experience for me, as a young flight lead, to have to come home without my wingman, I can only begin to imagine the pain of Jim's loss to your family. I sincerely hope that in some small way, knowing these details will provide you with some comfort and solace.

With Best regards,
Jim George
Firefly 32, 10-27-69

*

Took off at 5:00 p.m. in the right seat on the wing with Dave Friestad in the left seat and Daryl Heusinkveld leading. We were ten minutes late because Hoisy's airplane had a flat tail wheel tire. Dave and I were in a G model, and our takeoff weight was calculated to be 24,997 pounds, only three pounds under max gross weight for the airplane. We were notified of a weather hold ten minutes after we took off and directed to return and land. But the max landing weight for the airplane was 21,000 pounds, so the SOF said, "Burn off fuel and land." We had only 4,000 pounds of fuel, which meant landing with zero fuel—a tricky maneuver under good conditions made trickier with a full load of external ordnance.

We finally were directed to go to the jettison area south of Udorn to drop our ordnance. Hoisy had electrical failure on the way, so we took over the lead. It was still light when we were over the jettison area and I got a good look at it. It was very thick green jungle, with no sign of human life anywhere in the area. Unfortunately, with what we were dumping, it would be unfit for any kind of life for a long time.

Chapter 13

Steel Tiger

October 28, 1969. Tuesday. Took off at 4:45 p.m. in the right seat of a G model with First Lieutenant Rick Chorlins on his third night dual ride in the left and Stu Bischoff leading. Rick was a good pilot, which made it easy for his IP. We armed reccied Routes 7 and 61 with no results because of bad weather. We were directed to go to Lulu, but the weather was bad in that area, too, so we went over to White Rose at 025/31. White Rose said he had some tanks for us, but I think he just wanted an air show for his evening's entertainment. Four hours and twenty minutes on this mission.

October 29, 1969. Wednesday. Took off at 7:50 p.m. with First Lieutenant Frank Brown and Don Combs on the wing, and we went to Barrel Roll where the weather was bad in the entire area. We orbited at 090/20 from Channel 113—designated Control Point Charlie—for forty-five minutes. I could tell the weather was not likely to improve soon, so I called Alleycat and asked him to call Moonbeam to see if he had a target in Steel Tiger. After some delay for coordination, it was approved and we went to 095/67 from Channel 89 and struck with Nail 84 who had four trucks. We had briefed for a Barrel Roll mission and I wasn't up to date on ground elevation in Steel Tiger, so I released my ordnance 5,000 feet above the ground. The Nail said it all was within fifty meters of the target, which was pretty good considering how high I was. He didn't say if I got a truck, which probably meant I didn't. At least we did something. This was my 110th mission.

October 30, 1969. Thursday. Took off at 4:53 p.m. in the right seat with Frank Brown in the left and Stu Bischoff leading. We armed reccied Route 7, then went to Blue Moon at 025/33 and struck troops.

October 31, 1969. Friday. Armament crews painted all the ordnance orange today. Happy Halloween, bad guys!

We had a fifty-five minute delay because #445 had high carburetor temperature while we were taxiing out for takeoff. We finally got off at 5:45 p.m. with me in the right seat again, Frank Brown in the left and Noel Frisbie leading. We struck with Red Tiger.

I went to the Officers' Club after we got back and met some Air America pilots who had come in for the night. It was unusual for them to be at NKP.

*

In October and November we began to see a gradual shift of our mission from Barrel Roll to Steel Tiger, which involved a major shift in environment and tactics. In northern Laos, we were flying mostly in support of friendly native troops who were fighting to protect their land and families from domination by a foreign government, North Vietnam, and the North Vietnamese-supported Pathet Lao. Barrel Roll had antiaircraft artillery, but not nearly as much as there was along the Ho Chi Minh Trail in southern Laos. The major hazard to our type of operation in northern Laos was high terrain, especially at night.

In southern Laos, the terrain was less difficult for night attacks. Just east of the Mekong lies a mostly flat plain. Then with seemingly no warning, sharp limestone cliffs rise several hundred feet. The cliffs, called karst, are nearly vertical and sometimes covered with vines and other jungle vegetation and continue down much of the central spine of southern Laos. Farther east, the terrain flattens into a valley with streams and small rivers. East of this valley is the Annamite Mountain range, within which lies the border of Laos and Vietnam.

The Ho Chi Minh Trail, which was used by the North Vietnamese to send supplies around the Demilitarized Zone (DMZ) between North and South Vietnam, passed through the valley. The Trail was not just one road running through the jungle, but a series of roads. From above, the Trail appeared to be mostly free of jungle vegetation and pockmarked with thousands of bomb craters.

The northern part of the Trail lay just sixty miles east of Nakhon Phanom base and about fifty miles from the Mekong River. The highest elevation in this area was about 5,000 feet, so a collision with the terrain was not the major hazard; rather it was antiaircraft fire, of which there was a lot. The Trail had a large amount of truck traffic day and night, and our job was to make it as hard as possible for the North Vietnamese to get supplies through to South Vietnam. The job of the gunners was to make our task as difficult as possible, which they did well.

The type of fire we faced most often was 37mm antiaircraft guns that were easy to identify because they were fired in clips of seven rounds with red tracers that streaked to about 10,000 feet where they burned out. The shells continued upward about 2,000 feet more before they exploded—if they didn't hit something, such as an airplane. The firing procedure was to shoot a clip while swinging the barrel of the gun on its axis so the shells came up in different paths even if fired from one gun in one clip.

Since we extinguished our external lights about thirty miles east of the base, we were invisible to the gunners—at least we thought we were. I sometimes wondered how they could not see us on a bright moonlit night. They did not have radar for guidance, so they must have used sound tracking. They weren't very successful at hitting us at night, but it wasn't for lack of trying, and they were proficient enough to come frighteningly close at times. Larger guns were deployed near Mu Gia Pass.

Because American forces had stopped bombing North Vietnam, I didn't see any action on that side of the border during my tour of duty. During the time the United States was bombing the North, our pilots flew against all of the antiaircraft weapons the enemy could throw at them. It has been said North Vietnam was the most heavily defended piece of real estate in the world, and our pilots were facing the heaviest antiaircraft defenses ever flown against. But while they were making attacks in sophisticated high speed jets, we were flying old worn-out airplanes in which we sometimes couldn't even set up an appropriate dive angle because of cracks in the wing spars, and we were doing so *slowly*.

Fast we weren't—which put us at a real disadvantage in a high threat environment. We were told that earlier in the war, A-1s had been used in such areas with devastating results—high losses to the point of being unacceptable. The air force recognized the need to keep them out of high threat areas in the daytime except for SARs, when Skyraiders went anywhere necessary to pick up a survivor.

We could survive in those high threat areas at night with lights out, so the Trail belonged to the fast movers during the day, and A-1s and A-26s took over at night.

I seldom had time to count the number of guns firing at me during a pass, but they usually shot more than one.

It was not unusual to be directed to a certain point about thirty miles east of the base to wait in a holding pattern for our turn at the target. While in the holding pattern, I could see the guns fire, and from thirty miles away it looked like there was so much fire no one could possibly thread his way through it. After a while our call sign would crackle through the radio, "Firefly, they're ready for you now,"—just like a hygienist calls a patient into the dentist's chair—and it was my turn to thread my way through it.

It was especially unnerving to have to do it in the right seat while flying as an IP. In northern Laos, all I had to look out for were mountains and an occasional gun, and I usually knew where they were. But watching 37s come up from the right seat in Steel Tiger was no fun at all.

In November of 1969, the 609th Special Operations Squadron, the Nimrods, was phased out of the active inventory of the USAF. Two of my UPT classmates, Ray Russell and Tom Bame, were Nimrod pilots while I was in the 602nd. The squadron had been making the night strikes over the Trail that we were beginning to take on. Since Steel Tiger was much closer to NKP than Barrel Roll, the missions were shorter, and because we were working with airborne facs, tactics were different. The facs were Nails in their two-engine O-2

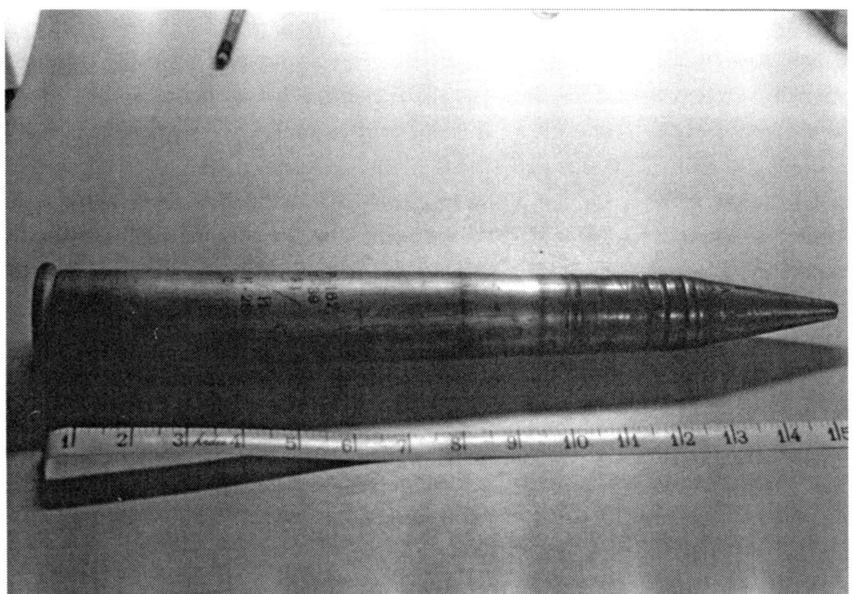

37mm shell (photo courtesy of Tom Coleman)

Cessna Skymasters and C-123 Candlesticks, both based at NKP, or Blind Bats, who flew C-130s out of Ubon. Nails usually flew at 8,000 feet and the Candles and Bats flew at 13,000 feet. All used starlight scopes.

A typical load for the Trail was six napalm canisters, four 500-pound Mark 82 bombs, and CBU-14 dispensers on two stations. While the flight leader was attacking the target, usually a truck, the wingman would watch with a bomb armed and ready. As soon as he could identify the location of a gun, the wingman rolled in on it. It was crucial for the pilot to not take his eye off the gun location for any reason, because if he did, he would lose its exact position in the darkness below. There were no identifying marks, no lights, no reference points of any kind, just darkness—until the guns spit out the red tracers. Then go get 'em.

It was difficult to tell if an attack against a gun was successful, because I was always pulling off the target when my bombs exploded. I would see only a momentary flash and then darkness again, so I was looking at the same dark hole I was looking at before I rolled in. Also, on the pull off, I was usually busy looking for tracers. We at least felt like we rattled their ears and made it harder for them to sound-track on the next pass. It let the gunners know they weren't getting a free pass out of the deal, either.

We had to have a means of preventing midair collisions. While it was part of the premission briefing, the wingman had primary responsibility to avoid a collision. The lead called out which direction he was coming from on his pass and the wingman had to judge from which way he could make his attack. Early on, some pilots thought the gunners were monitoring our frequencies. If they heard the lead say, "I'm coming in from the north," they would know where to aim the guns. So someone came up with the idea of calling out, "In from Detroit to Cincinnati," or "Chicago to Omaha," assuming a North Vietnamese gunner wouldn't know United States geography well enough to know what we were talking about. The wingman then knew where to position himself so he would be in a nonconflicting side of the attack circle to avoid a collision. It soon became apparent the code didn't matter because they were still shooting too close for comfort.

It was amazing how much better the airplanes responded to control inputs with each 500-pounder or nape release, so I was always anxious to get the first two napes or bombs off.

After the leader had expended his napes, it was time to change places, and then he had the responsibility to avoid a collision while the wingman was making his strike.

Don Combs reported, "One night a pair of Zorros had a midair (collision). They recovered and landed. It was a testament to our wonderful aircraft. One had a bent prop, the other had an 8 x 2 in. gash in the leading edge of the right wing. We all marveled at the sight of our sturdy flying machines that could 'take a licking and keep on ticking.'"

Only rarely did a truck driver keep his lights on when the fac had him spotted. They normally pulled over to the side of the road, hoping to be hidden from us until we left, so it was necessary for the fac to mark the target with logs.

It wasn't easy for the C-123 and C-130 facs to mark a target from their high altitudes because they were not able to make a diving pass to increase accuracy like A-1s could. They just kicked the marks out the back, usually three, and often they'd be scattered over a wide area. Frequently their instructions went something like this: "Draw a line between the two northernmost marks you see on the ground. Take a spot a third of the way down that line closest to the mark farthest to the northeast. Run a line perpendicular to the line between the marks from the one-third point to the northwest about one and a half times the length of the original line, and your target is right there."

If a pilot could understand that, the best thing to do was put a nape of his own in the general area to narrow it down a little.

That's the way it went over the Trail at night. No sweat, except for those ever-present guns. Somehow they managed to miss us most of the time, and our success rate against their trucks was not the best. We made our passes, they shot at us, we rattled their ears and then went home without much being accomplished—except for frequent applications of the pucker factor. And even though the gunners didn't have a very high rate of striking our airplanes, they came close at times, and I never heard anyone joke about how bad the gunners were. On the contrary, the jokes were about how good they were. A pilot might say, "A nine-level gunner was shooting at me tonight." Nine was the highest skill rating for air force enlisted-grade job descriptions, and a nine-level gunner was a good one.

The lack of accomplishment bothered me, and one day I asked Rich Hall about it. I said, "I can see how it is an inconvenience to them to have to haul the shells they're shooting at us all the way to Laos when it wastes a truckload that would otherwise be going to South Vietnam. They aren't accomplishing much by shooting at us and it doesn't seem like we're doing much damage to them. Why do you suppose we keep coming at them, and why do they keep shooting at us?"

His answer was simple and close to the truth. "They're keeping us 'honest' by not allowing us to press the attack lower, and we're keeping them 'honest' by forcing them to defend their shipments and by picking off a few trucks."

All that trouble, expense, and danger just to keep each other honest? It seemed to make a lot more sense to just call the whole thing off. But then Someone might not get his ticket punched for promotion. It was a dangerous game we were playing.

More than once I heard someone say in jest, "This is a crummy little war, but it's the only one we've got, so we've got to take advantage of it."

After several missions over the Trail, it became clear to me we could not stop the southbound truck traffic with the tactics we were using. If our government didn't see fit to throw everything we had at them, why try to do a job we couldn't do with the weapons we had? I realized American forces were not going to be able to prevail in Vietnam because the enemy was more determined than we were and they had the resources to carry out their determination.

It was the confirmation of a thought that had been gnawing at me for a while, and now that I had seen the situation first hand, I had no doubt about it. If we're in a no-win war, it will do no one any good if I get myself killed fighting it. I could do nothing more to keep myself out of harm's way that I hadn't already been doing, but it strengthened my resolve. Do the best I can. Get as many trucks as I can. Do whatever I have to do to rescue someone who might be shot down. But pressing another 500 or 1000 feet to try to get a little more accuracy just didn't make any sense. Fly it the way wing regulations specified, and don't do anything foolish. If someone else wanted to press, that was up to him. Advise against it, but I couldn't do much about it if he did, so let it go. The best award I could get from this place was a one-way ticket home. I knew if I got a truck it would save an American GI's life in Vietnam. But if we weren't resolved to get in and win, then we should do as Senator George Aikin of Vermont said, "Declare that we won, and bring everyone home."

Since I didn't make those decisions, and since I was still stuck there, the only thing I could do was my best, and do it as safely as I possibly could.

*

November 1, 1969. Saturday. Harry Dunivant and Tommy Tomlinson had their last flights today.

The engine on #455 failed about thirty-five minutes after takeoff this morning seventy-four miles up the Mekong from the base and crashed fully loaded. Major Pete Williams was in the right seat. His ejection seat worked like it was supposed to, and he was picked up unharmed. In the left seat was Major Dick Lytle on only his second mission—his very first in the left seat. His seat failed to work, and he rode it in and was killed. He was so new to the squadron that I barely knew what he looked like. And now he was gone, just like that. I'll bet no one had emphasized to him that if he had a double failure—both engine and then the seat—he should first get rid of the ordnance before attempting to go over the side. He probably just ran out of time before the airplane hit the ground. He was the fifth guy from the 602nd to be killed since I've been here. I didn't like the way things were going. I last flew #455 on October 13.

*

During the rainy season, if six or eight trucks were moving each night on the Trail, it was a big night. Sometimes none would be out on the muddy roads. But one night recently, 110 trucks were spotted, and on another night, 200 were moving supplies south. The rainy season was winding down, but frequently the targets were obscured by clouds, and we could do nothing. The clouds didn't have as much moisture and not as much rain fell, but they still prevented us from doing our mission.

I had another right seat ride tonight, and we were diverted from Barrel Roll to Steel Tiger because of poor weather in the north. We had a weather delay of an hour and a half before departure. Larry Dannelly was in the left seat and Tony Wylie was the flight leader. Tony struck at 104/77 from NKP and he got two trucks. When it was Larry's turn, the target was changed and we found ourselves in an area with several gunners who were eager for a fight. We had nine clips fired at us on each of three passes. Tony must have really stirred them up!

Our new squadron commander decided daily scheduling would be done by flights, and my flight would be going to day missions in two weeks. I had more missions at night in Barrel Roll than anyone in the wing. I was comfortable with the night mission and wanted to stay on it.

November 2-6, 1969. Sunday-Thursday. My missions were canceled because of target weather four out of the five nights. My only flight during that period was on November 4 in the right seat with Major Al Preyss in the left with Lieutenant Colonel Lucky Lowman leading. We were diverted to Steel Tiger from Barrel Roll and didn't do much good because of crummy weather.

November 7, 1969. Friday. Took off at 4:55 p.m. with a newer pilot in the left seat and Tony Wylie leading. My left seater was all lined up on the runway for takeoff with his flaps up until I reminded him an A-1 needs flaps extended for takeoff when fully loaded. That's another way to get killed. He knew better and was not very happy with himself when I pointed it out. That kind of simple error is one reason why IPs were assigned to the first five flights. A new guy had a lot to learn and it wasn't hard to overlook something very basic. The weather was poor, so we jettisoned our ordnance.

November 8, 1969. Saturday. Took off at 8:55 p.m. in the right seat and Noel Frisbie leading. We struck with Blind Bat 09 on Route 61 just north of Ban Ban. Noel got a truck.

*

November 9, 1969. Sunday. I went to church this afternoon in the new base chapel.

Took off at 8:50 p.m. with Chorlins in the left seat and Frisbie leading again. We had to return with all our ordnance because Alleycat couldn't find a target, and we ran low on fuel.

The weather has been very nice at the base but poor in the target areas.

*

November 10, 1969. Monday. After twelve consecutive nights in the right seat as an IP and a complaint to the scheduling officer, I finally got to lead a mission. Took off at 9:05 p.m. with Frank Brown on the wing and we worked with Lulu in Barrel Roll. We had a good mission, but a Mark 82 500-pound bomb hung on wing station #3, and no matter how I tried, I couldn't get it off. The #3 station was next to the end, and the extra weight caused noticeable wing down pressure.

I tried to release it on several subsequent passes and tried to pull it off manually, but it just wouldn't go. Had the armers forgotten to pull a pin? I had two choices: Eject and hope everything worked OK and I'd get picked up, or land and hope it didn't fall off, especially when I was on the runway.

The bomb had a valid time (VT) fuse that armed four seconds after it left the airplane. A sensor in the fuse would cause it to explode fifty to one hundred feet above ground. It was an antipersonnel weapon, as opposed to a bomb with a fuse that went off when it hit the ground, which was good for interdiction because it made a crater.

The thought of landing with a bomb that might release at any second wasn't very appealing, but it was about half a notch ahead of ejecting at night and having to wait until morning to be picked up. A 500-pound bomb would put a big dent in a runway (not to mention me) if it released at the wrong time, but with all my unsuccessful attempts to drop it, I felt it most likely would stay on until the dearmers could insert safety pins.

The situation wasn't dangerous until I got below about 1,000 feet, but from there on it could damage or destroy the airplane and me. I directed Frank to land first in case the bomb fell on the runway and closed it. At least he would be on the ground.

I declared an emergency and brought it in with fire trucks standing by. Many times when a person is under unusual stress he will perform even better than normal, and this was one of those times. I made a smooth touchdown and turn off the runway and was relieved when the munitions crew in the dearming area signaled the bomb was safe. I could get by without any more of those.

*

During briefing one night for a mission to Steel Tiger, the intelligence officer warned us to stay north of the 120° radial of Channel 89, which was well to the south of where we expected to be, because an arc light mission was scheduled. Arc light was the name given to B-52 missions that came in at high altitude and dropped 500-pound bombs. During my strike, I forgot about it because we weren't scheduled to be near that area. We worked with a Blind Bat who took us farther south than expected. After I made my strike, I changed places with the wingman. We had a lull in the action and I was orbiting the area with my four 500-pound bombs, waiting to cover the wingman, when I saw what looked like a giant string of firecrackers exploding to the south. I soon remembered why we had been warned to stay north of there.

B-52 saturation bombing must have been a terrible problem in the target area. They flew in high with little evidence of their presence apparent to those on the ground when all of a sudden the whole world blew up. Anyone who lived through it must have been left to wonder when it would happen again. It could make for sleepless nights.

Chapter 14

Poppy

November 11, 1969. Tuesday. Each pilot was assigned an airplane that he could name, and then the pilot's name and crew chief's name were stenciled under the cockpit on the left side. Aircraft #076 was assigned to me, the crew chief was Sgt. Ashley, and I named it Kawliga. My mission tonight was in Kawliga. Frank Brown was my wingman again, and we took off at 8:50 p.m. I was Firefly 40, and we worked with Poppy in Barrel Roll and had a good mission against troops. Base altitude was 7,500 feet.

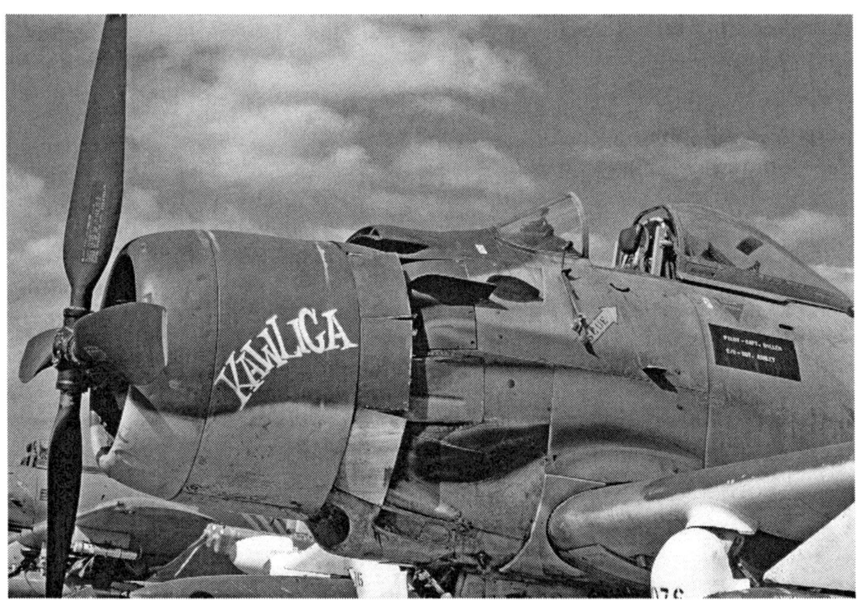

Kawliga

(I had a tape of this mission, and the following is a partial transcript. The tape started as we arrived in the target area and began trying to identify the target and the location of friendly troops. Poppy was the call sign of the ground-based Laotian fac and Blind Bat 06 was a C-130 fac who was providing support. The tape opened with a briefing from the night control ship, Alleycat, about the situation.)

Alleycat: ...and Blind Bat 06 will be there. He's at base plus two and your rendezvous is 074 at 42 off 108. You can contact Blind Bat on Charlie frequency.

Firefly 40: OK, 074 for 42 off 108 is where Blind Bat is and Poppy.

Alleycat: That's affirmative, sir, and the Bat will be at base plus two.

Firefly 40: OK, we're at base plus two point five and base plus three.

Firefly 41: Four One copy.

As we were flying in the direction of the target, Blind Bat 06 put out a couple of flares. He asked if I could see them, and I replied I was about ten miles away.

Blind Bat 06: OK. We're with Poppy who is on the ground here, and he'll be directing you as you strike.

Firefly 40: OK, we'll be there in about two or three minutes. Can you give us a terrain elevation briefing in this area, please?

Blind Bat 06: We're with Poppy down here, and we're flaring for him right now—those are the flares you see—he'll be directing you as to the strike. We'll provide a flaring service or a spotting service or anything else you want us to do around here to help you out.

Firefly 40: OK, I have you in sight—we're just off your left wing about straight north of you.

Blind Bat 06: Rog, understand. And I'm going to send you over to victor (VHF frequency) 123.2. That's the fac frequency, and that's the one where you'll be working with Poppy.

Firefly 40: OK, 123.2. And what's your altitude?

Blind Bat 06: We're at base altitude plus two. And if you'd like a terrain briefing once Poppy gives you a target, we'll give you that on uniform.

Blind Bat was doing a good job and was trying to be helpful, but this was *my* mission, the one I enjoyed the most, and I didn't need him. But since he was available, I decided to use him, and it was nice to know he was on the scene in case of trouble.

Firefly 40: Hello, Poppy, (this is) Firefly Four Zero.

Poppy: Firefly Four Zero, Poppy, go (ahead).

Poppy spoke English very well.

Firefly 40: We've come to work with you. We are just north of the flares that are lit now. Can you give us coordinates of the target, please?

Poppy: OK. Roger roger. Stand by.

Blind Bat 06: Firefly Four Zero, this is Blind Bat 06 on uniform.

I switched my radio transmitter to the UHF frequency and said, "Roger Bat, this is Firefly Four Zero."

Immediately after I transmitted, Poppy, who didn't know we were using another frequency said, "Firefly Four Zero, Poppy."

Apparently Blind Bat 06 wasn't monitoring our VHF frequency because he began to give me a terrain briefing at the same time Poppy was trying to talk to me.

Blind Bat 06: Your general terrain elevation is between three thousand and thirty three hundred feet.

Firefly 40: OK, thank you. Poppy is calling me on the other freq.

Blind Bat 06: OK.

Firefly 40: Poppy, Firefly Four Zero.

Poppy: Firefly Four Zero, Poppy.

Firefly 40: I just wanted to know if you have coordinates for me, please?

Poppy: Roger. Uniform Golf 625375. 625375. Over.

Firefly 40: UG625375. OK.

I had a writing pad strapped to my right knee and a pen in the left sleeve of my flight suit to write coordinates, keep track of passes and ordnance expended, BDA, takeoff time, airplane writeups, and anything else pertinent to the mission. Detailed notes were necessary for an accurate flight report.

Poppy: Charlie charlie.

Firefly 40: And that's the bad guys, is that correct?

Poppy: Yes. And the target is about 500 meters to the northwest of the first flare.

Firefly 40: OK, 500 meters to the northwest of the first flare. Can you give me the coordinates of the good guys' position, please?

Poppy: OK, roger. I have many good guys around these coordinates. The good guys are one klick to the southeast to one klick to the west and also two klicks to the northwest.

Firefly 40: OK, I copy the positions of the good guys.

Poppy: Roger roger.

It sounded like we were going to have to be precise with ordnance delivery.

Blind Bat 06: We're orbiting in a left turn to the south of the flares, and we'd like to make another flare pass. We're at base plus two. What's yours?

Firefly 40: We're at base plus two point five and base plus three.

We were invisible to each other in the darkness and altitude separation was critical. We were separated by five hundred feet.

Blind Bat 06: OK, how does that work out? Do you mind if we make another flare pass?

Firefly 40: We're just fine for right now. I have flares on board, so I'd like to do my own flaring. I'll only put out two at a time, so it will be easier to keep track of what Poppy's talking about.

Blind Bat 06: Also on these flares. They've got two green markers between the number two flare and the number three flare. When they burn out, you'll probably see them on the ground and they mark the good guys.

Firefly 40: OK, that marks the good guys.

Blind Bat 06: I hope so, yes. Poppy, this is Bat 6, how are these flares here?

Poppy: They are south of—north of friendly locations. North of friendly locations. The bad guy location is about 300 meters—correction, about 400 meters to the northwest of the first flare.

Blind Bat 06: Four hundred meters northwest of the first flare.

Poppy: Charlie charlie.

Blind Bat 06: OK Firefly, how about if we make one more pass over that position to see how it works out?

Firefly 40: OK. (After a pause.) Bat, I've been looking at my maps, and I do not have a good map of this area, so I'll be relying on whatever you have for letting me know about the elevation. What I would like is the highest elevation within three miles.

I knew about where we were and about what the elevation was, and if I hadn't had the Bat nearby I would have done just fine. We were about thirty miles east of the southern tip of the PDJ and almost twenty miles east of Xieng Khouang. The terrain rose rapidly to the southeast to a peak of almost of 8,600 feet. I needed to be wary.

Blind Bat 06: Stand by. We'll be working up that for you.

Firefly 40: I see your flares coming out now.

Blind Bat 06: They should be right over the gun. I picked up the bad guys. I picked up our two markers on the ground. (He meant he was able to see them well.) Let's see how they work out. We'll see what Poppy has to say.

Firefly 40: Poppy, do you see the flares that are lit now?

Poppy: Charlie charlie. I see the flares. Stand by.

He was checking with his people on the ground who were closer to the flares to see if they were near the target.

Poppy: I show the target is about 500 meters to the southwest of the first flare, over.

Firefly 40: OK, 500 meters southwest of the first flare, and the first flare is the farthest one south, is that correct?

Poppy: The target is 500 meters southwest of the west flare.

Firefly 40: OK, 500 meters southwest of the west flare.

Poppy: Charlie charlie.

Firefly 40: OK, I'm going to put out a flare in that position, and you tell me how I did, OK?

Poppy: Roger roger.

Blind Bat 06: Firefly, this is Bat to the south. What do you want me to do?

Firefly 40: You're below our altitude, so if you'd just hold down there for right now, I'd appreciate it. As soon as you get the target terrain information, I'd like to get that. You have the coordinates, don't you?

Blind Bat 06: Yeah, we're getting that right now.

Firefly 40: Very good.

Once again, the Bat was trying to be helpful, but the best thing he could do at this point was stay out of the way. I just needed to find the target that was not far from the good guys and high terrain. The moon was not up and I couldn't see anything without the flares.

Blind Bat 06: There is a 4,500 foot peak three miles to the south southwest, a 5,600 foot peak four miles to the north northeast. That's the high terrain in the area.

That voice was different from the earlier one from the Bat. I knew if I just stayed at the wing's minimums, 7,000 feet and was careful about the high terrain—and I knew where it was—I'd be OK. I was not going to go as low as 5,000 feet at night in this area.

Firefly 40: And what about the target itself?

Blind Bat 06: Target elevation, 2,400 feet.

Firefly 40: Four One, are you still in the area here?

Firefly 41: Yeah, I'm just off to the south.

Firefly 40: I'm right over the flares heading southwest. (After a pause) Poppy, I have two flares coming out now. Let me know if they are over the target, OK?

Poppy: OK.

Firefly 40: Are the flares over the target?

Poppy: Stand by one.

He checked again with his guys who were farther forward.

Poppy: Did you put out two flares or one flare?

Firefly 40: It looks like one flare popped its chute as soon as it left the flare pod instead of dropping a bit first. One flare is very high, and the other is on the ground.

Poppy: The target is about one klick to the north of the high flare.

Firefly 40: OK, one klick to the north of the high flare.

Blind Bat 06: Where are you from the flare?

Firefly 40: I'm about zero six zero (degrees) from the flare, maybe a klick or two. (After a pause) Poppy, I have another flare out. Is that where the target is?

Poppy: Stand by while I check.

Firefly 40: I don't know what's with those flares, they're lighting immediately without descending.

Poppy: The target is about 500 meters east of your flare.

Firefly 40: Five hundred meters east of the flare. And I just saw a flash on the ground to the southwest of the first flare. Is someone shooting in that area? (After a pause) Poppy, I'm going to drop two more flares 500 meters to the east of the last flares. Will you tell me if that is where the target is? (Pause) OK, there is a flare about 500 meters east of the previous one.

Poppy: Yeah, I see. It is right over the bad guy location.

Firefly 40: Understand, it is right over the bad guy location. I'm going to put down a ground mark now, Poppy, you tell me if it is in the target area.

Poppy: The target is still about 500 meters south of the flares. You can put the mark in that area.

It seemed like the target was moving, as we couldn't make Poppy happy about our flare location, and the wind was not strong enough to displace them. Maybe if I put a mark on the ground we could pin it down. Patience was needed for a mission like this because I didn't want to hit the good guys by mistake.

I pushed the mixture and RPM levers up to full rich and 2600, moved the intervalometer to the correct station, and flew into position to make a pass. Maybe if I got a mark down, we could find this target. I didn't have to be extremely accurate with this one as I was just trying to get the mark in the general area. When the left stub lined up with a black spot on the ground about 500 meters south of the last flare, I rolled in to the left, nose down 40°, pipped off a mark, and pulled out, careful to not pull over 4 Gs.

Firefly 40: Four Zero is in hot with a mark. (After a pause) I'm off to the east.

I climbed back to my altitude. Kawliga was still working hard for the altitude because I hadn't dropped much weight with the mark.

Firefly 40: Poppy, there is a white marker on the ground to the southwest of the flares that are lit. Do you see it?

Poppy: Charlie charlie. I see that. Stand by while I check. (After a pause) OK, that's where the target is.

Firefly 40: That's where the target is, is that correct?

Poppy: That's correct.

Firefly 40: And I can come in on that mark? And that's the one just southwest of the flares. And the friendlies are one klick to the south, is that correct?

Poppy: Yes, the friendlies are one klick to the south and also one klick to the west and one klick to the north. Or two klicks to the northwest.

Firefly 40: OK, one klick to the south, one klick to the west, and two klicks to the northwest.

Poppy: Charlie charlie.

Firefly 40: Now I see three lights on the ground—three in a row, and one of them is in the trees. Is that the correct one?

I was being extra careful because of the close proximity of the good guys and because of the difficulty in locating the target. I wanted to make sure I had the right spot.

Firefly 40: It's almost straight southwest of the flare about 300 meters southwest of the flare.

Blind Bat 06: Firefly, we have a couple of green marks on the ground there.

Firefly 40: That's what I'm afraid of. I can't tell which one is mine for sure. I think the one in the middle is the one I put down, isn't it?

Blind Bat 06: If you're asking us—we're way too far to the south to be any help in your area.

Firefly 40: Poppy, I'm going to put out another flare right over where the target is, and you tell me if that is the place. OK?

Poppy: OK

Firefly 40: Because I can't tell exactly if that one is the mark I just put down. Is the mark that I put down in the trees?

Poppy: Charlie charlie. It is in the trees.

Firefly 40: I think that I see the right one. I'm going to put out a flare here. The flares will be ready in a minute now. (After a pause) Do you see the flares now? Is that right over the target?

Poppy: Stand by.

Firefly 40: The target should be about a hundred meters south of the location of the flares.

Poppy: OK, the target should be about two hundred meters to the southeast, over.

Firefly 40: I see it now. I'm going to come in and hit it in just a minute. (After a pause) I'm going to wait until the flares go out. It's easier to see with the flares out. (Pause) I'm going to come in hot now and hit the target in the trees.

Poppy: Roger roger.

Firefly 40: Four Zero is in hot.

Firefly 41: OK, I've got you covered.

After a long search for the target, I had finally found it. Now the actual strike began. I pushed the RPM up to 2600 again, mixture rich, made sure the fuel selector was on the main (I didn't want to have the engine die of fuel starvation as I was climbing off the target), selected the correct station for a 750-pound canister of napalm on the intervalometer, set the mil setting on the gun sight, lined up the target with the left stub, and rolled in. Hard over left, nose down 40°. I had to be accurate because of the proximity of friendlies. They were trusting me. Not much time to line it up. There's the mark. It was the only thing I could see in the darkness. Release. Pull back on the stick. Pull! Four Gs max. Seven thousand feet. No lower. Pull back. Watch the attitude indicator. The airplane climbed better now, but was heavy on the right wing with a nape off the left and the combination of weight and drag gone. Back to 10,000 feet. Take a look. How close did I come to the target?

Firefly 40: I'm off to the west.

Firefly 41: Roger.

Firefly 40: Poppy, do you see the napalm on the ground?

Poppy: OK, this is very good. Very good, over.

Firefly 40: Do you want more in the same place?

Poppy: Charlie charlie. I want some more in the same place.

Firefly 40: OK, I'll be coming around in a minute, as soon as I get my altitude. (Pause) Firefly Four Zero will be in hot in about fifteen seconds. (Pause) Firefly Four Zero in hot.

I armed up the airplane just as in the first pass except for the intervalometer station, which I made sure was selected to the outboard napalm station on the right wing. I rolled in.

Firefly 40: Four Zero is in hot. (Pause) I'm off to the south. Do you see that one, Poppy?

Poppy: OK, I see that one, also. That's very good. Will you please put the next one to the south about one hundred meters more, over.

Firefly 40: One hundred meters farther south.

After all this, I was still not sure where the target was, but Poppy was providing directions, and I could only do what he wanted. I didn't know for sure if I had already hit what he wanted and he had something else to the south or if I was too far north to start with, but he had told me he had troops 1,000 meters south of the target, so I had to be careful.

The ordnance delivery system on the A-1 was very basic, with nothing high tech. Rolling in at 10,000 feet MSL with a target elevation of 2,400 feet and releasing at 8,000 feet MSL meant a slant range of about 6,000 feet to the target at the point of release. Just about one nautical mile. Had I compensated for the wind? Did I have the correct dive angle? Was the mil set correctly? Was the ball in the turn and slip indicator centered? A small detail gone wrong would cause a bomb or nape to be off target.

It was more common to find an error in length of delivery than a sideways error. With friendlies close to the target, it was best to make a pass parallel to a line running between the ground forces. But here, friendlies were to the south, west, and northwest. The bad guys were almost surrounded, and I had to put napalm in the middle.

On my next two passes I dropped 550-pound canisters of napalm, one on each pass.

Firefly 40: How do you like that one, Poppy?

Poppy (in a very calm voice): That one very good. Hit in the same area.

Poppy was so low key, and so matter-of-fact about the location of my napes that I wondered if I was doing any good, or if he was just enjoying the fireworks. The target was in dense forest, so the napes were hitting the tops of trees, and the fire trickled down. It was interesting to watch, but I wouldn't have wanted to be on the receiving end.

Firefly 40: Do you like that one, Poppy?

Poppy: That one very good. You hit south some more. About 200 meters.

Firefly 40: OK, 200 meters south. I'll be coming in with bombs this time.

I was out of napes, but I still had two 500-pound Mark 82 bombs with VT fuses. Poppy certainly had me wondering where the target was, but at this stage of the strike, I figured if I was anywhere near his troops, he'd let me know.

Firefly 40: Do you like that bomb? That's a little farther south.

Poppy: Charlie charlie. You can hit there some more. The last bomb very good.

Firefly 40: Last bomb very good.

Poppy: You hit the same place some more.

Firefly 40: Hit the same place again. Four Zero in hot. (Pause) Off to the south. Do you like that bomb, Poppy?

Poppy: Roger roger, I like that. Very good.

Firefly 40: I'll be in with CBUs this time.

Poppy: Roger roger.

By this time I wasn't very confident of Poppy's directions, and I was ready to just have some fun dropping my ordnance and get out of there. Who knows, maybe I actually *was* doing some good after all.

Poppy: Hit to the south 200 meters more.

Firefly 40: South 200 meters more.

But then again, maybe I was just making charcoal and toothpicks out of trees. Maybe Poppy and I needed to get together to discuss what 200 meters means.

Firefly 40: Do you like those CBUs?

Poppy: Very good.

Firefly 40: I'll be in with rockets this time.

Poppy: You need to go a little bit more, about 200 meters to the southwest, over.

Firefly 40: I've got rockets this time, I'll put them about 200 meters southwest. Those last ones should have been just about in the target area, about 200 meters south.

Rockets were fun to shoot, especially at night because the smoke and fire went right back onto and over the wing of the airplane. Even though I couldn't see them strike the target, I had seen impacts from other airplanes, and they were fun to watch. I don't think they did much good. I think they load them so we could have fun shooting them.

Poppy: Those were very good, over.

Firefly 40: I'm all done working with you now, Poppy, and Firefly Four One will come in and help you, OK?

Poppy: Roger roger, OK.

Firefly 40: Four One, I'm coming off target, I'm off to the east right now, and I have my lights back on. Do you have me in sight?

Firefly 41: Roger, I'm southwest, and I've turned my lights on.

Firefly 40: OK, if you've got me in sight, I'll climb up to base plus three point five, and you can have base plus two point five and below.

Firefly 41: Base plus two point five. What were you using for release altitude?

Firefly 40: Release at 8500 and pull out about 7500.

My wingman, Frank Brown, then checked in with Poppy and made his strike. Poppy directed him 400 meters south of where I had dropped my bombs. His next pass was directed farther south again. Maybe we should have started about a kilometer south of where we actually did, but we were told good guys were there.

Poppy directed each of Frank's passes 200 meters south of the previous one. After Frank made his passes and was out of ordnance, I called Poppy.

Firefly 40: Poppy, Firefly Four Zero, we're going to have to go home now. We're all out of bombs.

Poppy: Roger roger, copy, thank you.

Firefly 40: Four One, head out south one eight zero and climb to base plus four. Blind Bat, are you still on the frequency?

Blind Bat 06: Yes, we're still here.

Firefly 40: Poppy, do you have any BDA for us?

Poppy: Roger. UG625375. One hundred persons killed.

Firefly 40: UG625375. And one hundred persons killed, is that correct?

Poppy: That's correct. One hundred.

Firefly 40: Understand one hundred KBA. We'll see you tomorrow night, Poppy. We enjoyed working with you.

Poppy: That's one hundred percent.

Firefly 40: One hundred percent, is that it?

Poppy: Charlie charlie.

Firefly 40: Oh! I understand. OK. One hundred percent. And thank you very much, Poppy. And Bat, thank you for your help, too.

Blind Bat 06: OK, we'll see you, Firefly.

Firefly 40: Four One, go to 134.6.

By one hundred percent, Poppy meant one hundred percent of our ordnance hit in the target area.

On the way home, Frank had generator failure about thirty-five miles north of the base that caused his UHF and VHF radios to fail. The FM still worked, so when I checked in with the tower, I relayed his landing clearance to him. He landed about six minutes behind me.

This mission lasted three hours and ten minutes. It was typical of missions where we worked with ground facs, but most of the time we had better luck finding the target.

Someone went down in Steel Tiger tonight and I heard the beeper on the way back from my mission.

Chapter 15

Funny Bomb

November 12, 1969. Wednesday. Zorro pilot Captain George Porter bailed out of his airplane just southwest of the Birdshead in Barrel Roll last night when his engine quit. George was en route to the target area as I was on my way home and was working not far from where I had been.

The beeper I heard last night was from an F-4 that went down just south of Mu Gia Pass. A search and rescue effort was under way early today. One of the survivors reported enemy helicopters were trying to bomb him, and another F-4 crashed while trying to chase off the helicopters. During the SAR, an F-105 crashed, but the pilot was rescued. Then an A-1 from Pleiku went in. The original guys were picked up OK.

George had to wait his turn to get picked up because of all the activity on the Trail and early morning fog, but he was recovered OK—just not quite as soon as he might have wanted. He was uninjured.

*

Harry Dunivant left for home this morning, and I didn't even get to say goodbye. His next assignment was to be an A-1 instructor at Hurlburt.

Took off at 4:40 p.m. in the right seat with Rick Chorlins in the left. We struck at trucks just south of the Birdshead. The North Vietnamese have recently moved 57mm radar guided guns to just east of the border. This was my 120th mission.

November 14, 1969. Friday. Took off at 4:40 p.m., call sign Firefly 36. Frank Brown was 37. We went to Barrel Roll and armed reccied with not much happening, so I called Alleycat and told him it was too hazy to armed recce. Alleycat said a Candlelestick fac was en route, but still forty-five minutes away. Frank and I had been in the area for quite a while and didn't have the gas to wait, find a target, and strike, so Alleycat looked around for a ground fac and sent us to Bad Man. Bad Man said he had bad guys about 800 meters from his position and directed us in on them with napes and 500-pound bombs. After Frank made his passes, he called me on FM and said, "Bad Man doesn't seem to be very excited. Why don't we take our CBUs home?"

I agreed, so after Frank made one last pass I said to Bad Man, "We're out of ordnance and going to go home."

Bad Man said, "OK."

I asked for BDA and Bad Man reported, "Ninety-five KBA," which sounded inflated. We turned south. About the time we rolled out of the turn,

Bad Man called back with more urgency in his voice. "They're attacking my position! They're coming up the hill!" Big mistake.

The bad guys obviously had a radio and heard me tell Bad Man we were out of ordnance, which wasn't the whole truth. We were out of napalm and bombs, but we had enough CBUs, rockets, and guns to provide a nasty surprise for the attackers. Frank had two CBU-14s, each with six tubes. I told him to pip off three tubes a pass. I had flares and lit the area while Frank was CBUing. Bad Man loved it. When the CBUs were gone, I rolled in with LAU 59 white phosphorus rockets, one at a time. Bad Man said, "Oh, yes. That's where they are." When I was out of rockets I came in with my 20mm guns, but on the first pass my inboard guns jammed, so I armed the outboards. Lately we've had simple ball slugs with tracers most of the time, but tonight I had incendiary shells that sparkled when they struck the target or the ground. The incendiaries didn't have tracers, but we could tell where they hit. After several passes, Frank said they were shooting back. He thought it was about twenty rounds of automatic rifle fire, but I was bottoming out high enough above the ground that it didn't seem to be much of a threat, so I kept at it. We stayed until we had less than bingo fuel then turned for home. I called Alleycat to tell him of the situation. Bad Man gave us ninety KBA on the second half of the strike. Not bad if we could believe 185 KBA on one mission.

November 15, 1969. Saturday. Since Harry was gone and I had an empty bed in my room, I asked Jim George to move in with me, which he did today. We were classmates at the A-1 training school at Hurlburt Field last January and we had lived three doors apart in the same apartment building on the beach at Fort Walton Beach. Our wives had become friends and we flew together frequently, so it was natural for us to be roommates.

*

Took off at 4:45 p.m. in aircraft #053, call sign Firefly 35, with Russ Keeling leading. Russ's VHF radio didn't work very well, so I did most of the work with the fac, Black Lion, who had had a hard day. He was under heavy attack in the morning and a flight of Fireflies had worked with him. He reported bad guys within fifteen feet of his position. A Raven fac and the Fireflies were overhead just itching for a fight, so the bad guys must have been pretty anxious to get at him in broad daylight. The A-1s had a good day and managed to break off the attack. As the Skyraiders were leaving, Black Lion said they were going out to count bodies. This evening we struck in the same area, about a klick and a half (1500 meters) from Black Lion's position.

*

I was scheduled to fly with the wing commander the next afternoon. He didn't fly nights, so I hadn't flown with him; indeed, I had only met him briefly when he presented me with my DFC, and I didn't remember him very well, which didn't exclude me from flying a mission with him. I was comfortable with the concept of not knowing him, as I didn't see any advantage in doing so. I was content with my status of being a lowly squadron pilot doing my job the best I could, and I asked for nothing more than to be left alone by the powers who ran things. I felt if I was ever invited into the squadron commander's office, it was probably because I was in trouble, and if I ever was invited to see the wing commander it probably meant I was in BIG trouble.

*

The number of sorties assigned to our squadron each day had recently seen a big increase. We were up to twenty-two, counting Sandies. We had been flying eighteen and not too long ago were as low as twelve. Everybody was flying every day. The guys who came from Pleiku had gone back TDY, so while the squadron had them on the books, they weren't really here. Not that it made much difference to me, because I was on the flying schedule every day since I returned from leave October 10—except for my midterm instrument check the first day, the day I spent at Udorn, and two days ago when I was duty officer. I had four weather cancellations—one of which occurred after I had already taken off, and one day I was canceled because of a SAR.

Russ Keeling came by with food and we cooked supper. Noel Frisbee set up my tape decks so they would record from one to the other.

*

As the days rolled by and the season progressed, the monsoon gave way to what the Thais called the cool season, and the skies gradually became cloud-free. December was the coolest month of the season, and it felt good. Even in mid-November, the morning temperature was close to 50° F, and a jacket was needed. Sometimes I walked outside at night just to feel the chill air and enjoy the sensation. Someone said the coldest temperature ever recorded in Bangkok was 57° F, which was the cause of some wonderment. We even heard a rumor that once in a while the temperature on the mountain peaks of northern Laos reached the freezing level.

The enjoyment of the cooler weather was not unanimous, however, as the Thais who worked on the base and whom we had gotten to know were uncomfortable and shivered most of the time in the cool season.

The air in mid- and late-November and December was crystal clear. East of the base from an altitude of 10,000 feet, if I looked hard and used a little imagination, I could almost see all the way across Laos and the southern panhandle of North Vietnam to the Gulf of Tonkin. The clear, cool air was brought in by northeast winds that were stronger than we had previously experienced, and they caused weapon delivery errors until we got used to it.

*

November 16, 1969. Sunday. I went to church in the morning and was scheduled to brief with the wing commander at 12:15, but the mission was canceled because of a SAR for an F-4 crew who went down at Ban Phanop. Ban Phanop is seven miles south of Mu Gia Pass and about fifty-eight miles east and slightly north of the base. It was a heavily defended area along the Trail. Jim George was Sandy Three, and this is his account of the action that day:

> Boxer 24 A/B, 69/11/16. Sandy One was Major Dick Novak of the 22nd with Sandy Two being First Lieutenant George Driscoll (22nd). Sandies Three and Four were First Lieutenants J.G. George (me) and Noel Frisbie, of the 602nd SOS. The location of the SAR was immediately west of the Ban Phanop Valley, just south of Mu Gia Pass. Mu Gia was a steep mountain pass between North Vietnam and Laos and was one of few such passes, making this area the major north-south route structure on the Ho Chi Minh Trail, down which the North Vietnamese shipped war materiel through Laos to support the war in South Vietnam.

Mu Gia Pass

The crash site was barely west of the Valley and up in a large bowl in the karst. Fortunately, the pilots had stayed with the aircraft long enough to get clear of the route structure—almost too long. The orientation of the crash scene was what we described as "parachute, parachute, airplane."

Very shortly after arriving on scene, Lieutenant Driscoll, as Sandy Two, drifted out over the valley a bit, and took a serious hit by what was probably a 37mm. His aircraft was not flying very well and was full of holes, with the main hit located below and behind the cockpit, the round having come upward from the bottom of the fuselage. Not wanting to jeopardize the rescue, Lieutenant Driscoll jettisoned his external stores, said he was flying OK and decided to RTB to NKP alone. (My understanding is that the aircraft was so badly damaged, it never flew again...Class 26ed is the term!)

Sandy Three (me) immediately sent Four down to be the low wingman, to provide cover for Sandy One. As I made the call, Fris, who was capable and experienced, was already on the way down. He and I had been holding with two rescue Jolly Green helicopters about seven or eight miles to the southwest. I had decided to hold there, over an area we called the Roostertail, which was a formation of high karst in that shape, and was pretty safe from enemy guns due to the nature of the terrain. Realizing I would be escorting the rescue Jolly in by myself, I eased over closer to the SAR area to get a handle on the situation and locate the safest run in for the chopper, and while I was there, I dropped a one hundred pound willie pete bomb in the safe mode. This made a nice, dense, white, long-lasting mark for the Jolly to aim at on his run in, and I placed it so as to keep him out of the worst areas on the way in.

Major Novak had located the survivors, and first he and George, and now he and Fris, had been trolling unsuccessfully for ground fire and opposition up in that high karst bowl. When he deemed it was safe, which was pretty quickly, he called for the helicopter, and I escorted the Jolly in for the pickup. During the pickup sequence, we were in our usual daisy chain of A-1s, flying a counter-clockwise pattern around the helicopter while he was most vulnerable in his hover over the survivors, raising each up individually on the winch-driven rescue hoist. Our technique in the daisy chain was to have someone always rolling in and expending ordnance fairly close to the survivors, to keep the bad guys' heads down, and to allow us to have at least one Spad in a position to roll in and attack any significant threat that might come up.

But instead of four A-1s in the daisy chain, we had only three, such that there was a noticeable gap, which I was doing my best to split. As the chopper reported he had both survivors on board and was coming out, it happened that I was the only one eastbound, toward the bad guys and the valley. I started to turn back left to the west, and just fall in behind Sandy One and Four, who were now headed almost west, but I felt it would be a good idea if I made one more covering pass for the Jolly.

Up until this point, despite Two getting hammered, the rescue had been slick—almost textbook. The whole thing was over in probably thirty minutes total, from arrival on the scene until we had both survivors on the Jolly headed for safety. As I finished my pass, strafing and firing rockets into the area the Jolly had just exited, I pulled off to the left and started west to catch up with the others. Just as I rolled out, I took a clip of 37mm, in the standard five to seven round burst, which started detonating right at my altitude and close aboard off my right wing. I instinctively ducked, and the aircraft shuddered noticeably. I knew I had been hit bad, called a "Mayday," and reached back to pull off the external ordnance with the two pull handles, located back and to my left in the H cockpit. As I finished releasing the external stores, my eyes came back around to the oil pressure gauge as my hand reached for the ejection handle. The oil pressure was holding, although the engine was running extremely roughly. As I looked out through the now oil-covered windscreen, I saw why. The top of the fuselage cowling, just aft of the prop, was bent up in an ugly mess of torn metal.

Thinking it wouldn't run for long, I made about a 30° check turn to the left to head back toward the high ground of the Roostertail where I knew it was safer to bail out and where the other Jolly was holding. Just as I rolled out of that quick turn, another clip of six or seven rounds passed just off to my right side, almost in formation with me, and just where I would have been without the turn.

I vividly remember, to this day, being really pissed off at that, thinking "You sonofabitch, you already got me, I'm out of the game!"...but this was a poignant reminder that this was, in fact, no game.

Only later did I find out just how lucky I had been. One round from the clip of 37mm had passed between the rapidly turning blades of the prop, right near the prop hub, and exploded against the upper right portion of the cylinder bank, knocking out three cylinders. But the force of the blast was mostly up and outward, ripping the large ugly hole in the top of the forward fuselage, and causing the streaming oil. The old girl was not running too well, but she was running.

Very shortly, Fris joined up on my right wing and said two things, the first of which was helpful, the other not. "You've still got your centerline tank." (We normally "locked it" on, to preclude accidental release of valuable fuel, I had forgotten to release the lock to jettison it, which I now did, making me a bit lighter. Fris' other comment was something like, "There's oil all over the side of the airplane!"

"Thanks a lot, Fris," for just the reassurance I needed!

Since the aircraft was still holding together, I tried powering back to reduce the stress on the engine, but at any reduced setting, I didn't have enough power to climb, so I winced a bit, eased it back up and hoped for the best. Thankfully, she held together long enough for me to do a slow climb to about 13,500 feet. By then I was within sight of the runway at NKP, so I pulled the throttle to idle and set up for a flame out pattern, never touching the throttle again. Good thing I didn't need to, because it quit running as I was rolling down the runway after touching down.

One final postscript...We knew we were lucky that the crew had stayed with the aircraft as long as they had. If they had ejected just seconds earlier, we would have been forced to try to rescue them just a few klicks east, right in the floor of Ban Phanop Valley. The valley, and the truck convoys going through it, were so often attacked that it looked like the surface of the moon—sandy, pockmarked by bomb craters, with hardly a living piece of vegetation. It was heavily defended with countless entrenched gun positions and had been the site of many aircraft losses throughout the war. Little did we know that less than three weeks later, another F-4 would be shot down, and this time we weren't so fortunate. The crew ended up right in the middle of the valley floor, touching off the largest SAR effort in our history, a three-day effort known simply as "Boxer 22."

Note: Boxer 24 Alpha was Major Larry Davis, a friend of Major Pete Williams of the 602nd, whom we visited in the NKP hospital that afternoon.

*

Later in the day, another F-4 from Udorn went down seven miles east of NKP town and they were picked up OK. Before it was all over, yet another F-4 was hit and headed for water. They were picked up in the Gulf of Tonkin. Everyone made it back, but there was a lot of ground fire.

So my schedule was changed. I took off at 4:55 p.m. in aircraft #444 with Jim Monk leading. We were assigned to work with Lulu and I struck first. When it was Jim's turn he was diverted to Blind Bat 07 who had eight trucks cornered in Ban Ban Valley. Jim got four of them. Outstanding!

November 17, 1969. Monday. Took off at 4:50 p.m. in the right seat of aircraft #546 with Al Preyss in the left and Stu Bischoff leading. I took along a starlight scope to see for myself how well it worked. Using it was difficult because it was bulky, had to be held steady, and everything showed up in various shades of green. We armed reccied for over an hour with nothing to show for it, then hooked up with a Blind Bat fac who had a truck spotted in Ban Ban Valley. Al put a nape right on it. This mission lasted four hours.

*

November 18, 1969. Tuesday. I was up at 4:30 a.m. to brief at 6:15 and took off at 7:50. Ron Marzano was on his first mission as flight leader with an IP (me) on his wing. My flying duties included being an IP almost all the time. The weather was beautiful. I could see the mountains north of the bend in the river almost as soon as we took off. But low-lying clouds covered all the valleys in Barrel Roll and the PDJ, so at the fence, about seventy miles northwest of NKP, Cricket, the daytime control ship, called to divert us to a Nail in Steel Tiger. The Nail had some bad guys' hooches identified about twenty-four miles east of NKP, and I got two of them. My bombs were right on target. We each had six Mark 82s and two napalm canisters, but we weren't allowed to use the napes in that area because of the rules of engagement. I wondered if that made sense to anyone—why we could use the napes up north, but not against the enemy east of the base. After we struck with the bombs, we orbited for over an hour trying to get authorization to hit with the napes, but permission was denied, so we brought them back.

*

A listing with pictures and circumstances of all the guys who had been shot down and were either MIAs or POWs arrived at Intelligence today. I went through it page by page—maybe 500 pages—and I knew quite a few of them.

I was especially interested in Jack Swanson, an F-105 pilot who was shot down June 15, 1967. He turned toward the water and ejected just off the coast of North Vietnam. He was seen alive with a North Vietnamese patrol boat coming out to pick him up, but has never been heard from again. Jack's younger brother, Jim, had been my classmate in first and second grades, and I knew them because their grandmother lived across the back yard from us in Princeton. The listing had no new information about him. He was a graduate of the nuclear engineering program at the University of Illinois and was licensed to operate the university's nuclear reactor.

I received a letter from John Francis today. John was a C-124 pilot who had been a part-time roommate when I was at Dover and was now a pilot for Delta Airlines. Flying for Delta was at the top of my to-do list when I got back home, although I would be happy flying for practically any airline. Those guys didn't get shot at very much and having a job like that seemed to me to be almost magical.

*

The following was published in the June, 1993, issue of the *A-1 Skyraider Association Newsletter* and attributed to an anonymous A-1 pilot's diary.

The holiday season is here, and I'm working on my fourth month. I'm one-third through my tour, but I'm not suffering. I'm a night fighter now, qualified to skulk and to peer out of my cockpit into the darkness. On my first sortie rolling in on a spot in the dark, we took 200 rounds of 37mm. But it was too pretty to be ominous and threatening. In fact, I found myself staring at the stuff—a little boy with wide eyes. I forgot to be afraid. That will come, but not yet.

Night flying is the rage now. The rainy season is over and the Ho Chi Minh Interstate is dry enough to run supplies out of North Vietnam to the legions in the south. They are like so many ants scurrying from the hill in all directions. The squadron patiently orbits the exits out of the north with cans of napalm to trade for their rice. Reminds me of a cat waiting for a mouse by the hole in the wall.

My roommate just got a bunch of stereo equipment and we don't know where to put it. Right now it is strategically located on my desk, thus changing the desk from a useful entity with some sort of character to only something to keep sound equipment off the floor. Put it on the floor and save the desk from debasement.

I put the paper Santa Claus on the door that sister Bonnie sent me. I hope I can get in one more quick trip to Bangkok before Christmas for some last minute shopping. Also, I am determined not to let Christmas go by unheralded just because I am geographically displaced from home for the holidays.

Coming back from a mission over the Trail two nights ago was a beautiful experience. The moon was full and we were flying above a cloud deck that made a silver floor, reflecting moon and starlight. The visibility was unlimited. Man, safe and comfortable out of his element, relaxed enough to feel such protected things as sensitivity to beauty. The cockpit at night is twice as sensuous as in the day. The red glow from the cockpit lights, your reassuring instruments, the radios—your only link with other men. From all this you peer out into the night. Sights and sensations are much more unnatural than in the day. Alien is not the correct way to describe the night because twinkling stars and reflected moon beams are not unfriendly. I don't think it is possible to go "ho-hum" at night. To do so would be to become a nonchalant lover, to have shallow passions, and to never breathe deep again.

I scared myself on my last night ride. Evil vertigo clutched my inexperienced (though vertigo is benevolent for it clutches the experienced as well) self and had me in a near inverted dive while I was admiring the explosions my napalm was setting off. I wonder what my last act on earth will be. Whether it shall be generous or grave or selfish or desperate. I only hope it will be a truthful one reflecting who I am.

*

November 21, 1969. Friday. The time swaps from late night to early morning briefings and flights made it difficult to get adequate rest. Fatigue was a frequent problem, and I'd often go into sleep deficit and then catch up all at once. Yesterday morning was one of the catch-up days. I slept twelve hours.

I briefed at 10:30 p.m. last night and took off at 12:50 a.m. in the right seat with Lieutenant Colonel Art Linn in the left for a Steel Tiger mission with Pete Williams leading. Part of the Trail was covered with clouds, part was clear. Most of the movers were under the clouds, so there wasn't a need for a full complement of strike aircraft and we found ourselves stacked up in a holding pattern between thirty and forty miles east of the base waiting to be called in for a strike. The moon was bright. On the eastbound leg, we could see 37mm tracers going up whenever an A-1 made a pass at a target. They would arc up gracefully in clips of seven like sparks coming off a metal grinding wheel. The red tracers burned out, then a second or two later, the shell exploded in a white flash. A lot of metal was going up and showering back down onto the land. I wondered why they never seemed to hit any of our airplanes at night. They obviously couldn't see us even on a bright moonlit night, but it seemed like the law of averages would see to it that sooner or later someone would get hit and be unable to get home.

At forty miles we began a right turn to the west and while inbound to the station we could see the great Mekong in the moonlight. On the west bank of the river was the city of Nakhon Phanom with its bright lights and a few miles beyond was the base and safety. The contrast between the peaceful setting of the westbound leg and the violence and danger on the eastbound leg was profound. At thirty miles, we made another right turn to the outbound leg. The strike was thirty or thirty-five miles east of us, and at 9,000 feet we could see it clearly.

I felt relaxed and relatively safe. The hum of the engine was monotonous, and it was getting late. Suddenly a voice shot into the headset of my helmet and it got my attention with a start. It was Colonel Linn asking a question. I drifted off again and again was awakened by the voice in the headset. I guess all the extra sleep this morning still wasn't enough. At times, flying in the right seat, having a lieutenant colonel chauffeur me around had its advantages—now if he would only be still and let me rest a little....

It was a beautiful night and the views were spectacular, but after two hours of orbiting Someone decided they didn't need us, so we made the short flight back to the base and landed with all our ordnance. Why couldn't they have known before we took off they wouldn't need us? It was an enjoyable evening to fly and I got credit for a combat mission because we were east of the river, but nothing was accomplished. Colonel Linn received no practical experience toward being a safe night pilot and there was an inherent danger making a takeoff and landing in an old, fully-loaded airplane that had a less-than-completely-reliable engine.

*

I left for Bangkok on the afternoon C-130 for a CTO.

<u>November 25, 1969.</u> Tuesday. This was the last day of my CTO, so I left before dawn to go back to NKP on the morning C-130 flight. Years later, Emily told me she would watch as I walked under the overhead lights toward the street to hail a taxi, and each time she wondered if she would ever see me again.

Upon arrival back at at NKP, I had a tape in the mail Dad had started on November 15. He said they had just read an article in the local newspaper that I had received a Distinguished Flying Cross. I had been notified about it just after I returned from leave in October and it had been officially presented to me about a month ago. I hadn't mentioned it because I wanted them to be surprised when they read about it. They were!

The temperature had been down to about 54° F each of the past two nights with a high of about 75-78° F in the daytime. Beautiful weather, but our rooms were not heated.

November 27, 1969. Thursday. Happy Thanksgiving, but I'd never know it here by my schedule. I had two missions over the Trail with a full moon. I took off at 2:30 a.m. with Jim Matthews on the wing. We had to hold for an hour and a half, watching the 37s hose down someone else. Waiting and watching while flying in circles. If my nerves hadn't had a chance to act up until now, this was an excellent opportunity for them to do so. The air was very clear and it was an absolutely beautiful night with the moon providing illumination all the way to the horizon. But what was it doing to us? Would they see us? Was it that bright? It sure looked like it from our position just thirty miles away. I had to remember to not roll in with the moon directly at my back. But how do I do that? The moon was always at my back to someone.

Once again, on the westbound leg of the holding pattern I could see the base, the town of Nakhon Phanom, and the Mekong River shimmering in the moonlight. It looked so peaceful. Then I turned back to the east and saw the guns firing again. It wasn't peaceful over there. I looked at the instrument panel. The engine was running smoothly, and all the gauges looked as if they were frozen in the dim red back-lighting of the panel. The karst was easy to see in the moonlight, but there were no lights on the ground east of the river. Not even a camp fire. Didn't anyone live there? Even the deserts of the southwestern United States have occasional lights. So do the Rocky Mountains every few miles in all but the most inaccessible areas. But here, nothing.

I permitted myself to wonder briefly if any captive Americans were down there looking at us, longing for a way out, but those thoughts were not a good way to get mentally prepared for the job at hand. Occasionally a good song came over Radio Saigon.

Finally our number was called and we were assigned to Candlestick 41 who had five trucks spotted one hundred miles southeast of the base. This was my first left seat mission in about ten days and I wasn't very accurate on my first pass, putting my first two napes only in the general vicinity of the target. The next one wasn't very good either. But the bad guys didn't very much like what we were doing, because a lot of guns were firing. It looked like they were getting target practice and I was the target. Of the five trucks the Candle had for us, we destroyed two and damaged the other three. In addition, we started three small fires and cut the road once. According to the Candle, one of my 20mm gun passes started one of the fires beside the road. The Candle said we took 245 rounds of 37mm fire. I had a three-G airplane tonight and over-G'd it with four, so I had to write it up. It seems to me to be foolish to fly three-G airplanes in such an environment. Jim did most of the damage to the targets.

I dropped my first M-36 funny bomb tonight—a new weapon to us. Pilots called it a funny bomb because none of us had ever heard of it before, because it was different from anything else we carried, because of what it did when it hit the ground, and for lack of a better name. To us, it was a mystery bomb. Funny bombs weighed 926 pounds and had to be carried on the inboard stub because they were so heavy. A high drag item with a flat nose, it was designed to be carried internally in a bomb bay. The only delivery instruction given to pilots was that they were to be released about 4,500 feet above the ground for most effective dispersal of the munitions. We received no instructions on what mil setting to use in either a 40° dive or a 30° dive and no instructions on the aerodynamic characteristics of the weapon on its way to the ground. The only information came by word-of-mouth discussions with other pilots. It was designed to open about half way to the ground and release its 182 bomblets of magnesium balls wrapped in thermite that would spread out to cover an area "about the size of a football field." The bomblets would explode and burn on impact, and, sure enough, covered a large area. The really nice thing about funny bombs was they didn't require the pilot to be unerringly accurate. Somewhere in the neighborhood would do just fine, thank you. It was not a weapon for cratering a road, but if anything was in the road it would get burned. It was a very effective weapon and interesting to watch. Normally, we used them on the Trail east of the base, but once in a while we took one north. The first time I dropped one with a ground fac he got very excited and said, "Ooh, Firefly, do you have another one of those?" I laughed and told him I had only one.

*

Turkey was on the menu at the Officers' Club today and it was actually pretty good.

I had a 9:00 p.m. takeoff on Thanksgiving night with Dave Friestad leading. We had to hold for an hour and twenty minutes and then went to Candlestick 42 who had two trucks spotted westbound only fifty miles from the base. I wonder where they were going. We had a stronger than usual wind out of the northeast, which we weren't used to, and it blew our ordnance off to the side. We didn't do much good.

The ground fire was much lighter in that area. I took only twenty-one rounds, one clip on each of my last three passes. But the second one came pretty close. As I was pulling off the target and had the nose high climbing back up to altitude, I looked over my right shoulder and saw it coming—one clip climbing up toward me. Each shell came a little closer until I saw the seventh go past near enough it seemed I could reach out and grab it. Close enough so that if a clip had eight rounds instead of seven, it would have hit me. I could have turned out of the way, but I could see it would miss. I was fascinated by the sight of the shells coming up, ever closer, and then zooming past on their deadly journey. That gun was only fifty miles from the base! I took a deep breath, lined up the target, and went in for one more pass. I certainly had something to be thankful for on this Thanksgiving Day.

The northeast wind blew our bombs and napes south of the road. I dropped another funny bomb tonight and it missed the road where it was offset to the south for a mile or so. I was really upset with the way it missed.

November 28, 1969. Friday. Took off at 5:30 p.m. with Ron Marzano on the wing. We held for an hour and a half then went to Candlestick 44 who had four trucks. But it was their lucky night, because a strong wind blew out of the east again and we missed. The gunners missed, too, but not by much. The shooting didn't start until my fourth pass, but it was pretty accurate—the shells were just under my airplane. They came close to Ron, too, and we were glad to get out of that area. The Candle reported we got sixteen clips of 37mm fire—112 rounds.

November 29, 1969. Saturday. I got back to the room about 11:30 p.m. last night and was able to sleep for only an hour when it was time get up for breakfast and report for a 5:45 a.m. briefing to give Ron Marzano his IP check out. The plan was for me to fly in the left seat with Ron in the right, around the local area without ordnance, and I would make a couple of dry passes and intentionally screw something up to let him catch it. I'd make a shallow angle dive and a steep angle dive attack and then let him get three landings in the right seat. My IP check out was not like that.

When we got to the briefing room, the plan had been changed, so we took off at 7:50 a.m. with Ron in the lead on a combat mission. About forty minutes after takeoff Ron's engine had high carburetor air temperature and we had to RTB. After landing, we discovered my plane had fuel leaks, so I wouldn't have been able to fly much longer either. We landed heavyweight in a stiff crosswind.

Chapter 16

Boxer 22

December 1, 1969. Monday. Two pilots from the recently phased out A-26 squadron stayed at NKP to fly A-1s and I was assigned the responsibility for their airplane check out. They were the former Nimrod squadron commander, Lieutenant Colonel Jack Douglas, who had flown P-51s in Korea, and Captain George Luck.

This afternoon I set up a ground school for the basic airplane engineering. When that part of the training was completed, I was to take George as a student to teach him how to fly an A-1. After the aircraft check out, he was to be assigned to another pilot for his combat experience. Being an IP for transition flying was different from being an IP for night check outs because it involved teaching someone how to fly the A-1 who had never done it before.

I saw several advantages in this plan. I would get to make some lightweight takeoffs, fly in clear morning air, and do a few fun things I hadn't done in a while—aerobatics, stalls, instrument approaches, and landings. All with no one shooting at me. I was also promised I would not be on the combat schedule as long as George was in transition—a promise that didn't last very long. I had never been an IP for a transition student, but fortunately, George was a good and experienced pilot who didn't need much help.

*

December 2, 1969. Tuesday. At 12:06 a.m. Rick Chorlins ejected seven miles from the northwest end of the runway because of control problems and was picked up quickly. He was in aircraft #546, the same airplane he and I flew November 12. It was an old fat face G model, and I was glad to see it gone, although I'm sure Rick could think of better ways to dispose of old airplanes. It took all the strength he had to turn right, and it wouldn't go left at all, so he switched off the hydraulic aileron boost and it went completely out of control. He landed in a tree and the choppers made a night recovery.

*

I took off at 1:55 a.m. with Larry Dannelly on the wing. We orbited until 3:50 a.m., when I told the controller we were going to RTB. Just then a Candle said he had two trucks, and I said, "We're on our way. What direction?"

He was only about thirty miles from us. My bombs were right on target, but the Candle would give us only one truck killed and he wouldn't say which one of us got it. He said I had one hundred percent of my bombs within fifty meters of the target.

I flew again on December 2 with a 5:36 p.m. takeoff in the right seat of aircraft #514 with First Lieutenant Tom Coleman in the left and Colonel Lowman leading. Forty miles southeast of the base, the airplane started to make funny noises and pounding, so we turned back.

December 3, 1969. Wednesday. I conducted ground school for Colonel Douglas and Captain Luck. I was scheduled for a 6:00 p.m. takeoff in the right seat, but didn't fly because a big SAR used all the airplanes.

*

For many years, civilian groups and individuals have had a practice of sending boxes of goodies and supplies to servicemen who were away from home, which we called care packages. Care packages were always welcome and we were anxious to see what they contained. I received one today sponsored by radio station WZOE in Princeton and packed by local ladies. Packages included cookies, which didn't last very long. The box was intended as a Christmas gift, which I appreciated and sent a thank you note right away.

December 4, 1969. Thursday. For the second day in a row, I conducted ground school for the A-26 pilots, then had a combat mission with a takeoff at 8:05 p.m. in aircraft #028 with Lieutenant Colonel Al Martin on the wing. We went to Steel Tiger where Candlestick 41 said he had a lot of trucks moving and had facced a flight of fast movers in on them with little success. After the jets left and just as we were arriving on the scene something exploded right on the road that looked like a nape. But we hadn't dropped it and no one else was in the immediate area. All the trucks stopped moving for about ninety minutes and we couldn't find anything.

Then I saw one truck moving fast, so I rolled in on it and dropped two napes, but he was moving too fast and I wasn't in a very good position, so I missed. When my second nape hit, he pulled to the side of the road, turned out his lights, and disappeared, so we RTBd with most of our ordnance.

December 5, 1969. Friday. Took off at 11:20 a.m.in the left seat on TR-1, a transition training mission with George Luck in the right. It was an orientation flight to show him what an A-1 flew like. We flew for an hour and twenty-five minutes, at which time we were directed to RTB because our airplane would be needed for a SAR.

*

Just before we took off Sandy alert pilots were scrambled for an F-4C that had been shot down east of NKP on the 085° radial at sixty-two to sixty-five miles, right on the main route structure of the Ho Chi Minh Trail, a bad area with a lot of guns that had to be knocked out before a helicopter could be brought in. Jim George was Sandy One. The front seater had a broken ankle. Fast movers were facced in on the guns all afternoon and just before dark a rescue attempt was made. As the helicopter moved in a 23mm shell penetrated its side and killed a parajumper (PJ), Airman First Class David Davison.

By then it was too late to do anything else in the remaining daylight, so everyone RTBd with a promise to be back early in the morning to try again.

<u>December 6, 1969.</u> Saturday. At first light, A-1s were back on scene with Colonel Tripp flying Sandy One, but only one survivor was still alive. The one who came up on the radio said he heard shots and a scream just before dark. The call sign of the airplane that had been shot down was Boxer 22 and the back seater was the survivor, so he became Boxer 22B. His position was along a river with karst formations on both sides. The enemy didn't have to bring in guns overnight because they were already there to protect the route structure. The guns that hammered the airplanes all day yesterday were mostly 23mm and were positioned in caves at the base of the karst where they were safe from almost anything except a direct hit, which made them very difficult to knock out. Some pilots speculated the survivor was allowed to live overnight so he could act as bait to try to lure a few more airplanes into the guns.

A couple of the guns were repositioned overnight and a Nail was brought in to fac F-105s on them. F-105s and F-4s used laser and TV guided bombs for the first time in combat and were unbelievably accurate. It was a big battle today.

Rex Huntsman and I sat cockpit alert for an hour and ten minutes before we were launched at 11:20 a.m. The load was light, as we were carrying only CBU-30, an incapacitating gas, and CBU-14.

As soon as we arrived on scene we struck. We came into the area at 12,500 feet, rolled in from that altitude and pulled out about one hundred feet above the ground as we crossed the target. Three flights ahead of us dispensed gas and I was right behind Rex. After us, three or four more flights came in with smoke screen to protect the survivor from the still active guns. Quite a few were left, mostly small arms and ZPU (14.7mm).

Eventually Sandy Lead determined a helicopter rescue attempt could be made. Rex and I still had quite a bit of ordnance left, so we moved out of the way, but stayed on scene. The Jolly came up the river at very low altitude and got closer and closer to the survivor until he was within five feet of the hoist when all of a sudden the pilot pulled out. I could hear the survivor crying out on his radio, "Why did he leave? Why did he leave?"

The tail rotor of the helicopter had hit a tree and the pilot thought he had been hit with ground fire and decided to pull out. What a disappointment for all of us! It tore me up to know we were *so close* to getting the survivor out, but hadn't succeeded.

Rex and I heard and watched the drama unfolding, knowing if the survivor had to be left on the ground he would need protection while the rescue forces reorganized. Most of the air activity ceased temporarily after the failed pickup attempt because the airplanes needed to be refueled and rearmed and crews changed. Our mission became to keep the enemy occupied during the lull so they didn't have open season on the survivor. Rex and I knew where he was and we went in low, attempting to cover him and keep the bad guys away. We could kick out CBUs anywhere except for the survivor's location and be safe, which we did at nothing in particular, just away from him to try to get the enemy's attention.

Although we must have been fat targets, being low and slow, we didn't observe any ground fire. Both of us unexpectedly got secondary explosions with CBU 14, which we both observed. The gunners must have been rearming, too. When we were out of CBU we strafed the area, making several passes trying to buy time until the next group of airplanes arrived. As we pulled off the target to the east, we were turning out very close to North Vietnam. I could see the rivers and lowlands next to the Gulf of Tonkin, but not quite to the gulf.

We stayed until a new force of Sandies arrived and then RTBd.

*

The rest of the afternoon was spent with facs bringing in fast movers to knock out guns.

The wing launched 131 sorties today, not including the fast movers who came in for fuel. Just about everybody flew in support of the mission. Unfortunately, the survivor was stuck for another night, and things didn't look good.

We didn't lose any pilots or airplanes today, but Tony Wylie had a 37mm hole in his left elevator and another pilot took a round in one of the wing-mounted 20mm guns. The shell came from the side and might have gone into the cockpit if it hadn't been stopped. Some of the helicopters were hit. The ground in that area really looked bombed out.

It was reported the air war in Southeast Asia came to a halt everywhere except sixty miles east of NKP as all resources were expended in an effort to extract the survivor. On the other side, the enemy must have taken a terrific pounding. We have no way of knowing what their toll was, but I wouldn't have wanted to be in one of those caves. The guns getting the attention were all sizes: 12.7mm, ZPU, 23mm, and 37mm. It was not possible to attempt another pickup today due to the intensity of the action.

We went to bed discouraged because it didn't seem possible the survivor would be alive in the morning.

December 7, 1969. Sunday. Someone beat on the door before 4:00 a.m. with the news that contact had been made with the survivor—he had indeed lived through the night. Jim and I came straight out of our beds with the news and immediately went to the command post for our assignments for the day we hoped would be the day of the recovery.

The command post was buzzing. It wasn't long before we received our assignments, and the rescue briefing began. Initially, the area of the survivor had to be checked over and then dragged for guns. That is, someone would have to go in low and slow again to see if he could draw fire. When guns came up, facs and fast movers would be called upon to knock them out.

Jim Monk was the first Sandy One of the day, but on the first pick up attempt there was too much smoke for the chopper pilot to see the survivor, so he pulled out. Again the survivor asked, "Why did he pull away?" Another try was made and they still didn't get him because of ground fire. One of the Jollies saw a camouflaged truck with a gun mounted on the back shooting at them, so they pulled away.

Major Tom Dayton, who was in the class after mine at Hurlburt and was in the 22nd, took over as Sandy Lead at midday.

I briefed to be part of a flight of four A-1s armed with gas and willie pete (white phosphorus smoke) and was scheduled for a 10:00 a.m. takeoff, but had a mechanical problem. One of the other guys didn't have a tachometer and also had to go back.

Two A-1Hs armed and ready for takeoff

So two took off and two had to wait. We taxied back and waited for maintenance to fix the airplanes as no spares were available. At 11:45, we finally took off and immediately turned east. My call sign was Fruit 50 and Dave Friestad was Fruit 51. Pilots who took off five minutes before us were included in the action, but Dave and I were too late because it had already started when we arrived. When I checked in with Sandy Lead, he said to climb up high and hold. "If we need you, we'll know where to find you."

I brought my camera on this mission not knowing whether I would have an opportunity to use it. As things turned out, I had an excellent location from which to record the action of Boxer 22. My pictures are one-of-a-kind of any SAR, let alone the actual pickup of one of the biggest in the history of the war.

A river flowed south through the middle of the area, and the survivor was on the east bank. The Skyraiders had smoke, gas, guns, CBUs, and bombs. When Major Dayton had everything ready to go and everyone briefed, the daisy chain began on both sides of the river. One circle of six A-1s was on the east bank and another of eight was on the west. I was overhead, watching it all from 11,000 feet, looking almost straight down. The sky was clear.

The daisy chain has begun. Boxer 22B is on the near side of the river. Incapcitating gas is on the near side and willie pete on the far side.

Jack Hudson escorted the helicopters up the river at very low altitude. When the daisy chain began, willie pete smoke billowed up to obscure the view of the gunners. I could see the guns start firing. Jack started moving the

Jollies up the river from the south. They were down between the banks of the river just above the water. But the chopper went too far—past the position of the survivor. Jack said, "OK, Jolly, slow down, slow down." Then, "Do a one eighty (degree turn) and come back."

A hole in the billowing smoke.

Someone called out, "Fill in the gaps in the smoke!" On the west side of the river, a gap in the smoke allowed the bad guys to see enough to shoot through it. Jim Costin came over and laid couple of "big eggs"—500-pound bombs—right in the gap. Along with the gas, CBU-14, white smoke, and bombs, it was just enough to keep the bad guys' heads down. The Jolly managed to get in and make the pickup with action all around—guns firing, smoke, gas, and confusion.

As soon as he was aboard they called out, "We've got him!" Then they had to get out of the area, south, down the river.

Fewer guns to the south allowed them a safer exit route. The survivor's position was about as bad as it could have possibly been, but the extraordinary skill and courage of the A-1 pilots, the Jolly Green Giant helicopter pilots and crews, the Nail facs, the fast mover (F-4, F-105, A-4) pilots, the dedication of the support people back at the base, and the determination of the commanders for this one man's life allowed us to save him from certain death at the hands of the enemy.

Twenty-four Skyraiders all turned for NKP at once, which resulted in a traffic jam with everyone trying to land at the same time. Entering the traffic pattern wasn't easy. Dave was out on my wing and I had my head on a swivel trying to figure out where everyone was. I had to enter the traffic pattern twice, and the second time, I had to do a 360° turn to get spacing on the downwind. When I did finally get on the ground, the dearming area had A-1s backed up to the runway. About that time two Marine F-4s from Chu Lai diverted in for fuel. Earlier, before we even took off, two A-4s from a carrier somewhere off the coast had arrived. Some OV-10s also landed. It was like a big air show with a lot of excitement and was fun to be a part of.

A crowd met the survivor when he got out of the helicopter, and he was taken straight to the hospital for a checkup. I thought the first thing he would do was go to bed for a couple of days to make up for the two nights he had spent in a cold and dangerous place. The air temperature was down to 56° F this morning at NKP and must have been about the same on the Trail, so he couldn't have been very comfortable in his cotton flying suit in that chilly weather.

Everyone on the base was exhilarated because we were so glad to see him safe and sound. Unfortunately, we lost two of the air force's finest—Airman Davison and Boxer 22A, Captain Ben Danielson.

For leading the successful pickup effort Major Tom Dayton was awarded an Air Force Cross.

*

This is the second half of the diary of the anonymous A-1 pilot in Chapter 15.

> The greatest rescue effort of the whole war has taken place since I last wrote. Two F-4 pilots were shot down and had to bail out over the most heavily defended part of the Ho Chi Minh Trail. For three days, the air war in Southeast Asia stopped as every resource was made available to make a successful pickup possible. For three days, we pounded embedded gun (em)placement(s). The survivors ran and hid, ran and hid, as the North Vietnamese beat the bushes for them. After the first day, they caught one of the pilots. If I had known where the enemy were I would have flown my plane and its full load of bombs into the middle of them. I just wanted to kill every one of them. It was the most overriding passion I have ever had. For three days, the lone survivor hid from the

Vietnamese. And for three days, we hammered the area trying to make it safe enough for the helicopters to make the pickup. At one point, the survivor jumped in a river and breathed through a straw to keep from being found. A grimness settled over the base as the rescue effort went on. No one talked of anything else, no one laughed, no one got drunk at the bar at night. On the third day, I was just getting ready for another takeoff against the guns when the Operations Center called that the helicopters had made the pickup. I shut down as fast as I could and commandeered a jeep. I picked up everybody at the squadron who wasn't flying. Driving across the base, I couldn't believe the magical transformation. Everybody was hanging out the windows shouting and laughing.

Champagne corks were popping like fireworks on the Fourth. The news had passed around the base faster than I could believe possible. By the time I arrived at the helicopter landing ramp, everybody on the base was there to greet the rescue helicopter. Of the 5,000 people on the base, over 4,000 of them were waiting. I had never seen such a wild, joyful crowd, even those manufactured in the movies. Laughing and shouting and hugging each other—mechanics, secretaries, sergeants, colonels, pilots, civilians. And then the rescue force appeared on the horizon—first the strike aircraft and then the escort with the helicopter and survivor. As the helicopter hovered for a landing, I'll never forget the reaction of the crowd. The wild melee suddenly, without a signal, became completely quiet. The big blades quit turning and there was a silence ordered unspoken that was almost unnatural. The door swung open and every eye turned, every face full of expectancy. There wasn't a sound from any of the 4,000. And then the rescued pilot appeared. He was unshaven, dirty, his flight suit torn. He blinked once and stared like a man emerging from a dark room. And not a sound from the crowd. But when a weak smile tugged at the corners of his mouth, the crowd went wild. I'll never forget those few minutes as long as I live. Drama at its highest. Every emotion was real. There have never been that many honest people at one time feeling the same thing ever before. The joyous celebration carried on into the night. New Year's Eve will seem like a church social.

*

The crew of Boxer 22 was from Cam Ranh Bay. NKP generated 220 sorties in support of the SAR, 171 of which were A-1s, the rest were Jolly Greens and Nails. Ron Marzano returned with ground fire damage to his airplane and another pilot was down so low his airplane was hit by rocket shrapnel from the airplane behind him. Boxer 22 was the largest SAR in the Southeast Asian war to date. We were told the previous biggest SAR was a couple of years ago for Captain Dale Pichard, an F-105 pilot whose brother, Brent, was in my class in pilot training at Laughlin. Many other sorties were launched from other bases all over SEA and from navy carriers in support of this SAR.

*

Today, December 7, was my first wedding anniversary.

The New Christie Minstrels were putting on a show in the amphitheater behind the Officers' Club when I got back, but I was there to see only the last ten minutes of it.

*

December 9, 1969. Tuesday. I got to meet the Boxer 22 survivor and I've never seen a happier guy in my life. He had a cut on the bridge of his nose where his helmet had come off and something struck him when he ejected. They were around 500 knots when they ejected he said, and he had a couple of bruises, like black eyes, and the bridge of his nose was swollen and bruised. Other than that, he was in good shape. His name was First Lieutenant Woodie Bergeron, an air force navigator from New Orleans. Boxer 22A was Captain Ben Danielson, who was from Kenyon, Minnestoa, and a graduate of St. Olaf College.

Woodie ran out of water after the first day and a half, so he began to drink river water. Back at NKP, as he got off the helicopter, he gave his canteen to the flight surgeon and said, "Here, analyze this. I want to know what kind of germs I got from drinking this water."

Yesterday I listened to his very interesting taped interview. He said it was devastating to be on the ground while the ordnance exploded around him. A CBU-14 went off on the other side of a tree he had his back against. It shook his head when it hit the tree. He said it was quite an experience to hear bombs go off nearby. He was asked if it would have been better to have had the bombs going off all night and he replied, "It would have been easier to sneeze." He had to be very quiet. The second night he moved about seventy-five yards north of where he had been the first day and a half.

Just at sundown and again at first light before air cover arrived were the worst times, because the gomers came looking for him. He said as soon as the A-1s came, they moved away. They didn't have flashlights and weren't equipped to search in the dark, so they left him alone at night.

But at sundown, he could see silhouettes come over the nearby ridge as they went down to the river to search for him. He left some things behind because he didn't see any sense in hiding them since they knew approximately where he was. When they found where he had been they shot up the area while he watched. If they had turned around, they would have seen him. A couple of gas canisters dropped by A-1s had not gone off, so they picked them up and threw them into the area hoping to flush him out. At night, he said he got in the river under some foliage and stayed there until dawn, hiding. After dark they didn't bother him at all, but in the daytime they would have had it not been for the constant air pressure they were under. He was almost certain they killed Ben and their object was to kill rather than capture him. He didn't see Ben's body, but he saw them shoot right into where he was and he knew they had seen him. He also heard the scream. So much for our theory that they kept him alive as bait to draw us back.

At least twelve rescue attempts by helicopters were made before Woodie was finally picked up.

Woodie said when the Paveway 2000-pound guided bombs went off at the foot of the karst (estimated by Sandy One to be about 300 meters from his position), it really shook the ground. It wasn't so much an aural concussion as it was the ground shaking.

He was between two river fords—one to the north and one south. At night the enemy had a signal to cross the river—every time a truck went across, two shots were fired from one side and then six from the other. They did it every time. A mystery object hit about six to eight feet from him in the dark and made a hole in the ground about the size of a shoe box. He didn't investigate because he was fairly well hidden, but it came from the air and he heard the sound of a propeller until it hit the ground with a thud, like a shot in track and field.

*

The following is a statement by Airman Bob Dennard on his recollections of Boxer 22. Bob had been a weapons loader in the 609th SOS, the A-26 squadron, and he stayed at NKP for a few weeks to complete his year after the squadron went home:

> At the time it happened, I did not know the magnitude of the Boxer 22 SAR. I didn't even know it by Boxer 22. I just knew that we worked day and night supporting a SAR and that in the end we got someone out. It was the last time I worked the flightline at NKP. It was only a few years ago that I found out just how big the total effort had been...that we only got 22B out and that 22A was shot by the bad guys...and that A1C David Davison, a PJ in one of the Jolly Greens, was killed by the bad guys.
>
> Now that I've had years to reflect on it, the Boxer 22 SAR was a microcosm of our war. We won every battle, but too many young guys didn't have the chance to grow old.

Chapter 17

R&R

Yesterday morning I was scheduled in the right seat with George Luck on his first left seat ride, but we canceled at the end of the runway because of a strong direct cross wind. We were scheduled again this morning, but maintenance couldn't provide an airplane for our 8:00 a.m. departure. The winds normally didn't pick up until mid-morning, so we tried to get our mission in early. A 10-knot crosswind was blowing when we took off at 8:20. As soon as we were airborne the crosswind was reported to be 10 knots and it was gusting to 16 by the time we landed. So we didn't complete a mission today, although we did get to do some air work.

A-1s flew differently in a crosswind compared to the airplanes most of us had flown. I had about 500 hours in Skyraiders, but had made very few cross-wind landings and none from the right seat. I had forgotten how different A-1s were to fly until I tried to explain it to someone.

The biggest difference was the conventional landing gear. All airplanes had conventional gears in the early years of aviation and nobody thought much about it. But pilots who trained more recently learned to fly in tricycle gear airplanes and the transition to tail draggers was a new experience.

Tail draggers had unpleasant surprises for those unaccustomed to them. For example, if a pilot panicked and applied the brakes too hard, the tail might come up and the airplane could nose over onto its engine—or go all the way over.

Directional control, particularly at high speed on the ground while taking off or landing, was critical, too, because it might ground loop on an unwary or inexperienced pilot. That could be very hard on the landing gear and particularly dangerous with a heavy load of bombs and napalm. The pilot needed to "stay ahead of the airplane," meaning not let it even begin to drift off the assigned heading. If it did, a slight change could be made early when a small adjustment was all that was needed, instead of letting it drift into a need for a larger, more dangerous correction.

Even taxiing was different because of the tail wheel. Directional control while taxiing was accomplished by differential braking instead of using rudder pedal deflections as in modern conventional-gear airplanes. While taxiing in a straight line as along a taxiway, the pilot engaged a tail wheel lock to help keep it going straight. Once established, only small corrections were needed.

A-1 brakes were designed for tight maneuvering on the deck of an aircraft carrier, not for absorbing the energy of an aborted high-speed takeoff.

Added to the difficulties of directional control was the problem of engine torque that pulled the airplane to the left at high power settings, especially at low speed. It was dealt with by setting the rudder trim to five units (marks on the trim wheel) nose right for takeoff. Even at that setting, immediately after releasing the brakes, more right rudder was required as full power was applied to the engine. As explained by physicists, torque was the result of the gyroscopic effect of the rotation of that big propeller and engine, and was a force to be reckoned with. As speed increased on the takeoff roll, right rudder was gradually decreased until at about liftoff, none was required. As airspeed increased to cruise speed—140 knots—rudder trim was reduced to zero. The rate of airspeed increase after takeoff when heavily loaded on a hot day was very gradual.

It was not unusual to hear someone say, "You must be an A-1 pilot because your right leg is bigger than your left leg." Said in jest of course, but those who knew the A-1 knew about its torque.

Taking off and landing in a crosswind compounded the inherent trickiness of flying a Skyraider and doing so on a pilot's first flight was especially difficult. I had almost no crosswind experience, so I didn't want to try to teach George in those conditions.

The wind was gusting to 20 knots in the afternoon, but was calm early in the morning, so we scheduled a 6:30 takeoff, which meant a 5:00 a.m. brief. I was also scheduled for an 11:45 briefing for a 1:45 p.m. takeoff for a combat mission to Barrel Roll. George had been wanting to go on a combat mission just to see what it was like in an A-1, so he asked to be scheduled in the right seat with me.

*

A mission that had become popular recently was called a rice shoot. Farmers in Ban Ban Valley stacked hay after the harvest and our object was to destroy as much of it as we could with low level skip bombing of napalm into the hay stacks to deny the enemy the use of that food for their animals. Colonels and lieutenant colonels from the wing wanted to fly rice shoots, and it was what I hoped to do tomorrow. The skip bombing missions were fun, but I doubt if we really did any good. Sometimes the farmers shot at the Skyraiders with small arms as they made those passes, and who could blame them?

The mission lost some of its popularity a few days ago when a squadron commander was in the valley skip bombing napalm and his airplane was hit by small arms. The bullet came in the right side of the windscreen, which shattered and caused glass to fly into the cockpit. A piece of it hit him on the bridge of the nose and opened a little cut, which was all he needed to earn a Purple Heart. It wouldn't have taken much for him to have lost an eye. I can't imagine why he didn't have his helmet visor down to protect his face, but apparently he didn't. (He should have been given a Dumb Cluck award instead of a Purple Heart.)

Getting on the schedule for one of those missions was much easier after that. It was a rude reminder that even the most fun and seemingly safe missions were inherently dangerous, and the careless had better beware.

*

December 10, 1969. Wednesday. I took off at 6:50 a.m. with George Luck on a training flight. The training program for our two A-26 pilots was seriously delayed, first because of the big SAR on December 5, 6, and 7, and the last couple of days because of crosswinds.

While doing check out duties, I was assigned daytime missions. I had forgotten how much easier it was to fly in the daylight compared to night missions. It wasn't hard to see why guys liked them. I could get used to this!

So I took off at 1:45 p.m. with Lieutenant Colonel Douglas in the right seat and Rex Huntsman in the lead on his next-to-last mission. I was a little surprised to have Colonel Douglas flying with me today because I expected George, but here he was. It was nice to have someone ride along—especially since I was assigned to fly a two-seater anyhow.

The mission took us to Ban Ban for a rice shoot. Skip bombing napalm was part of the curriculum at Hurlburt, but I last did it ten months ago and I had done nothing even close since. I was out of practice, and at first I was a bit uneasy at being so low—we were coming in at fifty feet or less—and I kept releasing the napes too late; in other words, I missed. About the time I was starting to get the hang of it I ran out of napes.

I thought, "OK, let's see what I can do if I fire some incendiary 20mm shells into that elusive enemy haystack." I wanted to see how accurate I could be on a low angle strafing run, which I had never done in Asia. Although we had not seen anybody on the ground and had not seen any ground fire, there was a certain amount of tension involved in making passes when we were many miles from friendly territory, especially at low altitude.

When the 20mm guns in the wings of the Skyraider were fired they made a tremendous clatter, and the airplane vibrated to the beat of the guns firing—the fact of which I had never before been aware because whenever I shot them, I *knew* I was going to shoot them and I *expected* a certain amount of noise. Twenty millimeter guns are big guns, and if someone didn't know it was coming, the noise could be quite startling.

Which brings me to Colonel Douglas who had never been in an A-1 when the guns were fired. I was concentrating so much on what I was doing that I forgot to tell him what was coming next. I hadn't had an opportunity to get to know him very well, but I liked him and had no intention of scaring him, but that was just what happened. The instant I fired the guns, I saw him out of the corner of my eye as he nearly jumped out of his seat, threw his hands over his head, and ducked. The guns were never shot for more than a second or two—and as soon as I saw him duck I had finished firing and was pulling out of the pass. I apologized, and he took it in good humor. We laughed about it afterward.

It was a bright sunny afternoon with little wind and cool temperatures. A nice day to be alive and on an easy combat mission.

*

A constant point of discussion around the hooch was the menu for the day at the Officers' Club—the only place on base approved for officers to eat—and when was a good time to go. Nearly all the food was flown in from the States, so very few items on the menu were fresh. With almost nothing fresh to offer, the food ranged from monotonous to dreary and eating became a matter of necessity rather than pleasure. Even so, I still had to eat, and I made a point to bulk up before I left for a mission. With briefing two hours before scheduled takeoff, it took some careful planning to be sure I was properly nourished. Occasionally I took a sandwich along on a mission.

Sometimes my schedule was such that I ate only one meal a day, but when I did I usually made up for the fact that I hadn't eaten earlier in the day. The menu usually had four entrees, and after eating one, I'd sometimes still be hungry, so I'd order something else. The other guys got into the habit of checking with me to see what was good and what was not, because I probably knew what to avoid.

On most air force bases, maids and waitresses at the Club were civilians and NKP was no exception. Young Thai women who could speak English had jobs where that was a requirement, such as waitressing. The waitresses were very pleasant and sometimes their command of English was limited. The best way to avoid confusion about what we wanted was to simply point to the desired item on the menu. If there was some left she would say, "Yes." But if the kitchen was out of that particular item, the reply was, "No have." Many days "no have" was the best and most plentiful item on the menu.

If we got tired of eating at the Club, we could buy something at the commissary, which was just a block from our hooch. But the selection at the commissary was so limited, it frequently made "no have" look good. They offered plenty of canned soups, popcorn, soft drinks, and canned meat, but no fresh food.

By far the best place to eat on base was the enlisted men's dining hall, which was off limits to officers. The only exception was the Officer of the Day was allowed to eat in the enlisted mess hall, ostensibly to inspect to make sure the men were being treated properly. The real reason the OD ate in the enlisted men's mess was the food was good, it was inexpensive, and it made a tour as OD somewhat bearable.

One other place on base that had good food was the Thai Restaurant. It was not cheap, but the menu was varied and the food was fresh. The biggest problem with the Thai Restaurant was the constant warnings we received from the base veterinarian, who was the food inspector, of the possibility of gastric discomfort. Indeed, every once in a while someone would experience an intestinal emergency, but it was hard to pin problems on the Thai Restaurant any more than on the Officers' Club. A man could only hope he was not too far from a relief facility if gastric discomfort should arise.

I was fortunate in that I had very few emergencies of that sort, but one of the pilots (who shall remain nameless here) did, and it occurred at a very inopportune time—on the way to Barrel Roll not too long after takeoff. He told me, "I gritted my teeth and held on for as long as I possibly could, but it finally became too much." For the rest of his mission, he had his oxygen system set at one hundred percent. But how would he explain to the crew chief what happened? What if he had had to bail out? What helicopter crew would have welcomed him aboard?

The local women who couldn't speak English were hooch maids, which must have been very good jobs because there was no turnover in personnel during the year I was at the base. Communication opportunities were limited and if we wanted to have something done a little differently, we were mostly out of luck in getting it changed.

One day I was having a hard time remembering what happened to a pair of my flight boots, which the maids kept shined for us. So I went to the Thai man who served as bartender and janitor in the Sandy Box and who spoke English pretty well, and I asked him to ask my maid about my boots. She was very upset and glared at me the next time I saw her and I could tell she was angry. I asked him what the problem was. It turned out that somewhere in the translation she thought I had accused her of stealing my boots. What use could any Thai possibly have for size twelve boots? It took awhile to get that one smoothed over and when I left at the end of my tour I gave her a generous tip for having been a good maid. I doubt if she understood anything I said, but I hope she understood the money I gave her.

*

I enjoyed visiting Nakhon Phanom, but the town was nothing special, except it was Thai and very different culturally from anything I had ever experienced. Some of the guys never went to town, but for me it was an opportunity to experience things I might never do again.

Civilian taxis were not allowed on base, so I had to walk about a half mile to the main gate. Roadside scenes of farmers and water buffaloes working in rice paddies were of great interest to me as were the houses built on stilts to stay dry during the monsoon.

Once in town, the way to get around was to walk or engage a rickshaw driver who supplied the power to take me anywhere I wanted to go. A downtown section of three or four streets had shops and restaurants of interest to us Americans.

Immediately north of the downtown area was a small park that looked out over the Mekong, and from that vantage point a person could get a full grasp of how big the river was. I managed to see it from the same spot in both the dry and the wet seasons and got a good perspective of its change in size. It is big, even in the dry season, but during the monsoon the level of the river was twenty feet or more higher and the current was much swifter. It was a very impressive river, indeed.

On a prominent corner of downtown Nakhon Phanom was a large clock given to the people of the city by Ho Chi Minh himself during a visit in the 1950s. It felt strange to see that clock and hear the people talk about it and Uncle Ho, knowing he was the leader of the enemy I was fighting against every night. Although I never got into any political discussions with the locals, it was apparent that Ho Chi Minh had some measure of goodwill in the community. Politically and comercially, they seemed to be our friends.

Ho Chi Minh clock in Nakhon Phanom

We were told many of the samlar, or rickshaw, drivers lived in the town of Takhek, Laos, just across the river. In order to get back and forth to work each day, they took the river taxi. I always wondered what Takhek was like, but saw it only from the air or from the Thai banks of the Mekong.

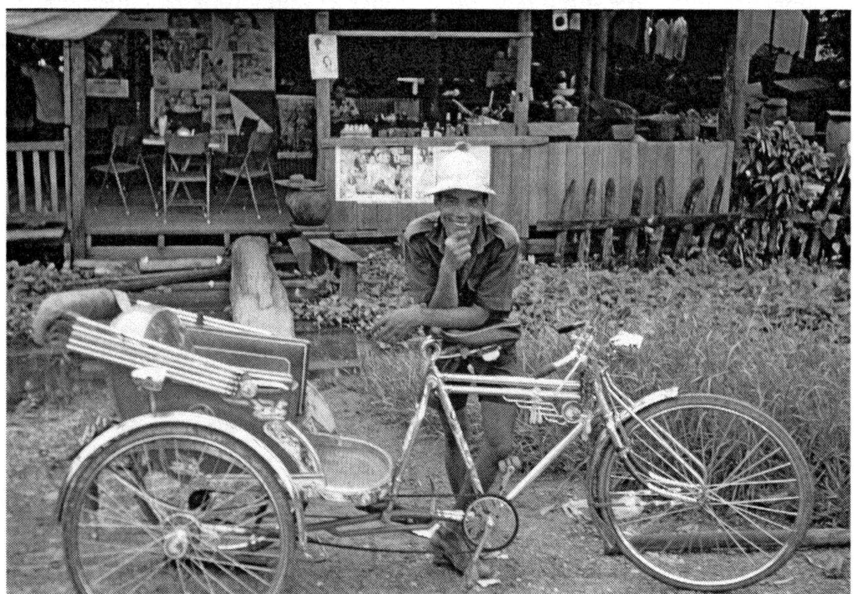

A samlar driver in Nakhom Phanom

In Nakhon Phanom the food was reasonably good in any of several restaurants, Singha beer was good, and the people were friendly. Just don't drink the water.

*

After the diversions were over, one hard fact was constant: Soon it would be time to go brief, put on the equipment, get in that big airplane loaded with bombs, rockets, CBUs, and napalm, and go back to war. Flying A-1s was better than having a ground job, but it wasn't pure fun like flying T-38s and F-106s, and I didn't particularly enjoy it. If I stopped to analyze why, I would have to say the mountains at night didn't really concern me too much—all I had to do was keep track of where they were and not go too low. The threat of the guns didn't overwhelm me, although they provided enough thrills to last a lifetime. (Maybe I'm too dismissive of the threat they posed.) I felt our mission was morally correct and had no problems with that either, even though I recognized our efforts would ultimately be futile. Deep down inside, I was most afraid of engine failure and cracks in the wings. We didn't lose anybody or even any airplanes to wing cracks as far as I know (possibly J. B. East), but we did lose people and several more airplanes to engine failures. I always felt I was playing a form of Russian roulette each time I flew a Skyraider because of that problem, and I did everything I could to stay alert. I was one of the lucky ones because, except for the sump light on October 21 and a rough engine on January 4, I didn't have any engine problems. For that I'm thankful.

*

The monsoon had a pronounced effect on the fortunes of the ground troops fighting the war in northern Laos. The roads were dirt that became impassable in the monsoon and that prevented the North Vietnamese from keeping their supply lines open for a significant part of the year. During the dry season, when supplies could get through, the NVA and Pathet Lao were successful on the battlefield, but during the wet season, the tide turned in favor of Vang Pao's troops who were able to recover large amounts of ground that had been lost earlier in the year. Almost overnight, the PDJ returned to friendly hands and many areas on the fringe of the Plain were captured by the friendlies.

When the good guys captured the land, they also captured several 37mm antiaircraft guns and many rounds of ammunition that had been menacing us in the northeastern PDJ around Roadrunner and Arrowhead Lakes. A short time later, a 37mm gun arrived at our base and was parked in front of TUOC so we could see it every time we went in the building to brief for a mission. It was a gangley, strange-looking thing with four metal wheels, a metal seat for the gunner, a gun sight, and instructions stamped into the metal in an Eastern European language.

Previously, we could see the areas around the two lakes from a distance, but had been continually warned to stay away during the day because of the threat of ground fire. I can attest to the presence of guns in those areas from nighttime experience. By the end of November the good guys owned those areas and it seemed strange to fly over them in broad daylight and not be threatened. Soon some of the long unused airstrips in the PDJ became active again and I actually felt safe there, too.

Another effect of the success of the friendlies in northern Laos was less need to provide night air support. And since the A-26 squadron was phased out of active duty about the same time, it was only logical the emphasis of our activities would shift eastward. Although I still had an occasional mission in Barrel Roll, a large share of the flying in the last five months of my tour was in Steel Tiger.

*

One thing that didn't change, even in wartime, was the personalities of people. Most of the time, captains were on a first-name basis with lieutenants and majors, and we were very relaxed with each other. We all knew who outranked whom and there was little need to make an issue of it. But every once in a while, someone came along who thought it necessary to provide reminders, just in case anyone forgot.

Major Dan Denning and his roommate, Major Jack Collins, were quite a pair. They had been in the class behind me at Hurlburt. Jack had come from F-102s and Dan had come from Strategic Air Command (SAC) and had been a KC-135 tanker pilot before coming to NKP and the A-1. I liked them both and got along fine, but Major Denning was pompous and overbearing at times, perhaps because of the fabled influence of being "sacumcized" for many years. He didn't like the fact that he was referred to as Dangerous Dan. Once when I was in Bangkok on a CTO he gave a speech at a pilot meeting on why he thought captains and lieutenants should call him "Major Denning" instead of "Dan." Upon my return I was told about the speech, but pretended I never heard about it and continued to call him Dan. He never complained to me, but I was more careful to not refer to him as Dangerous Dan when he was within earshot.

Part of the protocol of the military was to let the senior ranking officer go through a door first, which I thought was a good idea because then I had someone to open the door for me—which I needed when I was loaded down with equipment just before or after a mission.

Dan liked beer and one night in the Sandy Box after a few extra brews, he decided to show me the scars from the vasectomy he'd had on a recent CTO in Bangkok. It was important to him that it had been quite inexpensive. "Lookit there, just two little scars," he said proudly.

I changed the subject as quickly as I could and we got into a discussion about being IPs and the fact that I had been scheduled recently for an IP mission in an airplane that didn't have a stick or rudder controls in the right seat. When I got to the airplane and saw what it was, I told the other pilot to take the night off, because I was not going to fly an airplane as an instructor in the right seat without flight controls.

Dan said, "I would have taken it and let the student be in the left seat."

"You would have taken it with no controls in the right seat?"

"Yeah. No problem."

"You don't have any flight controls in the right seat," I reiterated. "How would you fly it if the left seater became incapacitated?"

"I'd just reach over to the left side of the cockpit and fly it from the right side." He was very certain of himself.

I was flabbergasted anyone would even consider doing such a thing. "Do you really think you could do that—fly it from the right seat with no controls?"

"Captain," he said condescendingly, "I could do that if I had to. I have a lot of experience, and I'm certainly not going to cancel an IP ride for not having a stick in the right seat." With that, I figured the conversation was over, but I'd really like to see him try to use the rudders from the right seat.

Dan's roommate, Jack, was known as kind of a wild man in an A-1. His idea of fun when returning from a mission was to fly low and hunt for water buffalo to kill with his 20mm guns. A little target practice. It was within the rules of engagement as long as we were over enemy-held territory in Laos, but it didn't seem to me to be a very safe way to go home and it was no way to make friends with the local farmers who were caught in the middle of this war. He might find himself on the ground some day trying to make friends with someone whose water buffalo he had killed last week. It just didn't make very good sense to me.

*

<u>December 11, 1969.</u> Thursday. George Luck and I flew another training sortie. It was a contact flight stressing performance and included aerobatics and stalls.

I was duty officer in the afternoon, so I didn't fly a combat mission. Colonel Tripp, Colonel Linn, and Rex Huntsman had their last flights today. I was out to greet them when they returned, and a bullet hole was discovered in the back of Rex's airplane. We were all astounded that on his last mission he would be out fooling around low enough to be hit with small arms fire. He just grinned and said he didn't know how that could have possibly happened.

A going-away party was held tonight for the three of them at the Officers' Club, and we all wore our best party suits, gaudy orange jump suits with the squadron insignia sewn on in all the appropriate places. The guest of honor was Senator Barry Goldwater.

<u>December 12, 1969.</u> Friday. I had a cold and felt crummy, but stayed on duty anyway. Took off at 4:50 p.m. with Lieutenant Colonel Wilfred Gabel, who has been the squadron comander since Colonel Stueck left in September, leading. We flew for three hours and forty-five minutes and didn't accomplish much of anything. There just wasn't much activity in Laos this evening.

<u>December 13, 1969.</u> Saturday. I had another training mission with George in the morning, then a combat mission as an instructor pilot in the early evening with Major Ed Solley in the left seat. Pete Williams was the flight leader, and we worked with a ground fac named Shamrock who couldn't speak English. Another fac named Hunter interpreted for us. This was my 140th combat mission.

A twenty-five mile radius around the PDJ was off limits today because Laotian General Vang Pao was hosting a party at Lima Lima, one of the airstrips in his newly acquired territory.

A pilot meeting was held in the afternoon. I always thought it best to be flying when one was scheduled but couldn't avoid it this time. It was a time for the squadron commander and executive officer to pass along the latest bits of information about changes in local flying rules, performance data of the airplanes, keep your sideburns trimmed, and above all don't go to sleep during the meeting! We also had the opportunity to stand at attention when the squadron commander walked into the room and again when he left. All in all, it took about an hour to pass out five minutes' worth of information, and the meetings were good to avoid whenever possible.

*

December 14, 1969. Sunday. About five months before the end of an assignment, the base personnel office sent a request for each person to indicate his preference for his next assignment. The form was commonly called a dream sheet by veteran military people who knew better than to expect what they wanted, but who filled it out anyway, probably to make themselves feel good for a little while.

I was no exception and filled out a dream sheet a few weeks ago, duly noting I had only six weeks from the time I was scheduled to leave this assignment until my DOS, the date I was scheduled to become a civilian again. Of that six weeks, probably at least two would be leave time, so my usefulness wherever I might go would be limited.

My choice was Perrin AFB because I was familiar with it, had trained in F-102s there three and a half years ago, and because I liked the area. I was not pleased when my assignment orders came today for Dyess AFB at Abilene, in west Texas. Dyess was a Tactical Air Command Base, and their airplanes were C-130s. I had never flown an airplane with more than two engines. And now Someone in personnel wants to make a trash hauler out of me! The thing that saved me from that fate, of course, was my DOS looming over it all, but it gave me an indication of where my career was headed if I had decided to stay on active duty.

I wasn't the only one. Russ Keeling, who was one of our best pilots and who had come to the A-1 from F-104s, received an assignment to B-52s. Russ was a Texas Aggie and a career officer, so away he went.

"Russ," I said, "why don't you get out and get a civilian flying job?"

"My goal is to continue my education through AFIT (the Air Force Institute of Technology) and get a master's degree in engineering, and I can do that in the air force easier than I can in civilian life," was his reply.

Another example was the one received by Major Ron Marzano, a topnotch officer and pilot. His assignment after A-1s was to go to Columbus AFB, Mississippi, to be an air police officer. Ron had a degree in police science, but to me that assignment made a C-130 at Dyess or a B-52 in SAC look good. And so it went with assignment after assignment of our guys at NKP.

I decided to not give in without a fight and appealed up the channels about the assignment. I pointed out every step along the way I had only six weeks left on active duty and the air force would receive little advantage in sending me to Dyess for such a short time. Not that Abilene was bad—I had never been there—but it became sort of a game to see if in some small way I could overcome the bureaucracy. Meanwhile I had to wait for the wheels to slowly turn out a decision.

*

I had another flight with George this afternoon, this one an instrument training flight, and then a combat mission to Barrel Roll with Bob Bohan leading. We armed reccied Route 7 northeast of Ban Ban Valley just after dark and didn't find anything, so we struck at a fire on the road. One of my napes hit where it was narrow and elevated compared to the surrounding terrain, and burning napalm splashed down both sides like floodlit water over a waterfall. I don't know if it did any permanent damage, but at least for a little while all truck traffic was stopped.

I also had about 28 rounds of 37mm tracers shot at me on four passes at the target. He was a pretty good gunner and didn't miss by much. It was a reminder that even though Vang Pao's troops owned the PDJ, the enemy still had a presence in the area. Maybe the gunner was a farmer who was friendly until Jack Collins killed his water buffalo.

The next few days were spent flying with George Luck, being duty officer, and serving as instructor pilot for a new guy getting his first flight in an H model.

*

<u>December 17, 1969.</u> Wednesday. Jerry J. Jenkinson was killed today in a T-37 at Webb AFB, Texas. He had returned home to be a UPT instructor pilot in air training command. When I heard this news, my thoughts turned to my first flight on April 21 when I flew with Jerry and Jim East. If someone had told me last April that of the three of us, two would be dead as the result of aircraft accidents within eight months, I probably would have taken a bus to Bangkok and a boat home. It was a situation similar to that of R.D. Watkins and Gray Warren. I first met Jerry when he came to Dover in November of 1967, to bring the 95th's new squadron commander, Colonel Robert Sowers, to visit after he received the assignment. Jerry was from Waterloo, Iowa.

*

<u>December 19, 1969.</u> Friday. One hundred days to go until I return home. I flew an FCF for an airplane that had an engine change. Then I aborted another for excessive magneto drop. I was duty officer for an hour and a half then went to brief for a mission that was canceled because of target weather.

Someone tried to sneak onto the base this evening, so we were issued guns and everyone was placed on alert for a while. Nothing came of it, but it was a bit of excitement we weren't used to. At certain places in Vietnam I suspect that sort of thing happened frequently, but for us, it was an unusual and unsettling experience. We were told to be very careful in unlighted areas and to check our doors extra carefully before going to bed. It wasn't any fun thinking that behind every tree a bad guy might be lurking.

*

<u>December 20, 1969.</u> Saturday. I went to Bangkok this morning on the C-130 for my R&R that was a part of everyone's tour of duty in Southeast Asia. R&R locations differed, varying from Hawaii (which was very much desired), to Malaysia, and the Philippines. I was happy to go to Bangkok because Emily was there and because my parents were taking advantage of the opportunity to make an around-the-world trip. Their itinerary had them in Bangkok during the holidays, so it was almost like being home for Christmas. Doug Scroggs was on leave, so he was also in Bangkok for Christmas.

My parents had arrived about two days earlier and had settled into the spare bedroom by the time I arrived. We spent the afternoon together and Emily cooked supper for us. We all went up to the roof of the building and enjoyed the sights of the city. The moon was full and bright.

*

<u>December 21, 1969.</u> Sunday. Bob Bohan ejected from aircraft #811, a Zorro H model, today and was picked up unharmed.

*

We went to the Sunday Market in Bangkok, which was an open air bazaar where people came from the country to sell what they had produced. The displays of fish, poultry, fruits, and vegetables were remarkable because of the way the farmers arranged their products in artistic patterns on large trays. We were unfamiliar with many of the tropical fruits, but when we tried them they were delicious. It made me wonder why we couldn't have access to fruit like this on base. Probably because of Someone's lack of imagination or too many requisition forms had to be filled out.

Vendor preparing rice bugs for sale

Vegetables for sale in the Bangkok Sunday Market

We went to church at 5:00 p.m. and then to the Erawan Hotel for supper. Bob Hope and Neil Armstrong were staying at the Erawan while they were in Bangkok as part of the Christmas program tour for servicemen, and Mom and Dad were excited when they saw them in the hotel lobby. It was another experience for them to tell people in Princeton about.

December 22, 1969. Monday. Mom and Dad went to Johny's Gems where Mom bought a few things to show off back home. Emily and I went to JUSMAG to mail packages. Mom and Dad had purchased several things on their trip prior to their arrival in Bangkok and needed to send them home and Emily had packages to be shipped. We made several trips on different days to the JUSMAG post office.

At night we went for dinner at La Rotunde at the Narai.

December 23, 1969. Tuesday. Johny's Gems gave Mom and Dad a free Floating Market Tour because Mom bought so much stuff yesterday, so they went on the tour this morning. Dad went to the Bangkok Rotary Club meeting at noon. Emily and I went to JUSMAG again. In the afternoon, we went to the BX and commissary for last-minute Christmas purchases and food for Christmas Eve dinner.

December 24, 1969. Wednesday. We had a small artificial Christmas tree in the apartment under which we put our gifts to each other. I bought Emily a Seiko watch with a silver band, wrapped it, and put it under the tree. She promptly guessed what it was—what she really wanted—a Seiko watch with a gold band. Oops! So when she wasn't looking, I took it from under the tree and hid it in my suitcase. On one of my trips into the city by myself I bought a Seiko watch with a gold band, wrapped it, and slipped it under the tree. The new present didn't draw much attention, but the disappearance of the original one did. "Where's that present?" she asked. I pretended like I didn't know what she was talking about, so she went on a hunt around the apartment. The apartment had only a few hiding places and nothing was safe from a determined hunter. She eventually found it and it made its way back under the tree. My intention was to return it where I bought it—the NKP BX, but I was foiled.

Included in the care package box I received from WZOE on December 4 was a small mystery package wrapped in Christmas paper that I decided would look good under the tree. It had no address label. It was just a small, nicely wrapped present. It became the object of Emily's intense curiosity and I just played dumb, even though I knew it was intended for me. When we passed out the presents to be opened, Emily, assuming it was hers, latched on to it tore it open and discovered a small portable battery-powered radio. She was mystified. "Who would give me this?" she asked with astonishment. We got a good laugh when I told her how it got there. She had just assumed it was hers and opened it even though it had no name.

For Christmas Eve, Linnea Bolin and Doug and Bonnie joined Mom, Dad, Emily, and me for dinner and presents. Emily gave me a beautiful black star sapphire ring. Later in the evening we went to the International Church, which was not far from the apartment.

December 25, 1969. Thursday. Christmas Day. We went to Linnea's for breakfast and then went home for a peaceful afternoon while Mom and Dad went back to Johny's Gems for more loot.

December 26, 1969. Friday. We had another quiet day at the apartment.

I found out many years later that navy Lt. (jg) Dustin Trowbridge was killed today in an A-6 on takeoff from the USS Coral Sea in the Gulf of Tonkin. Grandma Diller and Dustin's grandfather were siblings, which meant he was my second cousin. He was twenty-five.

December 27, 1969. Saturday. JUSMAG was closed on Saturday, so Emily and I went to the Chao Phya Hotel to mail packages and we had to wait in line for an hour. Doug and Bonnie asked us to go to Ayudia with them tomorrow, but it was an all-day tour and we declined. Dad and I went for a walk.

We barbecued spare ribs and pork chops for supper.

December 28, 1969. Sunday. Noel Frisbie ejected from aircraft #552 today and was picked up OK.

Mom and Dad got up at 5:30 a.m. to go to Chiang Mai, which was about 400 miles northwest of Bangkok and was a popular tourist destination.

Emily and I were invited to Doug and Bonnie's for lunch this noon and had a nice time. We went to the Edelweiss Restaurant at the Topper Club for supper, but the chairs were ladder-back and uncomfortable.

The review in *Time* magazine for the movie *Hello Dolly* was not very good, but we decided to see for ourselves. We had center aisle seats and found out *Time* was correct and left at intermission.

December 29, 1969. Monday. We went with Doug and Bonnie to the theater at the Petburi shopping center to see the movie *The Italian Job*, starring Michael Caine.

Mom and Dad arrived back from Chiang Mai about 9:00 p.m. and had had an interesting trip.

December 30, 1969. Tuesday. Dad went to the Bangkok Rotary Club meeting again this noon. Emily and I went to the Manhattan Hotel and rented a car and driver for thirty baht per hour and did several errands, including a trip to the BX, commissary, and JUSMAG to mail the last of our packages.

December 31, 1969. Wednesday. New Year's Eve was a time of big celebration in Thailand and people around the city were excited today with drivers honking horns and waving flags.

Dad got up early and went for a walk by himself because none of the rest of us were up.

My parents, Charles and Celia Diller, ready to leave for Chiang Mai.

The Two Vikings had a buffet on Wednesday nights and we made reservations for 7:30 p.m. for six people, including Doug and Bonnie for a fine New Year's Eve dinner. When we arrived at the restaurant we were taken to a semiprivate dining room we hadn't been in before and seated at a table. The other table in the room was occupied by a party hosted by a United States Army officer who was celebrating his promotion to brigadier general.

When the menu was presented to us, it was only a wine list. When we pointed this out to the head waiter, he told us that on New Year's Eve the food was a standard menu, and the only decision we had to make was whether we wanted this expensive wine, that expensive wine, or another wine that was not quite so expensive. After we decided on the third option, we received the menu for the evening, which was simply a notification of what was going to be served—no selection required.

The meal was presented with a great deal of flourish and started with liver pâté and crackers, smoked salmon, soup, and coffee. It continued with Waldorf salad, sherbet "to cleanse your palate," pheasant with a long feather inserted in the side of the bird, potatoes, peas, petit fours, and a dessert with a sparkler. It was elegant, even though the waiter accidentally poked Mom in the eye with the feather and Dad and I both found shotgun pellets in our pheasant. We also were mystified as to which spoon we were to use at which time, and it seemed like our place settings had an extra fork or two. It was not the $4.95 buffet we had expected for the evening, either, and when the bill came we had to pool our money and scratch around to come up with enough. I guess Thais really do like to make a big deal out of New Year's Eve. It was definitely one to remember.

We went back to the apartment. Then Doug, Bonnie, Emily, and I went to a nightclub called The Fox for the New Year celebration. The crowd was lively, well dressed, and happy, and we enjoyed the music of a live band.

Chapter 18

Old Airplanes

January 1, 1970. Thursday. My R&R came to an end today and it was time to return to NKP. We had had a marvelous Christmas and New Year's celebration together in Bangkok and hated to see it end, but time moves on, so I packed up and said goodbye.

I suspected I wouldn't be going back to the apartment again, and, since we needed a way to get the rug home, I took it with me so I could ship it with my goods when I left NKP. It was a wool 6 x 9 ft. rug that was too heavy to pack up and mail.

Since I was on my R&R, I had a guaranteed seat on the flight to NKP, but the rug didn't. So I went to Don Muang Airport early, found the NKP base C-47 about to depart, and put the rug aboard. The C-130 left an hour later and arrived about the same time as the C-47, so I went directly from one to the other, picked up the rug, and got a ride to the hooch.

I arrived at NKP about 5:00 p.m., just in time to cope with a fever, chills, and diarrhea.

January 2, 1970. Friday. When I visited the flight surgeon this morning I had a fever of 100.4° F which grounded me, but was not enough to keep me from work and I was assigned to be duty officer all day in the command post. A search and rescue effort was underway for an F-4 crew who were down a little north of where Boxer 22 was four weeks ago. Neither one survived.

January 3, 1970. Saturday. My fever was not as high (99.4) today and I felt better, but still not ready to fly. A rash the doctor called a viral eczema, which is common in children, covered most of my body. I was assigned to be TUOC briefer all day.

January 4, 1970. Sunday. I was duty officer in the morning and felt better, so I went to the flight surgeon who put me back on flying status. As a result, I was scheduled to fly late tonight. I went to church in the afternoon.

Briefing was at 8:15 for a scheduled 10:20 p.m. takeoff. While I was on R&R, the A-1 parking area was moved from the center of the ramp to the north end. Taking off to the northwest on runway 33, as we did tonight, required a long taxi from the parking area to the southeast end of the airport—about two miles. When I ran the engine up for the mag check before takeoff, it popped, and the mag dropped too much. With all the engine troubles we'd had, I decided to take it back to the ramp for a spare—two miles. The spare this evening turned out to be an old G model that used to belong to the Vietnamese Air Force, and it had just arrived from Pleiku. I began my takeoff roll on runway 33 about 11:30 p.m.

On takeoff, I could feel and see the engine afterfiring, which is similar to backfiring except backfiring comes out the carburetor and afterfiring comes out the exhaust stacks. The third time it popped I was close to 70 knots and it really got my attention. I decided if it did it again I would abort the takeoff. At 90 knots it afterfired again and, even though the tail wheel was up and the airplane was almost ready to fly, I pulled the throttle back. Something I had never thought of was the effect torque would have on directional control if power was suddenly removed at high speed during takeoff while still on the ground. Suddenly I had to deal with just that problem, as the airplane swerved sharply to the right. Somehow I managed to reverse the rudder in an instant to stay on the runway. Then I had to stop. The A-1, having been built for the navy, had an excellent tailhook system and I immediately reached for the lever and lowered it, hoping it still worked. The barrier cable stretched across the runway about 2,000 feet from the end and I felt with relief the gentle, but firm deceleration of the cable system. I didn't apply the brakes until I had come to a full stop.

My wingman was Dave Friestad and it was procedure for the wingman to release his brakes thirty seconds after the leader had released his. When I aborted Dave still had not begun his takeoff. He called out, "Tower, my lead has either gone off the side of the runway or taken the barrier." He couldn't tell which, but he knew something had happened. Maybe this was what happened to Bob Moore three months ago. It wasn't hard to imagine I might have been off the side of the runway upside down trapped in a burning airplane.

Ron Marzano was the supervisor of flying for the evening. He did a check of the runway, inspected the barrier, and said it went out 800 feet, which was a long way. The airplane weighed close to 25,000 pounds and engaged the barrier at over 85 knots—a lot of energy to stop.

*

I thought back to almost seventeen months earlier, August 13, 1968, when I was flying F-106s at Dover. The 95th had a night evaluation exercise on a clear moonless night, and I had just made a successful intercept of a target. I was about 150 miles out over the Atlantic Ocean at 3:00 a.m. when the throttle stuck at 90 percent RPM. Getting back to the base was no problem, but landing and stopping was. Whatever was blocking the throttle was solid, not spongy, and I didn't want to push the throttle forward to try to dislodge the obstruction because I was afraid it might stick at a yet higher power setting. I had a workable thrust situation in that I could use the speed brake and gear extension to create enough drag to descend, which might not be possible at a higher power setting. I just couldn't get it on the ground and stopped with the engine at 90 percent RPM. The procedure required the pilot to shut off the two fuel control switches in order to shut down the engine.

I called the squadron command post and asked the duty officer, squadron executive officer Major Walt Newton, to read out of the aircraft manual. The book said at 90 percent RPM it would take six seconds for the engine to flame out from the time I turned the fuel shutoff switches off.

I made a low approach to get an idea of what things looked like. I flew down the runway with the landing gear down and made a missed approach, then waited for a few minutes until all the other squadron aircraft were on the ground so they wouldn't have to divert to another base if I blocked the runway. All the while tension was building.

Finally it was time to bring it in. I made a faster-than-normal approach at 200 knots because that was as slow as it would go. Normal would have been 178. I turned off one fuel switch about five miles out and when I thought was just the right moment, I switched the other one off. I was over the approach lights. All too soon I was over the overrun with the engine still running. The runway end lights disappeared behind me and it was still running! I was committed to a landing and kept it coming down. Finally, just as I was about to push the panic button, the engine wound down. I forced the airplane onto the runway because the speed was still high, deployed the drag chute and the tailhook, and tried to slow it as much as I could before I got to the barrier. With relief I could feel the deceleration of the airplane as the tailhook engaged the barrier, and finally came to a stop. The nose wheel was just into the overrun with the main wheels still on the runway.

When I arrived at the command post that night the sergeant on duty shook his head and said, "I'm sure glad it wasn't me in that airplane with the stuck throttle!"

"I wasn't too wild about it, either," I replied.

That F-106 had recently returned from IRAN (inspect and repair as necessary) at McClellan AFB, near Sacramento, California. The obstruction turned out to be a small screw that had been dropped in the cockpit, managed to find its way into the throttle quadrant, and blocked the movement of the throttle. Better there than to have had it block the control column.

*

The A-1 had a retractable tailhook and all I had to do to disengage the barrier was raise the tailhook lever and taxi away. While in the dearming area I called the command post hoping they would tell me to give it up for the evening. But no.

"We've got another spare for you, tail #668, and the crew bus will be out to take you to it."

"Hey, man," I thought, "my knees are shaking after that one and I need a break. I'm in no condition to fly and it's getting late. When are you going to run out of spares?"

"Sorry, Firefly Four Zero, but we need you guys to get launched as soon as possible."

We finally took off at 12:15 a.m. on January 5 and were told to hold about thirty-five miles east of the base because the weather was too bad for a fac to find a target for us to strike. While orbiting and waiting, I listened to the live broadcast of the Cleveland Browns-Minnesota Vikings football game on Radio Saigon. It came in loud and clear and I listened to the whole game, so having to orbit wasn't such a bad deal tonight. The night programs were usually music, some of which I liked and some I didn't, so the game was a nice break from normal.

What a way to build combat time! But who needs combat time? At least I was in a single-seat H model. After about three hours, Dave ran low on fuel and we had to RTB. After all those problems with getting off the ground, we accomplished nothing.

We had to bring all our ordnance back and land over max gross weight again. How badly were we needed? Why did we launch for nothing? Surely Someone knew the weather was bad in the target area. Who's making these decisions? Were we just putting numbers on the board to make the wing commander look good on the report he filed to Saigon so he could get promoted to general? Was Someone in Saigon just putting up numbers to send to Washington? It was becoming clear to me the answer to the last two questions was probably yes and I was not happy. Helpless to do anything about it, but angry nevertheless. It was clear to me I was putting my life on the line just to boost Someone's career and I didn't like it one bit.

Trying to pin down the culprit was next to impossible and a battle I didn't have the stomach or the rank for, and I knew it would serve no purpose. But it forced me to once again consider my thoughts about what we were accomplishing in this part of the world.

Again I came to the conclusion that our motives were good and correct, but in the end we weren't going to be on the winning side. To come to the realization we were just putting numbers up for no real good reason took a lot of the spirit out of me. Just let me get out of here in one piece!

Overriding my misgivings was the fact that a soldier on the ground in South Vietnam was counting on me to kill a truck loaded with weapons meant to kill him, and if I could do that maybe we'd have one less casualty. That was the always-sobering reality and what kept me going. Somewhere, somebody's life might be saved if I knocked out just one more southbound truck. So I'll do it for him, but whoever's running the show can stick it. I was just the latest in a long line of American combatants who had become disillusioned with the way the war was being run and certainly not the last. For career officers it provided a nice opportunity to rack up some badly needed combat time for their resume, but a short timer like me didn't need the glory. Just a ticket home.

Those thoughts would lead to broader ideas of the enemy gunners we were dueling with nightly and the drivers of the trucks we were trying to kill. But wait—were we only after trucks—an impersonal piece of machinery? What about the drivers of those trucks? It seemed like a thought better left alone, but I felt I had to address it—as, I suppose, did most of the rest of the guys at some time or other. The answer that came out every time I thought about it was that the drivers of those trucks were our enemy just as much as the gunners and just as much as the ground forces menacing our allies, whether in South Vietnam or northern Laos.

We weren't just killing trucks, we were killing people in those trucks, but it was all so clean and sanitized from several thousand feet in the air. As long as the groundfire didn't get too close to threaten, we were far removed from the reality of it. We never had to look them in the eye and pull the trigger and see the look of terror on their faces. We seldom had to battle the elements except from inside our relatively comfortable cockpits. The reality of it was never the blood and the guts and the mud and the dust and the noise and the pain and the discomfort and the constant terror of war. For us, it was here now, gone in an hour. Like a lightning strike, a pilot was gone, but we didn't have to deal with the terror of the build up and the misery that went with it. To be sure, the pilots who died were just as dead, but none of us shared their deaths with them except in a most sanitized way. Essentially, they all died alone.

The rest of us who had survived to this point went to bed between our clean sheets in our air-conditioned hooch rooms with our maid-shined boots nearby. That didn't make the reality of the deaths of our fellow pilots any easier to take, but it might partly explain why few pilots need psychological counseling years after war hostilities have ceased.

The impersonal nature of war for a combat pilot was nothing new. It had been the case since the start of aerial combat in World War I and would probably be the case for wars in the future. It certainly was the reality for me in 1969 and 1970 over Laos.

*

I was scheduled for a 1:50 a.m. takeoff tonight and again tomorrow night, which I liked because the TUOC building was usually quiet so late at night. And I was scheduled to go to Barrel Roll where ground fire was not as much of a threat as it was in Steel Tiger, although the enemy was beginning to move some big guns in along Route 7 again. I knew and liked that mission the best.

*

We were way short of pilots, and guys were having to pull mobile control or duty officer the same day they were on the flying schedule. Until recently, mobile and duty officers switched positions between morning and afternoon and enough pilots were available to have a full flying schedule and have one or two standing by. When the Pleiku squadron shut down, we got more missions, but no more people. We were told Someone at Hurlburt decided that, because Pleiku closed, NKP would be overstaffed with A-1 pilots, so a couple of classes were delayed. The pilots in those classes were told to "get lost for a while," so they scattered all over the country. When NKP people figured out what happened they called Hurlburt and said, "Send us those classes," but the people at Hurlburt didn't know where they were.

The entire base received a total of about three pilots from Pleiku. Several went to a detachment at Danang. Each squadron at NKP picked up four sorties per day to make up for Pleiku being shut down, and a number of our missions were now going very far south in Laos. We needed thirty new pilots in the wing in the next thirty to forty days to make up for the ones who were going home.

Some in the wing hierarchy were not happy with me for going DNIF (duty not involving flying) as soon as I got back from Bangkok, but I couldn't do much about it. The people who were on duty through Christmas were pretty well worn out from the schedule they'd been flying.

My A-1 class at Hurlburt started a year ago yesterday. Of the twelve pilots in it, only five were left at NKP. Two, Shorty Hartz and Ralph Highmiller went to ABCCC, two went to South Vietnam on July 4 to be O-1 facs, one was at Danang, and one, Major Jim Pretlow, had finished his tour because he had only a nine-month requirement because he had three months credit in an F-102 four or five years ago. Jim Monk, Jim George, and I are in the 602nd, and First Lieutenants Al Williams and Don Travis are Zorros. Don came from Pleiku.

*

January 6, 1970. Tuesday. After an hour and thirty-five minute weather hold, I took off at 3:25 a.m. with First Lieutenant Dan McAuliffe on the wing. The Barrel Roll weather was bad, so we diverted to Steel Tiger and struck with a fac who had three trucks spotted on a road at 118/93 from NKP. We got two of them and were happy about that. We landed just as the sun was coming up at 6:00 a.m.

A-1 class 69-06. Standing L-R: Shorty Hartz, Dick Diller, Bob Karre, Vern Saxon, Jim Pretlow, John Williams. First row: Jim Monk, Ralph Highmiller, Gene Smith, Al Williams, Don Travis, Jim George. (USAF photo)

*

Today I received revised orders assigning me to Perrin AFB, Texas, when I return home in March. My complaints worked! In a small way I had beaten one part of the bureaucracy and it felt good!

January 7, 1970. Wednesday. Took off at 2:05 a.m. with Dan McAuliffe on the wing. Call sign Firefly 42. The weather was bad in Barrel Roll again, so we diverted to Steel Tiger, only this time without the long wait. We had to orbit for only about five minutes when we were assigned to a Nail fac who turned out to be my friend Jim Anderson. Jim had a truck park spotted about fifty-five miles southeast of the base, so we struck it. The mission was only an hour and forty-five minutes. I wished they were all short and quick like this one. No one shot at us for the second night in a row, although we could see a lot of ground fire to the east.

Jim had an assignment to Norton AFB, California, to fly C-141s in about a month.

A SAR was on for first light tomorrow for someone down in a bad area near Tchepone.

I was also scheduled for a 10:20 p.m. takeoff, but canceled because of mechanical problems. Our new squadron commander, Lieutenant Colonel Dick Michaud, was scheduled to go with me on his first night mission, but when the other pilot arrived at his airplane, he found a panel wouldn't fasten down properly, so we waited over an hour to get it fixed. Then my airplane had an inoperative fuel boost pump, so I went to the spare, but it had an inoperative left brake. By then we were two and a half hours late for our scheduled takeoff time, so the mission was canceled.

Jack Hudson diverted into Ubon because of a bad engine. It quit completely as he was rolling out after landing.

*

I received a letter from John Francis today who told me Delta Air Lines will hire 250 pilots starting in January. Dick Colby told me he had been hired by Delta, so he will probably be in the first class of 1970. Meanwhile, I was still getting shot at.

January 8, 1970. Thursday. Colonel Michaud finally got his first night mission in the right seat with me in the left and Stu Bischoff leading. We took off at 7:45 p.m. and struck with Candlestick 43 at 110/98 from NKP. The Candle didn't seem too sure of where he wanted our ordnance, so it was another wasted mission. On my last pass, the engine started to pop, so I immediately turned for home and jettisoned my CBU pods. The engine began running fine as we neared the base—the closer we got, the better it ran—but no harm was done since I was on my last pass. With all the mechanical problems we'd had lately I was quick to assume the worst when an engine began to make funny noises.

*

January 9, 1970. Friday. This morning Jack Hudson was striking with a Raven fac who was in a T-28 when he noticed his prop speed was not responding to commands. He began to lose altitude because of a lack of power from the prop and knew he had to turn south. He was north of the PDJ and a long way from home. He asked if the PDJ was in friendly hands and the Raven said he couldn't guarantee it. Jack knew he had to get as far south as possible. He had to cross the line of mountains south of the PDJ before he would be over the Mekong River Valley and lower terrain. That would allow more time to nurse his airplane along and a greater possibility of finding friendlies on the ground if he should have to eject. He also had the possibility of landing at LS 98 if he could just get over the mountains.

As he approached the high terrain south of the PDJ it became obvious he wouldn't be able to get over it. Terrain was higher to the east and was clearly not the way to go, so he turned to the right, west, hoping to be able to get around it. His airplane continued to lose altitude as he flew along parallel to the ridge. It was apparent that he wasn't going to be airborne much longer, so he made the decision to eject and hope for a successful pickup.

The ejection sequence was uneventful and the yank out of the cockpit was smooth and easy. He was close to the mountain ridge to which he had been flying parallel and drifted down in his parachute into a tree that was growing out the side of the mountain close to the top of the ridge. He was suspended with his parachute tangled in the tree. When he looked down, it was a long way and going up wasn't an option. Survival training included situations such as this. The parachute harness had a long nylon tape that could be rigged in such a way that a pilot could let himself down from the treetops if he became stuck in the jungle canopy. It worked well in training, but when Jack tried to use it he slid about four feet down the nylon tape and found himself stuck again. That was it, no way to go up or down, and down was a very long way.

Air America helicopter crews received a bonus if they recovered a survivor, enough to get them to take sizable risks. The drama of Jack's airplane's malfunction had been played out on the radio frequency as well as in the cockpit and by the time he had to eject, it was well known to anyone on the frequency that someone was in trouble. He hadn't been in the tree very long before an Air America helicopter showed up overhead with a crew eager to make the pickup. When Jack looked up, he saw a small helicopter, not the big CH-53s the Jolly Greens used. It was a model not really made for this kind of situation. Jack knew he was close to Lima Site 98, virtually just on the other side of the ridge where a Jolly crew was on alert and that one of them would arrive soon. They were the experts and could more safely accomplish this job. He used his survivor radio as he hung in the tree far above the ground and told the Air America crew thanks, but no thanks, he would rather wait for the Jolly.

But the Air America pilot was eager for money and glory, so he moved in with his penetrator hanging down to a position directly above Jack's tree. Being a smaller helicopter, it had a comparatively short penetrator cable, so the pilot was forced to hover lower than a Jolly would. The downdraft from the blades created a tremendous wind, shaking the tree's leaves and branches violently. Jack had no assurance the tree was not going to fall or break or that his parachute canopy would remain safely entangled in the tree. The tree was growing out the side of the ridge and was in a precarious position itself. Jack pleaded with the Air America pilot to go away before he was blown out of the tree. Finally, he left.

A short while later the Jolly Green came over the ridge and Jack knew help was at hand. But they still had the difficult problem of getting him out of the tree and into the helicopter. The helicopter flew into position next to him, hovered for a minute or two and they looked at each other eye to eye just a few feet apart while the Jolly pilot figured out how to solve the predicament.

The Jollies had a rail they could slide out the side of the cabin, so the pilot could hover above and off to the side of the survivor. The rail went out far enough that it was out of the downdraft of the rotor blades, which was just what was needed in this situation. A parajumper slid out on the rail and the cable was lowered. He was still just beyond Jack's reach, so the pilot began to rock the helicopter and the PJ on the penetrator began to swing back and forth like the pendulum on a clock. Jack took off his oxygen mask and hose and when the PJ came close he swung out the hose, keeping a tight grip on the other end. The PJ caught it and the linkup was made. When Jack reached the penetrator he latched on to it tightly. But he was still in his parachute harness, so the PJ had to lean over him and cut all twenty-eight risers on the parachute one by one. When the last one was finally cut, they swung away from the tree and were hoisted up on the cable and aboard the helicopter to safety.

Jack arrived at NKP after dark, and I was there when he got off the airplane from Udorn. He looked just fine except for a small cut on his forehead. He was scheduled for his champagne flight in about two days and the decision was made to let him call this his champagne flight, which I thought was a good idea.

Jack was a superb pilot and, like Russ Keeling, had come to the A-1 from F-104s. Flying the F-104 was the dream of many students who went through air force pilot training courses in the mid 1960s, but very few were able to achieve that dream because the USAF had so few of them (most were sold to NATO countries) and because when they did appear on the list of assignments out of pilot training, only a few were available and only the top graduates in the class had a shot at it.

In the mid 1960s, the air force had eight pilot training bases and they were standardized as to curriculum, standards, and class starting and graduation dates. Jack and Russ were at different pilot training bases and each finished number one in his class. When assignments came for their class, six F-104 assignments were posted, which was very unusual, and the top graduates at each of the eight pilot training bases bid for them. So air force personnel people made a decision that should be applauded—they expanded the number of slots available for the F-104s to eight, and each of the number one ranking graduates got the assignment.

*

The wing honchos decided to classify Jack's accident as a combat loss, which meant the airplane was shot down by ground fire instead of classifying it as what it really was—mechanical failure—because a mechanical failure classification would require an accident investigation which would be too much trouble. Rank and file pilots were not happy about it. It was a bad habit Someone had acquired—masking mechanical failures. It helped the administrative work because no one had to go to the bother of conducting an accident investigation, and no one had to be held accountable for the fact our equipment was old and unreliable. I thought to myself, "Sooner or later someone's going to get killed if we keep jumping out of airplanes." (A person doing research on aircraft losses in Laos will see Jack's experience listed as a combat loss from small arms fire. If that had been the case, Jack would have known about it and would have told me.)

Some pilots even speculated that we might have been experiencing sabotage on the airplanes because, with so many mechanical problems, they thought it went beyond the coincidence stage. So far, we had lost one pilot in this siege of bad airplanes—Dick Lytle on November 1. Things calmed down for about a month, and then the mechanical failures began again. Since they resumed, we hadn't lost any pilots, but it was just a matter of time until something happened in a bad area and the pilot wouldn't be able to get to safety before having to eject.

Personally, I didn't think it was sabotage, but simply the price to be paid for flying old, worn-out airplanes. Anyone who drives an old car can attest to the lack of reliability of old mechanical things.

*

I took off at 10:55 p.m. in aircraft #077, call sign Firefly 40. Dave Friestad was 41. We were diverted from Barrel Roll to Steel Tiger again, this time to escort Lizard, an AC-123. When we completed that mission, we struck with Blind Bat 09 at 120/75 from NKP.

January 10, 1970. Saturday. Rick Chorlins and I had a pleasant visit this afternoon in front of my room. He told me he was going to Hawaii on R&R in a few weeks and was really looking forward to it. He said that he had gone to graduate school immediately after graduating from the Air Force Academy, and I could tell he was proud of that, because it was not the usual sequence of events. Most new grads go directly to pilot training before graduate school. He also said he was from suburban St. Louis. So it was nice to get to know him, something I had not done with any of the other pilots.

Took off at 8:25 p.m., forty minutes late because of maintenance problems. I was Firefly 30 in aircraft #570, and Rick was the wingman, Firefly 31. We had to hold for an hour and thirty minutes and finally struck with Candlestick 45 sixty-five miles from the base on the 105° radial. It was another one of those miserable holding patterns where we had to just wait and watch the ground fire come up. Around and around for ninety minutes, watching and waiting. When we finally made our strike, we damaged a truck and got a secondary explosion and a secondary fire. Not much for all the ordnance we dropped.

Jack Hudson and squadron commander Lieutenant Colonel Gabel had their going-away party tonight, but I couldn't go because I was flying. Such conflicts are a permanent part of the life of a pilot—military or civilian. The world is structured for nine to fivers, not for pilots, even in an organization of pilots. This was one of the going-away parties I really would have liked to attend. Instead, I was out getting shot at again.

*

Jack told me that one night Colonel Gabel went along on a mission with a Candlestick to see what it was like over the Trail from their perspective. Jack was one of the Fireflies being facced by the Candle and he had a bad night and missed the target—something that happened to all of us as often as not. When he got back, Colonel Gabel told Jack he was embarrassed by his performance. Jack was really sore about it.

With Jack and Colonel Gabel gone the only one left in the squadron who had been here longer than I was Jim Monk, and that was by only four days.

Two guys who were here almost as long would be leaving soon because one, Bob Bohan, had credit for fifty-six days in KC-135 tankers, and Dick Walter had a few days credit as a C-47 navigator back in 1964 or 1965.

Chapter 19

Fireworks

We weren't authorized to take many personal possessions on missions. Some guys put items that weren't allowed, such as a civilian driver's license, in a pipe tobacco pouch, which made it easy to keep everything together. About the only personal items allowed were a Geneva Convention card and however much money each pilot wanted to have with him. I also took along a calendar. College or wedding rings were taboo as were any insignia identifying the squadron, such as a patch on a flight suit.

*

January 11, 1970. Sunday. It was my practice to attend church each Sunday. Since I was flying late night missions so much of the time, I usually went to the 5:30 p.m. service and today was no exception. Part of the service was a time set aside for hymn requests and two of the most popular were "How Great Thou Art" and "Amazing Grace." It was a time of quiet reflection for me, and the peacefulness of the setting of the base chapel was a sharp contrast to what my environment would be in just a few hours—when I would be facing the enemy guns over the Ho Chi Minh Trail again.

*

My mission brief was at 8:20 for a scheduled 10:20 p.m. takeoff. About the time our briefing started, word came to the command post that Rick Chorlins was shot down at 8:08 p.m. He was not far from Mu Gia Pass, just sixty-four miles from the base on the 074° radial, a location known as Delta 30, about thirty-five miles from where he and I made our strike last night. He was Firefly 31, the same call sign as last night and Stu Bischoff was 30. Rick was in aircraft #570, the same one I flew last night. Stu returned to the TUOC building as I went out the door for my flight. I asked, "Stu, what happened?"

He said, "All I can tell you is Rick was hit by a 37mm shell as he was between passes preparing to roll in again and his airplane exploded." He was literally there one minute and gone the next. Pilots referred to this as getting hit by a golden BB. They didn't normally shoot at us between passes and I can't expain why they shot at Rick at that time.

Holy cow! We just lost one of our pilots and a friend. Can't we just stop this war for a day or two to pay our respects to Rick? How about a couple of hours?

"Sorry, G.I. We have a mission to fly and you have to go."

There was no time for grieving or mourning.

I had gotten to know Rick better and had flown with him more than any of the guys who had been killed during my tour. He was from the St. Louis area, was a graduate of the Air Force Academy, and had earned his master's degree from Georgetown, where he graduated cum laude before going to pilot training. It was an unusual sequence and he was proud of it. He was a fine, personable young officer. He was really looking forward to his upcoming R&R in Hawaii to see his wife. Now he, too, was not coming back. What a waste!

Rick Chorlins's Air Force Academy graduation portrait. (USAF photo courtesy of Toby Keane)

The circumstance of him being in the same airplane on the same mission I had flown last night was too close for me. Thoughts of The Closet beckoned me at times like this, and even though I'd been flying combat missions in A-1s a long time, I still couldn't get used to losing friends like Rick.

*

January 12, 1970. Monday. I was scheduled for a 10:20 p.m. takeoff on the 11th, but we were delayed almost two hours because of the weather and the actual takeoff was on the 12th. Russ Keeling was the leader and I was in the right seat with Colonel Michaud in the left. The weather was terrible, and we went into a holding pattern for a while and then jettisoned some of the ordnance and brought the rest back. This was my 150th mission, another useless one!

January 13, 1970. Tuesday. Took off at 7:35 p.m. with Dick Walter in the lead, but we air aborted because of a prop fluctuation in Dick's airplane. We were airborne for only fifty minutes, but it counted as a combat mission.

*

It was standard practice for the navigators in C-130 Blind Bats and C-123 Candlesticks who facced for us to lower the back deck door in flight and lie in the opening or sit near an open side door with a starlight scope, referred to as a night observation device, or NOD. During those missions, the navigators were also referred to as NODs, and they had unobstructed views of the ground below. They had a full communication hookup into their helmet earphones just as we in the Skyraiders had. Using their scopes, they could see what was happening on the ground much better than they could from any other vantage point. They could talk to their pilots to tell them where to fly for best visual advantage, and they could talk to the pilots of the strike airplanes to tell us where they wanted our ordnance. As was the case with all crew members flying over enemy territory, they carried full survivor gear and wore parachutes at all times.

Early this morning Murphy's Law reared its head, and the inevitable happened. A Blind Bat navigator who was a lieutenant colonel had just been relieved of his duties in the observation location at the side door of the airplane. With the side door and the rear deck both open, a strong draft was created. As he moved away from the door, his parachute manual deployment handle, called a D ring because of its shape, caught on something, popped his chute, and out he went over far southern Laos. It was not a good place to leave a perfectly good airplane, which is not to imply that such place or time ever exists.

One of the enlisted crewmen saw him go and in a panic called on the intercom to the aircraft commander in the cockpit, "Sir, we've lost our NOD!"

The pilot thought the reference was to the starlight scope itself—someone had dropped it out the back of the airplane—and he was going to have to account for the loss. He said, "You guys are screwing with me here. Which NOD did you lose?"

A big warm-blooded one.

Jim George was scheduled for Sandy duty that day, and he reported that when the Sandy crews showed up before dawn to set up the airplanes for the day's alert they were informed of a survivor down in southern Laos whose call sign was Blind Bat Four One K. He was talking on his survival radio and needed to be picked up. Four One A would be the pilot, Four One B would be the copilot and so on, but Four One K? Had a C-130 gone down and only one crewman survived? When the explanation was given, the guys rolled their eyes in disbelief. Sandies from Danang were assigned the task of leading the pick up with NKP Sandies as back up and Kilo was rescued without incident. It was not a good way for an officer to enhance his career, though.

What could have been another tragedy became a humorous diversion from the hard reality we were all facing.

*

January 14, 1970. Wednesday. I was duty officer this morning and scheduled for a 6:50 p.m. takeoff. But just after sunset, the base runway lights went out and without the lights we couldn't go. We were told they were on a circuit like a string of Christmas tree lights and if one burned out, they all went out. It seemed like a poor system for runway lights, but like everything else around here no one asked for my opinion. Nevertheless, I had to wait for an hour and a half before my mission was canceled. The lights weren't fixed until 1:20 a.m.
January 17, 1970. Saturday. Briefing was at 6:45 a.m., and I took off at 8:15 in the right seat on IP duty with Major Loren Evenson on his first left seat ride. We were Firefly 43 with Colonel Jerry Ransom and First Lieutenant Hester leading as Firefly 42. Loren did a good job and we had a good mission. We worked with Raven 46 who was faccing us for Kingpin near Lima Site 196. The sky was clear in Barrel Roll and I could see the entire PDJ, but the mountains to the north, where the target was, were covered with clouds. The mission went well anyway. It was nice to fly in the daytime again.

*

January 18, 1970. Sunday. I had an interview with our new squadron commander, Lieutenant Colonel Dick Michaud, this afternoon. I already knew him since we had flown together a few times, and I thought maybe he had something else to talk about, but it turned out to be just a formality. He was trying to get acquainted with all the pilots in the squadron.

*

An army chopper went down in South Vietnam and a SAR was launched to pick up the crew.

Took off at 10:40 p.m. with Larry Dannelly in the lead. We followed Nail 66 around sixty miles east of the base for two and a half hours before he finally found two trucks. When Larry rolled in on them, a 37mm gun came up to greet him. Since I was the wingman it was my job to go after the gun with a bomb. I was armed up and ready and rolled in without taking my eyes off the spot where I had seen the gun. As I was pulling off target and before my bomb even hit the ground the gunner almost got me. Close enough to scare me with some of the shells passing right over the canopy.

It was the only target available and we brought most of our ordnance home.

One of the tactics taught in training about how to avoid getting hit by ground fire was to make sharp turns while pulling off the target, first to the left and then to the right or vice versa, a maneuver called juking. The idea was to cause the gunner to try to lead the path of flight while aiming. When the shells finally arrived where he thought the target would be the pilot would be safely going in another direction. While it was probably a good tactic in a high threat area in the daytime when the gunners could get a good visual contact with their target, it didn't seem to me to be an effective tactic at night because the gunners couldn't see us and were shooting only at the sounds of our airplanes. The evasive effect of a slight movement of sound didn't seem very effective.

In my opinion, the best evasive maneuver was for a pilot to watch for ground fire and turn away when he saw it coming. This was often next to impossible because—especially on a moonless night—he had to keep his eyes on the instruments when pulling off the target. Even a quick check of the instrument panel served to break up the visual scan required to avoid the shells. Frequently, so many shells were being fired from so many guns that if the pilot fixed on one clip from a gun on, say, the right, he could miss the ones coming up on the left—not to mention the ones coming up from directly underneath the airplane, which he might not see at all.

*

January 20, 1970. Tuesday. I was scheduled for a department of special actions (DOSA) mission this afternoon, but it was canceled before I began to brief, so I was rescheduled for tonight.

*

I was assigned to the tower early this evening to act as IP for Colonel Michaud on his H model night check out. While in the tower, I caught up on some reading and discovered Mike Howard was killed at McConnell AFB, Kansas, on December 15 in an F-105. He had been my flight commander in the 95th at Dover, had left for his combat assignment after I departed, and he was still checking out in the Thud. It seemed like I would just get used to the fact that one guy was killed when I heard about another. Major Howard and I sometimes did not see eye-to-eye on things, but he was always fair in scheduling me for alert duty, flying, and leave time, and I appreciated that.

I had a briefing at 7:30 this evening for a scheduled 9:00 p.m. takeoff, but the first airplane was broken when I did the preflight, so I had to take the spare and took off an hour and ten minutes late. Tom Coleman was the wingman and we struck with a Candle 65 miles southeast of the base.

A C-123 came in with a 37mm shell in its side tonight, but no one was injured. They were lucky.

January 21, 1970. Wednesday. I got to bed at 3:00 a.m. after last night's mission and had to get up in time for an 11:15 briefing. The mission was to escort Durox 30-35, a flight of six helicopters who were picking up forty people from a forward base north of the PDJ and bring them back to their base camp about forty-five miles away. Daryl Heusinkveld was the wingman. Helicopters were much slower than Skyraiders, so we circled as we flew along, all the while keeping them in sight. We monitored their radio frequency and stayed alert for possible ground fire. It was an enjoyable mission.

When the escort part of the mission was over, we struck with a ground fac a few miles east of where the exfil had taken place. The cloud ceiling in the area was low, so we couldn't make our usual 40° dive angle attack. The fac had a target on the crest of a ridge away from any big guns and we made multiple passes. I got to shoot the mini-gun that was hung on the inboard station of the left wing and delivered 6,000 rounds a minute. My experience in firing the mini-gun was limited, and I discovered it was fun. It had a high-pitched whine and put out a lot of lead.

Because we were on an escort mission, we each had only one bomb. The rest of the ordnance was guns and rockets, which were forward firing, and CBUs, which were pickled out the aft end of the tubes. We lowered the nose just enough to fire and then pulled out low over the target, which we attacked for thirty-five minutes. The target was NVA on a ridge line with a friendly village close by. The villagers had painted some rocks white and fashioned an arrow on the ground pointing to where they wanted us to strike. We pounded it thoroughly.

I'm more impressed with the 20mm guns every day. We also had willie pete rockets that caused a lot of smoke when they hit the ground and burned. It was a fun, interesting mission because we were down low, no one was shooting at us, and I got to fire ordnance I didn't normally get to at night.

We flew lower than usual on the way home, about 6,500 feet MSL, and threaded our way through the mountains. A few months ago I never would have done that because of guns, but the area had become more secure and I was more familiar with it. It was not as threatening, foreboding, and mystifying as it was when I was new to Laos and combat. I also knew which valley led where I wanted to go and where home was—which I didn't know eight months ago. We looked up at mountains on both sides as we passed through the valleys. This was my 155th mission.

*

January 22, 1970. Thursday. The quality of the food was as bad as usual. Don Combs found some steaks and offered me one, which I accepted. It wasn't very good, but since he shared with me, I couldn't tell him it tasted like rubber after just a bite or two, so I managed to choke it down. Next time Don offers me a steak, I'll tell him I just ate, thank you. His heart was in the right place as usual.

I was scheduled for a late takeoff tonight.

January 23, 1970. Friday. I rejected the first plane because of an engine problem then took off at 12:35 a.m. and worked with a C-130 Blind Bat fac 145 miles southeast of the base. We didn't do much good, but we took about a hundred rounds of 37mm fire, which made me feel as if I was nothing but bait for the gunners. This was just under a four hour mission and we were on station (over the target area) for two hours.

I got to bed at 6:00 a.m. and had to get up about 11:45 for a squadron pilot meeting at 12:30.

*

I received a letter today from the commander of my new squadron at Perrin. He had been a pilot at Paine when I was based there five years ago. I also knew the officer who was to be my sponsor at Perrin from when I was a student in F-102s three and a half years ago.

I was scheduled to go to Steel Tiger late tonight, but one of the guys wanted to swap, so I went to Barrel Roll on an earlier mission. It would be a longer flight, but there would be a lot less shooting and I liked the mission better.

Took off at 6:55 p.m. with Colonel Michaud as my wingman. The sky was clear with no moon and the horizon was dimly visible. When we arrived in Barrel Roll, we were assigned to a Blind Bat who instructed us to hold while he found a target. The Bat was looking for trucks while we waited. And waited. It was dark and quiet. We were holding over a safe area and I was tired. The A-1 had a good autopilot and I really needed it tonight. Fortunately, I was the flight lead and could use the autopilot as we waited. Colonel Michaud, as the wingman, had to keep me in sight and pay attention to what was going on.

I put it into a slight left turn of about ten degrees to stay in the area. The engine was humming along smoothly and it was quiet. Suddenly the radio crackled alive, "Firefly, we've got some trucks up here and need you."

It startled me. Had I actually been asleep? It couldn't have been for more than a minute or two, could it? Next time a pilot meeting was scheduled for just six hours after I get in from a mission, they'll have to get along without me. My little reverie allowed me to feel more refreshed and alert, and the mission turned into a pretty good one.

We had been holding for about an hour when the Bat said he had two groups of five trucks each on Route 61 north of Ban Ban. He took a long time marking them. The moon had risen and I could see the road whenever I was in the right position. The atmosphere was very hazy. During daylight hours, haze made it especially difficult to see objects when looking toward the bright glare of the sun. It was the same at night with haze and a bright moon. I could see the ground target area when the moon was at my back, but not with it in my face.

The Bat had four marks down—the nearest one a mile and a half to two miles from the target, which was not good. Then he got his directions confused and told me the trucks were north of the marks when in fact they were south. Because of that, when he told me where the target was and described the situation on the ground I couldn't understand what he was talking about. I saw an area that seemed like it might be close to his description, so I decided to arm up a nape and throw it down to get things started. Just as I was ready to roll in he said, "Wait a minute, we've got it mixed up. The target is southwest of the mark."

What a confidence builder! "Oh boy," I thought sarcastically, "this guy is really sharp."

I knew his mark was way off the target, so I exaggerated the distance to the southwest and put down a nape. The Bat said, "OK, the target is southwest of your nape twice the distance between your nape and the marker I've got down." *Twice* the distance? I could tell his mark was way off target, but I never dreamed it was *that* far off.

So I selected another nape to narrow the target's location when he said, "Hold it, we have another change for you. The target is *between* your nape and the mark." Even though I was getting frustrated with him for being so incompetent, I decided to drop a 500-pound bomb, which landed on a ridge north of the road—just north of where he wanted it. So I came in with the second and it hit right where he wanted. At least I knew where the fac thought the target was, so I armed up my funny bomb, but missed the target by about thirty meters because of the strong westerly wind.

It was Colonel Michaud's turn next. His funny bomb hit just on the edge of the trucks and a fire started to burn vigorously. I went back in with CBUs, rockets, and 20mm guns. We worked the area over for quite a while until a flight of fast movers came into the area and said they had about ten minutes of fuel left and needed to make a strike. They said they had to hurry. Where have I heard that before?

Hey, that was *our* target! It wasn't the first time jets guys took my target just as I got something going and started to have some fun.

We were a long way north and flying home took over an hour. As we neared the base I was still talking to the Bat. I kept asking, "How many trucks do you have?"

He said the target was continuing to burn and explode. "There's another explosion! And another explosion! It's a secondary fire like I've never seen before," he said. "There may be one truck, and there may be five trucks. We don't know because the fire is too bright, so we'll just give you one truck."

I bugged him again, "How many trucks?"

Same answer. Finally he said, "There are probably three and maybe five, but I'll only give you one," which just confirmed my earlier opinion about him being a real blockhead.

The reason I wanted more trucks was because of a January competition among the Fireflies, Zorros, and Hobos to see which squadron would get the most trucks. As of last night, we had eighty-eight, the Zorros had eighty, and the Hobos had sixty-five. So we had a hot rivalry and I wanted all the trucks I could get!

About this time, one of the ground facs began to have trouble, so the Blind Bat went to his position to flare and we never did find out how many trucks there were.

This was a four hour mission. The nice thing about working in that area was the absence of big guns.

*

January 24, 1970. Saturday. One way to tell if it was Saturday or Sunday was the day annunciator on my Seiko watch had "Sat" printed in blue and "Sun" printed in red. The color for the rest of the days was black. Most of the guys had Seiko watches, so the saying was you could tell it was Saturday because your watch turned blue.

Took off at 11:40 p.m. with Frank Monroe leading. We struck about sixty-four miles east of the base in the heart of the Trail, and together we got four of the five trucks we were after, which was a pretty good percentage. Four guns shot at us tonight, but they were about mile and a half north, which was too far to be effective. Guns were usually much closer, and when they were that far away, it gave us a chance to see the tracers coming and turn away. I was happy with where my ordnance landed. Frank got off easy because the guns saved most of their fire for when I made my passes, and I really got hosed. The fac said we took 112 rounds of 37mm fire. The visibility was good and we had a good night.

*

January 25, 1970. Sunday. Even though I was flying in combat and based several thousand miles from home, I was still expected to file an income tax return and pay my fair share. Added to the federal obligation was a new-in-1969 state income tax in Illinois, my official state of residence. But the feds and state allowed an extension for those in my situation, so I didn't have to worry about it until well after I got home.

*

I went to church in the afternoon then briefed for a 10:30 p.m. takeoff. We were sixty-five minutes late because I ground aborted aircraft #058 due to a bad inverter. Larry Dannelly was the wingman and we struck with Candlestick 47 south of Mu Gia Pass. We didn't receive much ground fire considering where we were, but we did see some 57mm, 14.7, 23s, and a few 37s. It was a nice variety and would have been a good mission to show a new guy what it all looked like. We didn't do much good tonight.

We have five new pilots in the squadron—one of whom just arrived today—the first we've received since November. They replaced four who had left for home and one combat loss (Rick Chorlins).

*

January 26, 1970. Monday. I had the early mission to Barrel Roll this evening and took off at 6:55 p.m. with Russ Keeling on the wing. We had to hold for an hour while the Blind Bat looked for a target. He couldn't find any trucks, so he put us in on a picture target that Intelligence thought was a truck park. We were just south of the Birdshead in Northern Laos and took a lot of ground fire from five 37s and a ZPU. The area had a lot of new guns where there weren't any a couple of months ago.

January 27, 1970. Tuesday. About 12:40 a.m. today a Zorro pilot, Captain Chuck Kennedy, aborted his takeoff, jettisoned the ordnance, ran off the side of the runway, and collapsed the gear. He got out OK with no fire or explosion, but he had a pretty good scare.

At 7:40 this morning, an OV-10 fac arrived at the base all shot up and couldn't get his gear down, so the pilot had to eject off the end of the runway. He was picked up right away and turned out to be Captain Norm James who was in my UPT class at Laughlin four years ago.

Later that day I was surprised when I saw him at the Club. I said, "Norm! What are you doing here?"

He said, "Oh, I just dropped in."

*

I was scheduled to have a day off today, but was awakened at 8:45 and told to hurry to TUOC because a SAR was underway for an F-105 pilot who went down north of Ban Ban along Route 61 last night, and I might be needed to fly in case there was some resistance in the pickup area. Fortunately, when I arrived at TUOC, the pilot had already been picked up.

Because of the schedule change, I was assigned mobile control officer duty and while in the tower I got a lot of business. Ron Marzano returned with his engine smoking. When he retarded the throttle to land, he lost all power, but managed to get it on the runway and turned into the grass just before it came to a stop. He evacuated as quickly as he could. He was in aircraft #778, which I last flew three weeks ago.

Then another A-1 landed with zero engine oil pressure, and yet another came in with full nose up trim. The nose up trim occurred ninety miles from the base and the pilot had to overpower it manually for almost forty minutes, which must have been tiring.

As mobile control officer, I could do nothing for those emergencies except watch.

About 6:40 this evening, another A-1 took off and started to lose its engine right after takeoff, so the pilot, George Porter, brought it right around for an immediate landing. He managed to get it on the runway, but he said, "It started to come apart," so he ejected. The gear collapsed on the runway and it was still cooking off ordnance and burning an hour later, but at least George was safe. I could hear it in my room. The airplane was a complete loss, the runway was closed, and all flying was stopped. We had some real fireworks tonight.

George had had two other engine failures since his ejection on November 11. He had only a small cut on the bridge of his nose to show for this one, but he's had more than his share of problems in the six months he's been here. Maybe they should let him call his tour complete, give him a pat on the back, and send him home.

A lot of SAM calls (surface to air missile alerts) were made today (January 27). So F-105 Wild Weasels were sent in, and one of them, call sign Seabird 02, got hit. I hurried to the command post because a SAR was in progress and I was scheduled to fly on it. Al Preyss was Sandy low lead and he saw thirty or so people come out of the bushes and capture one of the survivors. The pilot in the other F-105 saw two chutes in the air, but the second one was never located on the ground and he didn't come up on his survival radio.

They were just across the border in North Vietnam and a lot of trucks were observed, but of course we couldn't strike them. For about three hours A-1s with gas, smoke, and Sandy loads, and Jolly Greens—the big Jollies from Udorn—were all orbiting over Laos about five miles from the border, in position and hoping for a chance to pick up a survivor. The control ship was a C-130, call sign King, and one of the Jollies asked King if there was a MIG cap. The answer, "Yes."

Someone asked, "What's the call sign of the MIG cap?" No reply.

The SAR was just about to be called off when two MIG 21s, one painted silver and one green, came in at high speed from the north. They fired two missiles then broke to the right, or west, right through where the A-1s were holding, turned all the way around, and took off back to the north. They were gone so fast that no one had a chance to shoot back and the A-1s couldn't match the speed of the jets. One of the helicopters was hit, exploded and came down in three pieces. All aboard were killed. Of course the news reports—if it ever hit the newspapers—would not mention that a helicopter was shot down over Laos, since the government hadn't acknowledged our presence there. The carelessness on the part of King or whoever failed to provide the MIG cap was inexcusable, and five men lost their lives because of it.

A brother of one of the guys in the chopper had recently been killed in Vietnam and he had just received a humanitarian reassignment home because he was the sole surviving son in his family. This was to have been his last mission. A photographer was also aboard the Jolly to take pictures of the SAR. He normally wouldn't have been there, either.

The pilot of the second chopper had to take evasive action to avoid a blade from the one that was shot down.

I was ready to go on this one, but was not needed. My mission for tonight was canceled due to the SAR.

<u>January 29, 1970.</u> Thursday. I was duty officer in the afternoon and then had a three and a half hour mission to Barrel Roll with Tom Coleman leading.

Chapter 20

NVA Offensive

January 30, 1970. Saturday. I attended a quarterly E&E review briefing this afternoon then took off at 10:50 p.m. with Tom Coleman on the wing. We struck with Nail 4 in Steel Tiger just south of Mu Gia Pass against trucks. I got one with a funny bomb, and the Nail reported we took 166 rounds of 37mm fire, 30 of 23mm, and 8 of 57mm. They must have been pretty sore about that one lousy truck because that was a lot of ground fire.

January 31, 1970. Sunday. CTOs were off again. I was scheduled to fly late tonight. We had a party for "Good Old Dan" Larry Dannelly, who was going to be married when he went home on leave.

February 1, 1970. Monday. Took off at 12:10 a.m. with "Just Plain Dan" McAuliffe on the wing. We went to Steel Tiger and orbited for a long time because the fac ran out of markers and no one could figure out what to do with us. I eventually dropped a funny bomb, a nape, and a 500-pounder and brought the rest home.

I was also scheduled to fly late tonight, but when we got to the airplanes, the other pilot, Dick Walter, had hurt his back and couldn't fly, so we had to cancel the mission. Dick had been to the doctor about his back yesterday, and he hurt it again as he was getting into the airplane.

*

The Thai government required Emily to leave the country every six weeks to get her passport stamped in another country—they didn't care which one. All she had to do was go across the border, get it stamped, and return. So this morning she left Bangkok on a bus bound for Nong Khai and Emily was the only passenger. When it got to Udorn the owner, a woman, berated the driver for driving all that distance with only one passenger, and canceled the portion to Nong Khai. After having lived in Bangkok for about eight months, Emily knew what she had to do. She told the owner she had contracted for transportation to Nong Khai, and it was her responsibility to provide transportation all the way. The argument must have made sense because the owner hired a car to take her, about forty miles each way, and back. The bus company paid for the car.

The border entry point in Thailand was scheduled to close at 5:00 p.m. and time began to get tight because of the argument with the bus company owner.

When Emily got to Nong Khai she went to the river, found a water taxi, went across to Laos, got her passport stamped, and went back to the water taxi. The water taxi had two other passengers, and when the driver pushed out into the river the motor wouldn't start. The current was swift, and they floated down river with no power as the driver continued to crank the motor. After what seemed a long time and many pulls on the starter, it finally came to life, and they arrived back on the Thai side just before the border agents left for the day at five o'clock. If they had been gone she would have had to return to Laos for the night.

The car was waiting and took her back to Udorn, where she checked in to a hotel after a long day.

*

I took off at 6:30 this evening with Jim Costin leading. We went southeast of the base about eighty miles and had to hold for a long time. When it was my turn to make a strike, I got the radios screwed up, thought I had radio failure, and turned for the base. By the time I realized my mistake, I was half way home and didn't have enough fuel to return and continue the mission. Just as I exited the runway and turned into the dearming area after landing, all the cockpit lights went out. It was no problem occurring where it did, but it could have been quite serious if it had happened right after takeoff or when I was pulling off the target on a pass. Maybe it was a good thing after all that I had messed up the radios.

February 3, 1970. Tuesday. I attended a pilot meeting at 9:00 a.m.

Emily flew on Thai Airways from Udorn to NKP and arrived at noon, so I went to the airport in town to meet her. The quarters for the 609th squadron pilots were trailers. Major Jack Maulden, one of the A-26 pilots who had yet to receive an assignment, was gone for a few days and invited me to use his trailer for Emily. That was nice of him and very convenient because their trailers were between our hooches and the Officers' Club. She was allowed to eat at the Club.

*

Took off at 8:20 p.m. with Frank Brown leading. Jim Anderson was the fac and we tried to hit trucks at 120/95 from NKP. It was the first time A-1s had been in that area in a long time because it was so hot, but we didn't take all that much ground fire. I could see the trucks on the road, but didn't hit them.

Bob Bohan had his last flight today.

February 4, 1970. Wednesday. I was still the 602nd's mobility officer and went to a meeting at 1:30 this afternoon.

Took off at 10:45 p.m. with Tony Wylie on the wing. We were assigned to work with a Blind Bat about 110 miles southeast of the base who had a nice juicy target lined up for us, but he had trouble marking it. It was one of those nights when his instructions were something like, "OK, Firefly, can you find the middle spot of the triangle formed by the three marks I've got down?"

Well, yeah, sort of.

"Then take a line from there straight south twice the distance of the line formed between the northern two marks, and then go west the distance between the eastern most marks, and that's where your target is."

Yeah, sure. Let's see if I can get a mark a little closer and work from it.

I had a funny bomb on the left stub that really weighed me down, so I thought I'd drop it first just to get rid of it as well as to establish a better mark. I rolled in, 40° down, lined up, and let it fly. Lo and behold, the Bat really got excited and shouted, "You've got it! A bullseye!"

"You're good at giving directions, Bat."

It was a POL (petroleum, oils, lubricants) dump which also had three trucks. It was a gas station. Joe's Truck Stop. Big explosions and a huge fire. We watched it burn for awhile, but then the Bat had a problem. He thought it was going to take most of our ordnance to find the target, but I got lucky and hit it on my first try. So now what was he going to do with us? He solved that problem when he went a few miles west, threw down a log, said he thought a truck might be down there, and told us to hit his mark. We didn't get shot at, we had target practice, and gave some trees a workout.

February 5, 1970. Thursday. Two new pilots arrived at the squadron today. We had a lot of new guys, but only six daytime sorties, which presented a scheduling problem in getting them checked out.

February 6, 1970. Friday. Took off at 6:30 p.m. in the left seat of aircraft #914 with Major Loren Evenson in the right on his night dollar ride. Dave Friestad was the leader.

Emily and I went to the Thai Restaurant on base when I returned.

A navy A-6 went down east of here today just before sunset, shortly before I took off.

February 7, 1970. Saturday. I was up early to fly a gas mission in the SAR, but both of the survivors were recovered before I took off. The enemy put up a little resistance, but nothing serious. One of the rescued pilots said he came down about fifty feet from a communications van, but didn't see anyone. Airplanes were sent back to blast it out of existence. It might have been used to monitor our aircraft conversations. The NVA had one less communications van than they used to have.

After I was released from the SAR, Emily and I went into town.

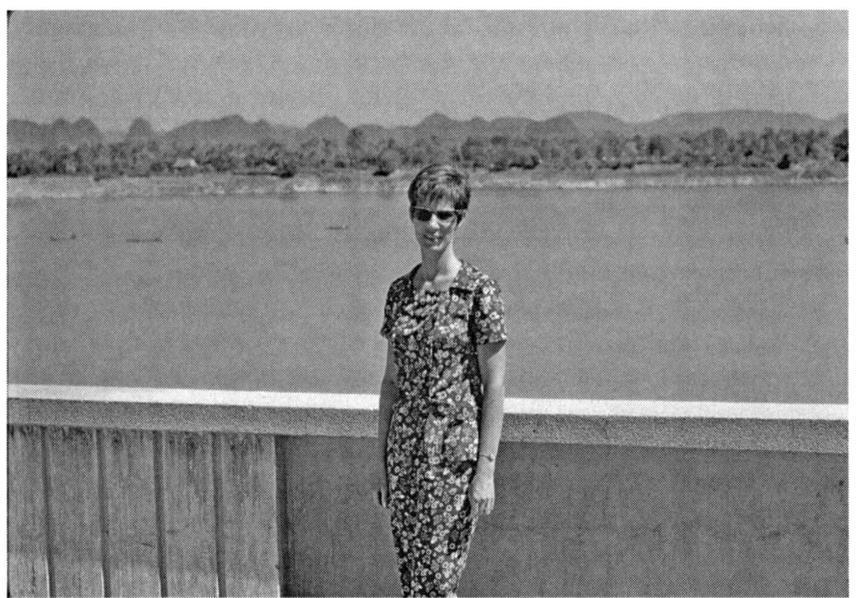

Emily along the Mekong in Nakhon Phanom

Took off at 7:25 p.m., fifty-five minutes late because we had to wait for two OV-10s that came in with emergencies. Noel Frisbie led and we struck with Blind Bat 41 at Delta 30 near Mu Gia Pass. I started to feel sick during the mission, but I got one truck. A 57mm gun fired at us, the first time I had seen a 57 up close. The Bat said the gun was coming very close and bracketed him at one point, so he left the area and couldn't give us BDA or a report of ground fire. He said my funny bomb went right where he wanted it. Fifty-sevens fired slower than 37s, had white tracers, and the shells went up much higher before they burned out and exploded. It was easy to distinguish between 37s and 57s.

After landing, I continued to feel sick and by the time I returned to the trailer it all came up—food from the Thai Restaurant I had eaten between 3:00 and 4:00 p.m. I felt much better afterward.

*

As a result of the North Korean capture of the United States Navy ship *Pueblo* in early 1968, F-106s were deployed to Korea to bolster air defenses. F-106 squadrons were rotated to Korea for 179 days TDY, and the 95th FIS, which was well into preparation for Korean duty when I left, was deployed in mid-1969.

Delta Darts were designed to intercept bombers, not for aerial combat with other fighters, but the air force discovered they were very capable air-to-air fighters. The airplanes were modified for aerial refueling, a new canopy was designed and installed that eliminated the metal bar across the top for better visibility, a gun was installed, and pilots were trained in air combat tactic maneuvers—in other words, dogfighting against other fighters. All this began shortly before I left the squadron, but I didn't get to participate in the training because I was on the way out the door. I was envious of the pilots who did because it looked like fun.

A 95th F-106 disappeared into the water off Korea in January. I found out today the pilot was one of my friends, Captain Frank Dahl.

*

February 8, 1970. Sunday. Emily left at noon on a Thai Airways flight for Bangkok. Since the Thai Airways flights operated from the base on weekends it was easy to get from the trailer to the terminal near the flight line. The next time I would see her was when I arrived home in about seven weeks.

*

Took off at 6:30 p.m. with Loren Evenson and Russ Keeling on the wing. We struck at 093/63 from NKP and got a big fire, but no trucks. This was my 170th mission.

February 9. 1970. Monday. Took off at 7:00 p.m. in the right seat with Loren Evenson in the left and Jim George leading, and we had to orbit in a holding pattern waiting our turn. Just as we were ready to roll in on the target, the sump light came on for about two seconds. I told Loren to dump the ordnance and RTB. When we got back to the base, we were number two in the emergency pattern because someone else had had the same problem and he was ahead of us, so we had to wait for a few minutes before we could land.

*

The war in northern Laos was heating up again because, as the monsoon season abated, roads dried and became passable and enemy supply lines opened to move armaments and supplies. For the past several months, the good guys had had things pretty much their own way, but now the enemy, meaning the North Vietnamese, were returning to claim ground they had lost, and our friends were starting to take a beating.

A feature of the weather in February and March in that part of Southeast Asia was haze. It was moderately bad at night, but during the day, haze was so bad that visibility was restricted to no more than a few miles, and a pilot had to be almost on top of a target before he could see it. Daytime temperatures increased as the cool season gave way to the hot season.

*

February 10, 1970. Tuesday. I had a daytime mission to Barrel Roll today that lasted only an hour and fifty minutes! That must be a record for me and I found it to be fun. Takeoff was at 12:35 p.m. with Frank Brown leading. Our attack was on Lima Site 46, which was reported to have been overrun by the bad guys this morning. LS 46 was only about thirty-six miles north of the bend in the river in very mountainous terrain and not far from where I saw the F-105 pass between my leader and me on my first solo mission so long ago. The target was covered with clouds about 2,000 feet above the ground and there was no ground fire, so we just worked it over and left.

*

February 11, 1970. Wednesday. The board that investigated the January 27 accident concluded that a partial contributing factor was pilot fatigue. Because of that, A-1 pilots would no longer be required to be duty officers at the squadrons, mobile controllers, or TUOC briefers. It was very timely for me because I was scheduled to be TUOC briefer from midnight to 8:00 a.m. today and I really didn't want to do that after a mission yesterday. Consequently, I was off the flying schedule today. But all it meant was off the *combat* flying schedule. I had an early training mission for one of the new guys and then I was on stand by for FCFs the rest of the day.

I took off at 7:30 a.m. in aircraft #038 in the right seat with Captain Bob Skelton in the left on his first ride—a local noncombat mission. The idea was to familiarize the new guys with the area and local flying rules in a nonthreatening environment and to let them just fly the airplane again before a combat mission. It usually had been quite some time since most finished training at Hurlburt. We were up for an hour and ten minutes and made a couple of dry passes, shot an instrument approach, and made a straight in landing. It was fun to fly in the daytime and not have anyone shoot at me for a change.

Dick Walter, who was to have his champagne flight next ahead of me, was scheduled for it today and the pilot who was next got to handle the water to hose him down when he returned. That's me! I was the project officer to make sure the fire trucks were out and to notify the wing commander of the last flight.

I was also on stand by all day so if anyone got sick I could cover his mission. I was listed as having a day off, but that only meant a day off the combat schedule. I was on stand by for everything else, flew a local training mission, and made arrangements for a last flight.

I attended the going-away party for Bob Bohan and Dick Walter this evening.

Lieutenant Colonel William Kieffer, a Zorro on his 17th mission, was killed when he was struck by ground fire and crashed this afternoon in the northern part of the PDJ. It was another reminder that this is dangerous flying.

February 12, 1970. Thursday. The rule against A-1 pilots being squadron duty officer didn't last very long, as I found myself at the squadron as duty officer from 7:15 a.m. until noon.

Took off at 6:35 p.m. in the left seat of aircraft #038 with Captain DeWan Madden in the right on his first night combat mission. We were sixty-eight miles southeast of the base when the sump light came on, so I jettisoned ordnance and returned to base. It was the same airplane in which I had a sump light Monday night and that I flew yesterday morning.

Jim Anderson stopped by today for a visit. He was to leave February 28.

February 13, 1970. Friday. I had a mission to Barrel Roll this afternoon because the bad guys had begun a big offensive. All of a sudden we were in a hurry-up mode to help the good guys in Barrel Roll because the bad guys were moving forward.

*

Jack Maulden and I were in the same flight at jungle survival school at Clark. He had been anxious to go along on a daytime ride to see Barrel Roll, so when I found out I was going to fly an afternoon mission I called and asked if he would like to go. He said, "Sure."

When we arrived at the airplane, we discovered an E model that didn't have a stick in the right seat. Jack was disappointed because he wanted to be able to fly in case something drastic happened to me and he wanted to know what it was like to fly an A-1. I apologized and told him it was OK with me if he decided to not go. To my surprise he said, "Oh well, I'll go along anyway."

We took off at 2:55 p.m. with Tom Coleman on the wing. Friendlies had been getting attacked by the bad guys in the PDJ, so we struck at a troop concentration on the east side of it. Raven 47 facced. We had a good mission to show Jack, and he enjoyed the ride.

*

February 14, 1970. Saturday. The English language newspapers *Bangkok Post* and *Bangkok Herald* were sources of information for our intelligence briefers as to what was happening in Northern Laos. The long-awaited offensive by the bad guys was now underway and even though it had been predicted, we had no air power dedicated to preempting it. All we did was react to the enemy's aggressions instead of initiating action. A friendly airstrip in the PDJ was attacked one evening recently by 600-800 men, but the good guys were well prepared. They had mined and sandbagged the defensive perimeter of the base and set off explosives. At least seventy-six bad guys were killed and the enemy was seen carrying off about one hundred wounded. Seven were captured and they revealed the attackers were the 144th Regiment of the NVA.

The next day artillery fire rained into the air base from the hills on the edge of the PDJ and cratered the runway, so A-1s were called in to deal with that development.

As of a week ago, seven flights of two A-1s were assigned to Barrel Roll with the rest of the A-1 missions assigned to the Trail. While we were useful on the Trail, fast movers could be effective there while A-1s go north. The friendlies had the territory and needed to hold it because it would be easier to hold it than to regain it after being pushed back.

Yesterday morning (February 13) was the first diversion of A-1 flights to Barrel Roll. I was scheduled to fly last night but got rescheduled for the afternoon.

*

I was Firefly 50 this evening and took off at 7:15 p.m. with Ed Solley on the wing. We were assigned to Candlestick 51 who was faccing with Red Hat who was in big trouble at Lima Site 2, eight or ten miles east of the PDJ. He was having a hard time and had to keep his head down until we arrived, at which time the enemy stopped shooting and we were back to locating them based on his directions. The visibility was poor, but we felt like we did quite a bit of damage to the bad guys.

This was my 175th mission.

February 15, 1970. Sunday. A new chaplain had recently arrived, a lieutenant colonel who was a very good preacher.

I received a letter from Northwest Airlines today that said they were hiring. They sent a pass from anywhere on their system to Minneapolis-St.Paul to interview when I get home.

*

I was scheduled in the right seat with DeWan Madden in the left, but ground aborted the first airplane because of an inoperative attitude indicator. The second one turned out to be a single stick E model, so DeWan got the night off and I went alone. We took off at 8:50 p.m., an hour and a half late. Tom Coleman was the leader.

We struck with Hilltop who was at Lima Lima in the PDJ. Hilltop did not seem to be under too much pressure, but had bad guys on a ridge near his position. The weather was clear at first, then clouds blew in and we were in and out of them. My airplane had a couple of funny bombs, which was normally a Trail load. It was a neutral ridge when we left.

Tom didn't have funny bombs. Before I rolled in for my first pass, I said to Hilltop, "Watch this."

"Firefly, what do you call that bomb?" asked Hilltop.

"We call it a funny bomb."

"Oh, I haven't seen one like that before. I really like that!" Hilltop laughed at the fact that we called it a funny bomb. He liked the second one as much as the first.

When we turned to go, he told us that the previous night he had A-1s strike and the next morning—this morning—he counted fifty dead, "...with my own eyes." So our strikes must be doing a lot of damage. When we left he gave us RNO BDA. Results not observed, bomb damage assessment—because of the darkness. They might find a few more crispy critters when the sun comes up.

Hilltop also told us that yesterday morning when the sun came up, he looked around the barbed wire surrounding the base and saw a North Vietnamese boy who was wounded in the leg. He went out to get the boy who blew himself up with a grenade rather than be captured. Hilltop said, "I was just going to take him to a hospital."

February 16, 1970. Monday. Two and a half months after he started, George Luck was still trying to finish his check out in the A-1. It wasn't George's fault, just the way the schedule went with higher priority demands on the airplanes delaying him. We got a formation ride in today for George with me in the right seat and Jim Matthews leading. We were up for an hour and a half and it was kind of fun, if I could call riding along in the right seat on any mission fun.

Took off at 11:15 p.m. with Russ Keeling on the wing. It was one of those nights when we had to hold for an hour and a half before finally being assigned to a target eighty miles southeast of the base. On the third pass, I felt and heard a thud and smelled gunpowder. I called out over the radio I thought I'd been hit and was turning for home. The fac was a Nail who said he saw a flash underneath my airplane just before I made my call. He confirmed it looked like I had been hit.

I did a control check, and everything seemed to be working OK. As the lights of the town of Nakhon Phanom and the base got closer my panic level began to subside. The thought was constantly with me of where I was and how far I could glide if my engine quit or, in this case, if the airplane would begin to have control problems. But as I crossed the river I knew I was safe and would soon be on the ground.

When I taxied to the ramp and shut the engine down, the crew chief climbed onto the wing to help me unstrap and asked, "What happened to the centerline tank?"

Pipping off the centerline tank, thinking it was a hit—and announcing it over the radio—was a sure-fire way to make a pilot feel silly. It was easy to do—just a simple error in selecting the station on the intervalometer—but I still wondered how I could do such a thing. How embarrassing!

*

February 17, 1970. Tuesday. I was getting near the end of my tour and my commitment to the air force and had a date of separation of May 12, 1970. So today at 1:00 p.m. I had my separation-from-the-air force physical and, as with any physical, I was glad to get it over with a clean bill of health.

We had a pilot meeting at 5:30.

Took off at 11:55 p.m. in aircraft #577, a single stick E model with Noel Frisbie leading. My call sign was Firefly 37. We orbited in the target area for an hour and a half until we got too low on fuel to be able to make a strike and brought it all home. We were up for three hours and five minutes.

February 18, 1970. Wednesday. An F-4 went down this afternoon near the Birdshead east of Ban Ban on Route 7, and crews worked the rest of the day to recover the survivor. He was the back seater and was in a high elevation area—about 6,000 feet—and even though a little Jolly was in the area, he was too heavy to hover at that altitude. The location was a long way from the base and the helicopters have to have enough fuel to return. A big Jolly can hover at that altitude, so one was brought in for the rescue. In addition to being a long way from the base, the area was hostile, so it was a long SAR and a lot of work went into getting him out. The front seater did not eject and was killed.

*

A-1 designers knew the airplanes would be flown on lengthy missions, so they were considerate enough of pilot physiological needs to provide a relief tube. It was never easy to use—even in the most favorable of circumstances—and with a full load of survival gear and parachute, it was a test of determination and a chore to be undertaken only when one was in distress. At best, it was an adventurous procedure as the parachute straps had to be unhooked and the flight suit unzipped from the bottom up. The pilot had to slide forward in the seat while keeping the top of the tube in the correct position. The top of the tube was about six inches long and slightly funnel shaped—that is, it had a larger opening at the top and tapered to a smaller opening at the bottom where it connected to the tube itself.

The autopilot was very helpful at such a time, and although a procedure was never mentioned in training nor in the manuals, I thought it prudent to insert the Yankee system's safety pin when using the tube to prevent accidentally pulling the ejection handle as that would really put one in a difficult situation.

A word-of-mouth-recommended procedure was to first pour a little water from the canteen into the relief tube to ensure it was not clogged.

One day Jim George found it necessary to use the tube and, time limitations being what they were, he didn't bother to pour water into the tube to make sure it worked—a decision he quickly came to regret. It didn't take long for the tube to fill. As a matter of fact, his chore was far from complete when he found himself with a tube full to the brim and a half empty bladder. Now what? "Necessity is the mother of invention," and Jim invented a procedure for his predicament, although I doubt if his procedure ever made it into an aircraft manual. He opened the canopy and poured the water out of his canteen, then filled the canteen with the fluid in the relief tube, screwed the lid on tight, and threw it out near Route 4. He said he hoped a Pathet Lao or NVA soldier would find it and assume it contained water. We'll never know.

Chapter 21

Haze

February 19, 1970. Friday. Took off at 12:55 a.m. with Dan McAuliffe on the wing. We escorted a C-123, call sign Peer, and RTBd. Escort missions were usually easy unless someone decided to shoot at the aircraft being escorted and no one did tonight.

February 20, 1970. Saturday. I took off at 12:50 a.m. with Tom Coleman leading. We planned to escort a C-123 gun ship, but somehow the assignment got screwed up, and we were too late to do the job. Maintenance had not had a chance to get the airplanes ready in time for the escort mission anyway, so we were reassigned to a Nail fac about 120 miles southeast of the base. We struck in a very hot area with a lot of guns, and a couple of clips came uncomfortably close. It was not a good feeling to have 37s passing so close.

A pilot meeting was held at 5:00 p.m. today.

I took off on the second mission of the day at 8:30 p.m. with Ed Solley leading. We struck with Candlestick 43 against trucks sixty-seven miles east of the base. Only two clips of 37s came up, which was unusally light ground fire for that area. We were in and out so fast it was almost like a day mission.

A few hooch rooms were raided today and some of the guys had things stolen, but Jim and I were lucky and didn't lose anything.

February 21, 1970. Saturday. I was scheduled to takeoff at 9:45 p.m. with Colonel Michaud as the leader on his first night lead. While cranking the engine to start, the side panel console lights on my airplane went out, so I called the crew chief who called an electrician. When I asked him how long he thought it might take to fix it, he said, "Fifteen minutes," and I relayed that to Colonel Michaud. After about fifteen minutes, I asked again how long it would be and he replied, "Fifteen minutes." It happened a third time. He had a weird sense of fifteen minutes.

He finally got it fixed, and we were ready to go. Then another light in the cockpit went out, so we gave up and the mission was canceled.

February 22, 1970. Sunday. I slept late then went to church in the evening. I was scheduled for a late mission. Jim Anderson and I went to see *Number One* at the base theater. It was a movie starring Charlton Heston who played the part of a quarterback with the New Orleans Saints.

The PDJ had been retaken by the bad guys.

February 23, 1970. Monday. I briefed at 1:30 a.m. leading Dave Friestad and took off at 3:25 a.m. in aircraft #586, a Hobo H model. The haze was really thick and I was on instruments just skimming the tops at 11,000 feet, so I climbed to 12,000 where it was clear. The haze was so solid it looked like a deck of clouds. About 125 miles north of the base, my attitude indicator warning flag began to flicker. I couldn't tell if I had an actual malfunction of the attitude indicator instument itself or if it was simply the flag providing an erroneous indication, but because of the visibility limitation due to the haze I couldn't continue the mission. I remembered being told if an attitude indicator malfunctioned, a good technique was to cover the unreliable instrument to remove the temptation of referring to it by mistake. So I put a piece of paper over it and forced myself to rely on the little stand-by indicator that was located by my right knee. I then went to the jettison area to get rid of ordnance and RTBd. Visibility went below VFR minimums by the time we arrived back at the base, so I had to come in under actual IFR conditions using the standby. I landed with no difficulty and when I uncovered the primary attitude indicator after landing, it had tumbled, so the problem was with the instrument and not the indicator flag.

This mission had been canceled two nights ago because the haze was so thick.

<u>February 24, 1970.</u> Tuesday. Takeoff was scheduled for 3:20 a.m. with Dave Friestad on the wing. I rejected the first airplane because of a mechanical problem and finally took off at 4:10 on what turned out to be an interesting, but frustrating, mission.

We struck with Red Arrow just southeast of Xieng Khouang as the sun was coming up. Red Arrow was not the usual fac in that area, and he was very difficult to understand. He said the enemy attacked at 1:30 a.m. and he had many dead and wounded. They had been under attack most of the night. Red Arrow's position was in a valley in an area of high mountains just southeast of the PDJ. The highest mountain in that area was 6,972 feet, and several others in the immediate area were over 6,000 feet, so we had to be very careful about how low we were bottoming out on each pass—especially since it was just before dawn and very hazy. Visibility was really bad. The target was tanks less than a quarter mile from Red Arrow's position.

A C-119 was on scene when we first arrived and he had a xenon light, which I hadn't seen before. It was a powerful light that was very effective for spotting a target on the ground. It was beamed from the bottom of the airplane to the target, and if it was where he wanted it, he would say, "Hit the light." It was a big improvement because we could tell exactly where the target was and where the airborne fac was in order to avoid hitting him. Of course, it couldn't be used in an area with anti aircraft guns; but in a permissive environment, he could beam the light right on the target, and if the ground fac liked it, he could say, "hit it," or "move it," whatever he needed. It worked especially well with the ground facs who didn't speak English very well and from whom it was difficult to get directions.

But the C-119 couldn't stay around and we were on our own with Red Arrow.

It was difficult to be accurate because of the mountains, and because of the haze it was difficult to see the mountains or the target. I put my first bomb right where I thought he was telling me to drop it, but because of the communication problem it wasn't on the bad guys.

We could see them shooting at each other including a 37mm being used ground to ground, but it was hard to tell the friendly fire from the bad guys. I asked him, "Where are the bad guys?"

He answered, "Nobody's shooting," which we could see was incorrect. We couldn't seem to get through to him what we wanted to do. So we went after the tanks, but didn't do much good.

*

The temperature reached 98° F at the base today. The hot season was back.

I had another mission today with takeoff just before midnight. I was in the right seat of the number two airplane flying as an IP. We were sent to Barrel Roll to work with a C-130 Blind Bat who told us he didn't have a target yet. The control ship told us to hold over Ban Ban and wait for further instructions.

Being the wingman and in the right seat to boot was not my idea of a good way to fly combat missions, but I recognized the need to train my replacements. We were told during briefing that Ban Ban had recently received more than its share of 37mm guns and it was a good idea to avoid it if we could. It was one thing to be over guns in the area of a target, but holding over guns when a whole sky full of safer places was available seemed sorta dumb to me. So I called the leader on FM and said, "Hey, Lead, let's hold about fifteen miles to the south." There were only mountains and no guns to the south. So we did.

We finally made the strike and the mission was uneventful.

When we got on the TUOC bus to go in for debriefing after landing the flight leader was already on the bus and even in the darkness I could tell he was angry. He said, "Dick, when you're an IP, you are IP only in your own airplane and not for the whole flight."

I was completely taken by surprise. "What's the problem?"

"You had no right to call me to move our holding area. That was my decision to make as flight leader."

I couldn't believe he was mad about that and I was really upset that he would be so stupid as to accept holding over guns and then blame me for wanting to move away from them.

"I'm sorry you didn't like it, but I could see no reason to hold over known guns when there is a perfectly good and much safer area nearby. As flight lead, you have a responsibility to conduct the mission in as safe a manner as possible, and you weren't doing that. Moving just seemed like common sense to me."

The leader had recently had his flight lead authorization reinstated. It had been withdrawn for an earlier serious mistake.

This was my 184th mission and I was experienced enough to not let an oversight on the part of someone else get me into any more trouble than necessary. We had enough hazards to deal with without blindly accepting more when a simple solution was obvious.

February 26, 1970. Thursday. I took off at 1:00 a.m. with Loren Evenson on the wing. I was Firefly 50 in a Hobo H model. Blind Bat 05 was the fac and he had a target as soon as we arrived in the area. We were airborne two hours and twenty minutes.

The temperature was 102° F today, which was reported to have been the hottest day on record at NKP in February.

*

February 27, 1970. Friday. Not only did pilots have to work with old worn-out airplanes, so did the maintenance guys, and it wasn't easy for them either. They did a fine job and did their best to have airplanes ready and in good shape when we arrived for a mission. All too often, pilots had a tendency to take the efforts of crew chiefs and other maintenance people for granted. We were the front line troops—the guys who were hanging it out every night and actually getting shot at—but we never went anywhere without a great deal of effort by a lot of people. About the only ones we saw regularly were the aircraft crew chiefs briefly before and after each mission and the weapons loaders who armed the ordnance before takeoff and disarmed whatever remained after landing. The rest of their work went on behind the scenes as far as pilots were concerned, but it was vital to the success of each mission.

Since I flew nights, I considered it my duty to be sure all cockpit lights were working, and the crew chiefs came to know me for writing up lights. They considered it an accomplishment when I brought back an airplane after a mission without a light write up.

The crew chiefs, who were enlisted men, were always polite and respectful to the pilots, who were officers, which was the way it was supposed to work. I can speak from the point of view of only one, but I suspect some of the pilots didn't give much thought to the efforts given by crew chiefs and other maintenance people who gave us the best airplanes they could for every mission.

*

The wing commander had recently decided to fuel the external centerline tank half full for Steel Tiger missions, which seemed like a good idea.

I took off at 12:50 a.m. in aircraft #622, a Zorro H model, fifty minutes late because maintenance hadn't had enough time to get the airplane ready. Ed Solley was the wingman in an E model.

We were assigned to a Blind Bat who had a target on the 130° radial 140 miles from the base. He had spotted a couple of trucks, and when he put his marks down, six guns fired and some of the rounds came close enough to scare him. It was unusual for a C-130 flying level at 13,000 feet to receive ground fire. Maybe that's a new tactic—to frighten the facs.

We were a couple of minutes away when the guns started firing and we could see the tracers. The Bat said, "Let's move north. Those guys are too eager." So we held off to the west for about twenty to twenty-five minutes while he looked for a new target. Two-seaters were less fuel efficient than single-seaters and Ed began to run low, so we had to RTB before the Bat could find another target for us. My fuel situation was still OK, but we were a long way from home, almost to South Vietnam.

The haze was so restrictive to vision that a pilot had to be on instruments as soon as he got airborne. It was not possible to see the stars from the ground at night and the moon was yellow.

I took off at 11:15 p.m. on February 27 for my second mission of the day. Al Preyss was the leader, and we escorted Roofy, a C-123. Visibility conditions were IFR below 9,000 feet because of the haze, and we could hardly see the gunship. We were airborne for over three hours and brought all our ordnance back.

The temperature hit 102° F again today.

March 1, 1970. Sunday. Took off at 2:50 a.m. in aircraft #028 with Dave Friestad leading. We went to Barrel Roll, where there was an undercast, but no targets when we arrived because Alleycat couldn't raise any of the facs on the radio. They must have been asleep. It was another example of Whoever was running the war not knowing what was going on, not seeing that the weather was bad. There was no reason for us to even take off because the guys on the mission ahead of us did the same thing. Dave suggested to Alleycat we might as well terminate the mission and they agreed to let us jettison and RTB.

About 3:30 a.m. a navy A-7 pilot ejected one hundred miles southeast of NKP. We could hear him calling on the radio and being told the Sandies would be out first thing in the morning. We needed to get our airplanes back so they could be used in the SAR if necessary.

He was picked up about 9:00 a.m. from high ground just south of Tchepone, which was about the worst place he could have been because of guns.

*

My parents had been reading in the newspapers about action in the PDJ and *Stars and Stripes* had recently had stories about it. Apparently a reporter had gotten his foot in the door in Vientiane or Saigon to find out what was going on in Laos and was reporting on it for the first time. The newspaper articles dealt with the North Vietnamese push into the PDJ with no mention of our bombing in Laos, but believe me, we were there.

The airfields in northern Laos that had been in friendly hands were now almost all controlled by bad guys. We could soften them up from the air, but it took ground troops to take and hold territory, and the Laotians just didn't have enough people to do that. We surmised the Laotians had lost a lot of men on the current offensive, but we really didn't know for sure. Many were missing, and we speculated some might have simply blended into the jungle for a while to E&E until they could make their way back two or three weeks later and show up at their HQ. At least, that was what we hoped.

March 2, 1970. Monday. Took off at 2:20 a.m. with Noel Frisbie leading. We orbited for a while and then RTBd with all the ordnance. The haze was bad again tonight.

I had another mission with a takeoff at 11:50 p.m. in a Zorro H model with Dan McAuliffe on the wing. I had UHF radio failure right after takeoff, so we orbited for a while and then brought everything back.

*

March 3, 1970. Tuesday. One year ago today I had a flight physical at Hurlburt Field, Florida, which was one of the last things I had to do before clearing the base and departing for a few weeks of leave before going to Travis AFB and southeast Asia and the war. The depth perception part of the vision check had always been difficult for me to figure out and that day was no exception.

In my role as the medical supply officer at Paine Field before I went to pilot training, I had had access to the eye exam apparatus in the dispensary. I learned the machines were the same at every United States Air Force base, so I spent several evenings by myself in the back of the dispensary where pilots took their vision tests trying for all I was worth to see the difference in the five little rings and why one would stand out from the other four. But I just couldn't do it, even when I had the answer in front of me. When I researched the subject, I found out the chart used by the air force relied upon interaction of the eyes and did not measure depth perception beyond a range of about thirty inches. Thirty inches! That wasn't going to help me fly an airplane! I also learned a person gauges depth beyond thirty inches by relative motion, the relative size of objects, and shadows. In other words, the air force depth perception test measured nothing useful for flying an airplane.

Meanwhile, I still couldn't determine which of the little rings was supposed to stand out from the others. I had only one option: Memorize the answers and hope the air force didn't change the charts for a while, so I could bluff my way through the eye test. A man who wants to fly badly enough will go to great lengths to get to do it. My solution had one problem: Each machine had two depth perception charts, #7 and #7a, which required me to pay close attention when the airman administering the test rolled the chart to depth perception, so I would know which chart was being displayed. Since all the machines in the air force were the same all I had to do was pay attention and then recite from memory the answer to #7 or #7a.

On that day, March 3, 1969, I got the charts mixed up and the technical sergeant at Hurlburt who administered the test allowed me to complete my exercise in memorization then about screwed himself into the ceiling. "Captain, you read the wrong one!" he sputtered. "You've got this memorized! I want you back, and I will give you this test myself and see just what the situation is with your eyes. You are to take this test from me personally! No one else."

Right. Now what? Maybe *he* had it mixed up. My little trick had worked in five previous physicals. I had top grades in UPT and hundreds of hours and landings in one of the hottest fighters the air force had. I was trained and ready to go to war and needed only this one little detail to be on my way. And this sergeant wanted to make a scene about a test that measures nothing of value to a pilot? How did I get the charts mixed up? I had to be more careful!

Air force hospitals kept ground hours that were pretty standard. I used to work in a dispensary and thought I knew a little about what their daily schedule might be. Hmmm. What time was it? Ten thirty. What time did the sergeant go to lunch? Probably noon to 1:00 p.m. What would happen if I showed up during the noon hour? Had he locked up my medical chart so he was the only one who could get it? There was only one way to find out.

So three days later I showed up promptly at 12:30 and found a young one-stripe airman on duty—a very pleasant young man who was eager to be helpful. I said, "I had a little trouble with the depth perception chart on my physical a few days ago and was asked to come back for a recheck. I'm all set to leave the base and just need to do this. Do you suppose you could give me a retest?"

"Just a minute, sir, and I'll see if your chart is here." He ruffled through a stack of files and finally found it on top of a cabinet. "Here it is. Come on back here." Maybe this was going to work! I looked into the machine before he began to rotate the charts and watched him crank it around. Number 7 came before #7a. Watch it! There it was. Number 7. The first three rings for 7 and 7a were the same. I slowly recited the next three. "I always have trouble with this," I said truthfully. "Did I get any of those right?"

"Yes, sir. That was correct," which was all I needed to hear. I zipped through the rest of #7. The airman said, "You got them all right, sir. I'll sign you off, and you can be on your way." (Air force people always carried their own medical and personnel records when transferring from one base to another.)

I signed out of the base, picked up Emily, and was gone within about thirty minutes. I was going to be on leave for over two weeks and my next obligation to the air force was on March 28 when I was to sign in at Travis AFB. What was that sergeant going to do, chase me down at Travis? And then what were they going to do, tell me I couldn't go to war? Fat chance! I just hope the airman didn't get into trouble on account of me. But he shouldn't because the sergeant obviously had not told him not to give me the retest and he probably forgot about me anyway.

*

<u>March 4, 1970.</u> Wednesday. Took off at 12:55 a.m. with DeWan Madden on the wing. We escorted a C-123 gunship with the call sign Doily about 175 miles southeast of the base. I was also scheduled for a 10:50 p.m. takeoff, but after we waited for an hour and a half, the mission was canceled because of target weather.

<u>March 5, 1970.</u> Thursday. The phone in the hooch area rang about 1:00 a.m. to tell whoever answered that Dave Friestad was down in Steel Tiger. We heard at first there was no chute or beeper, but then word filtered in that a beeper had been heard, meaning he had ejected and might be alive. It was not surprising that no one saw a chute at night.

Everyone who hadn't flown was ordered to show up at 3:00 a.m. at TUOC for a briefing for a first light SAR. Two groups of four A-1s were loaded with CBU-30, which was gas and two groups of four had smoke in addition to the Sandies.

Dave was eighty miles east and a little south of NKP in a bad area. When he spoke into his survival radio, he whispered because he could hear voices nearby and he didn't want to give away his position.

I was in the second group of four gas airplanes with Dan McAuliffe on my wing. We took off at 9:00 a.m. Dave was near several guns that had to be knocked out before a pickup attempt could be made. The best way to knock out guns was with fast movers—F-105s and F-4s—which worked the 37s over with their Vulcan 20mm cannons for three hours. They did a good job, and a pickup attempt was begun shortly after Dan and I got airborne. We orbited about thirty-five miles southeast of the base and listened to the action on the radio. We were above a cloud deck at 9,000 feet and could hear it all very well, but couldn't see any of it. It was like having a ring side seat at a boxing match without being able to see. Our mission was to be ready for a second try in case the first one failed.

A west wind blew the smoke over Dave's position when the helicopter came in for the pickup. The Jolly pilot almost had to pull out because he couldn't see, but he stuck with it and was successful on the first try. They didn't experience much groundfire during the pick up, but one of the A-1s had his right speed brake shot off by a 37. The speed brake on the single-seaters was located on the sides, instead of the bottom as on most airplanes. The airplane lost hydraulics and oxygen. He didn't know what was wrong, but it flew OK, so he came back and landed. Another A-1 took two hits and a third took one hit, but all came back and landed safely.

The dry season wasn't completely over, but the monsoon was coming and rain had been falling for an hour when I came back—raining so hard that I had a difficult time seeing the runway. I was airborne for an hour and thirty-five minutes. It was the first measurable precipitation since the first week of October, and the ground really soaked up the water.

Dave had been in aircraft #914, which I last flew on February 6. He said when he landed he got on his survival radio and talked to the guys in the air to let them know he was OK and that he would really appreciate it if they would get the Sandies and choppers out at first light. It was pitch black under the jungle canopy and he didn't have much to do, so he sat down on the ground and leaned against a big tree to wait for morning. He knew he was in a dangerous area, so turning on his flashlight was out of the question. It was dark and became very quiet. Sleep was not possible, of course. After a while, his hearing became very acute and he was aware of every little sound around him. Suddenly he realized he wasn't alone. Something was nearby. He didn't dare move a muscle. Whatever it was came closer and began to sniff him! Not only might he be captured or killed by the enemy, but now he had to contend with the very real thought that he might be eaten by a wild animal! Dave mustered up the courage to shoo the animal away. It growled and left.

*

<u>March 6, 1970.</u> Friday. Took off at 11:15 p.m. with Noel Frisbie leading. Our mission was to escort an AC-123 gunship and suppress any ground fire he

might encounter. I didn't understand why a well-armed gunship needed an escort from A-1s, but it was an easy mission. We followed him around for almost two hours and saw only one harmless little gun. We tried to put napes on it, but I'm not sure we succeeded. We were airborne for about three hours and fifteen minutes.

*

March 7, 1970. Saturday. I went to the dispensary today just checking to see if I needed anything done prior to leaving the base and was surprised when I came out full of holes. I received a cholera shot, a TB test, and a smallpox vaccination.

I attended a squadron pilot meeting from 4:30 until 6:00 p.m.

I was pretty hungry when I ate supper at the Officers' Club this evening. After I'd been eating for a while one of the Thai waitresses came to me and said, "You've had seven glasses of tea!" She had been counting because I had been asking for "More iced tea! More iced tea!"

She said, "Every thirty minutes you order something new and I think you're ordering for one of your friends and then you eat it all." Several of the Thai waitresses were standing around giggling and talking among themselves and I seemed to be the subject of their conversation. I suppose tonight was not the only time they had watched me eat. Tonight I had ordered a hamburger steak, and after I ordered, I decided I wanted a bowl of soup—the Club had pretty good soup. For dessert I ordered watermelon and said I wanted "mak mak," a big slice. She brought out a big thick slice I was barely able to eat, and the Thais marveled that anyone could eat so much. Prior to the watermelon, it really hadn't been very much, but the Thais thought so. They were good-natured people and we all had a laugh out of it.

*

The last time I had a cholera shot, I didn't have a reaction, but by evening I wasn't feeling very good. Reaction to a cholera shot was not a good enough reason to get off the flying schedule, so I took off at 10:55 p.m. with Noel Frisbie leading again. We were assigned to a Blind Bat in Barrel Roll who didn't have much of a target, so he threw out a mark and said, "Hit it." I still wasn't feeling well, so I took the easy way out and used a 20° dive angle and hit my napes right on the mark. Lucky. If it had been a good target I probably would have missed. Not only that, but I got two secondary fires and two secondary explosions.

Chapter 22

More Losses

March 8, 1970. Sunday. Took off at 4:25 p.m. in the right seat on a noncombat training flight with a new guy who hadn't flown in three months because of the lead time required to get here from the time he finished training at Hurlburt. It had been so long that the operations officer decided he should have a local training flight before being sent out on a combat mission. It was a good idea because he was really rusty and nearly flew us into the ground. I had to tell him to pull out on one of the practice passes and then he over-G'd it and I had to write it up. He wasn't used to flying in such dense haze and didn't cross check his instruments like he needed to in order to fly safely.

I was glad to have a stick and throttle in the right seat, but it really wasn't his fault—it's just the way his schedule worked out. It gave me a renewed appreciation for my own skills and how difficult it was to fly the A-1, let alone use it as a weapon of war with the much greater degree of difficulty that required.

I was scheduled for a 10:30 takeoff tonight, but I came down with a fever and felt sick, so I went to the dispensary. Sure enough I had a 100° F temperature, so the flight surgeon grounded me at the last minute, which upset some of the powers at the squadron because there was no time to schedule a replacement. I didn't have much choice. I didn't begin to feel badly until the last minute, and I sure wasn't going to fly with a 100° fever feeling as poorly as I did. I probably could have flown it OK, but what if I had gone down feeling sick? Flying in combat while sick was not a good idea and I resented the pressure to fly in such a circumstance.

March 9, 1970. Monday. I saw the flight surgeon this morning who said it was a continuing reaction to the cholera shot I had two days ago. You'd think I had crashed an airplane by the reaction. I told them what I thought about flying sick. If they want pilots to fly, they need better coordination between the squadron and the dispensary. I certainly didn't ask for that cholera shot.

*

Took off on a combat mission at 7:25 p.m., thirty-five minutes late because the airplane of my wingman, Ed Solley, had a prop regulator failure, and he had to take the spare.

We struck with Candlestick 41 just east of the M in the river in Ban Ban Valley. The NVA had brought 37mm guns into that area in the last few weeks, and we took a lot of ground fire.

I had a hung nape and tried to release it electrically but not manually because I also had two flare pods that would have gone. The base had a shortage of flare pods, which we were to bring back if at all possible because new ones for A-1s were not being manufactured. A hung nape was a serious problem, but in my opinion not as serious as a hung Mark 82 because of the difference in explosive power. Maybe I was beginning to get used to problems like this on these old airplanes. I made the decision to bring it back.

I declared an emergency when I first checked in with base radar upon my return. When I checked in with approach control, I was directed to call the supervisor of flying in the command post. The SOF told me to jettison the nape by pulling it off manually in a small jettison area near the base. The flare pods would be lost if I did that and the napalm might still be hung as had happened to me before. Perhaps the safety pin in the nape had not been pulled in the arming area before takeoff, and then we'd lose the flare pods for nothing. My feeling was if it wouldn't come off when I wanted it to over the target, it probably wouldn't come off inadvertently on landing. I asked the SOF to call the deputy commander for operations (DCO) to make the decision. The DCO was the colonel in charge of all flying operations, the ultimate authority, and he said to bring it in. So I landed, and it stayed on until the dearmers safetied it without incident.

When I taxied in, the microphone in my oxygen mask quit working and I couldn't call the command post to send out a truck to pick me up. It was a long way to the command post—too far to walk with all my gear—so I got a ride with a maintenance man. Just another day at the office.

Then the hungry monster grabbed me. Of course the Officers' Club wasn't open that time of night and all I had was a can of chili. It looked and smelled like something we used to feed our cat.

March 10, 1970. Tuesday. The Officers' Club had been losing $1200/month in its food account, so one officer from each squadron was tasked to audit the books to try to find the problem. I was selected to represent the 602nd, even though I didn't remember much of Accounting 101 from my sophomore year in college, and I spent three hours this afternoon checking food slips. At least I didn't get shot at while doing that.

*

Don Combs was flying an IP mission with George Luck this afternoon when they got a first-hand taste of the guns that have recently reappeared in the PDJ. They were in aircraft #445, took a hit in the engine, had to eject, and came down fairly close to each other. George had a small cut on his ear, but was otherwise unhurt.

This is Don's account of his experience:

> I just had two weeks left on my assignment. I would report to Moody to instruct in the T-38. Pete Williams said "Don, I have a good deal for you. I will take you off Sandy alert. All you have to do is check out George Luck." George had attended the air force Flight Safety School, and since we didn't have a safety officer, the decision was made to check him out in the A-1 at NKP. Another instructor had been given the job of providing transition training, that is, learning how to fly the A-1. I was given the job of getting George mission qualified; that is, how to bomb. The big drawback was that we weren't teaching him in a benign range like we had in the States. This had to be accomplished in actual combat. Not a safe or recommended procedure. What was fortunate was that George had gone through the complete A-26 program, so he was proficient in that platform. The A-26 had a navigator to call out dive angle, airspeed, release altitude, and a bomb bay that provided center-line delivery. Our machine had bombs on the wings, which was an offset problem in low level delivery.
>
> Our first two missions went well. On the third mission, we were assigned to a Raven fac who found a target on the PDJ. It was a lucrative but hot target, a North Vietnamese tank. We descended to 4,000 feet AGL and began a napalm run. He was in perfect position and dropped one of the napes. Unfortunately, he did not offset, and it impacted in perfect position, but right of the tank. I took the aircraft from him. He had flown a pattern that had been taught back in the states. I decided to demonstrate combat maneuvering. As I went into a series of jinking maneuvers, we ran into the "magic bullet." The enemy fire caught us somewhere in the propeller housing. Suddenly we had a lead sled, an aircraft with no power. The prop was just windmilling. I turned the aircraft toward what I thought was a safe area and told George to eject.

When he ejected, it was very strange watching a rocket take George up into the sky. Then I pulled the ejection handle. The Yankee extraction system worked perfectly. It lifted me out of the aircraft, the parachute blossomed, and I found myself in a surreal setting, gently settling earthward. I looked up at the parachute canopy and saw small holes appearing. I thought this was strange and suddenly it dawned on me that someone was shooting. I was the target! I pulled the red cords above me and initiated a system known as "cut 4." Four shroud lines separated and I began a faster descent and oscillated under the chute. My purpose was to make a more difficult target for the bad guys.

As I descended to about 500 feet AGL, I stopped the oscillations and set up for my parachute-landing fall. As the oscillations stopped, my left leg was hit and rose above my head. I slammed into a dry rice paddy. It felt like hitting a concrete road. My legs were spread and my head came down between them. I sat in a daze and realized that the dirt around me was being beaten up. I was still under fire. My back hurt severely and I could taste blood in my mouth. I managed to roll onto my stomach and make my way to a dirt mound. It was a dirt side of the rice paddy, my only protection. I continued to receive ground fire. I realized I had been shot and I thought my back was broken. I could not move or feel my legs. I managed to get my survival radio and .38 pistol out.

I contacted the Raven and my wingman, Lt. Col. Dick Michaud, my squadron commander. I told them I was taking fire from a ridge line about 500 meters away. I could not provide a cardinal direction, but asked if they could see my body. They replied in the affirmative. I said, "Use my head as a cardinal point. I am taking ground fire from a ridge line 500 meters on a line from my head."

My wingman made repeated passes at the ridge line with his bombs and guns. The Raven contacted the airborne command post, ABCCC, and they diverted A-1s and F-4s to assist. They hammered the ridge line and silenced the enemy.

There was a ravine 150 meters to my right and I thought I heard something. The Raven directed a flight of F-4s to hit it. I can remember the flight leader telling me to keep my head down because the area was dangerously close. The ground shook and rocks burst into flame. Just like being in the middle of a firework display on the Fourth of July. It was quite a display of precise bombing.

The Raven found other targets in my area and put in some more strikes. It was getting dark and he asked me if I could move. I told him, "Negative, I think my back is broken, I can't move my legs." I later learned his name was Fred Platt. He had planned to land his O-1 next to me and spend the night if the rescue helicopters didn't get to me. I heard the beating of helicopter blades as a CIA UH-1 Huey approached me. The parachute shroud lines were still wrapped around my legs. I was afraid of the helicopter landing next to me and those lines getting whipped into its blades. I warned the pilot, and he landed about one hundred feet from me. The side of the cargo doors opened and a crewman leaned out and said, "Get up, you son of a bitch, and run."

"I can't," I yelled back. He got out of the bird, unstrapped my chute, threw me on his back, and carried me to the helicopter. It hurt badly when he threw me inside, but it was a blessed hurt. We took off and picked up George in a tree line about a half-mile away. The door gunner hosed down the tree line to discourage enemy fire. I gave the helicopter pilot and the crew chief my .38 revolver, my survival radio, and whatever other valuables I had.

They flew me to Lima Site 20-Alpha, the headquarters of the CIA and Raven FAC program. I was taken from the helicopter to their infirmary and examined. Jerry Rhein, who had been one of my instructors at Hurlburt walked in. He was Raven 1, the commander of US Forces in Laos. With him was a short Laotian in uniform. Jerry said "Don I want you to meet Gen. Vang Pao." The general was legendary. He was the leader of the Hmong mountain people and a staunch ally of the United States. He thanked me for my sacrifice and shook my hand. I was surprised and honored. I looked up at the doctor and recognized him from Brown University. I do not remember his name.

I was flown to Udorn RTAFB, Thailand, in a Caribou aircraft. They popped a parachute to make me comfortable. At the field hospital, they gave me an X-ray and determined that I had fractured my pelvis. During the examination, I felt a hard object on my left side. I reached down below my buttocks and pulled out a scrap of metal. It was a spent AK-47 round. I had the heel of my boot shot away. Also a round passed through a Mod 0 Mark 13 flare in my flight suit pocket. This is a white phosphorus flare that had a day and night end separated by a piece of cardboard. The flare was ignited by pulling an O-ring and receiving contact with air. The round passed right through the cardboard. I have no idea why that flare did not ignite. If it had, I probably would have burned to death. I don't remember much about the next week. I remember being placed in a sling to reset the pelvis. I also remember a doctor injecting saline solution directly below my larynx to make me cough, puke, and expel fluid from my lungs to prevent pneumonia. I had two Laotian soldiers, horribly burned by napalm, as my roommates.

Don had had two previous assignments in Vietnam flying C-123s, had volunteered to fly A-1s, and in between each assignment had gone back to Moody AFB, Georgia, as a T-37 instructor.

*

Took off at 10:45 p.m. with Tom Coleman as wingman. Our assigned mission was to escort a C-119 who was up to something in Barrel Roll, but we didn't have the speed to keep up with him, so we orbited until we were assigned to a Blind Bat who had four trucks spotted on Route 61. The Bat had several marks down, and after listening to his instructions, I rolled in and put my ordnance right on target—except for one problem—I picked the wrong marker and missed the trucks by four miles. My napes were right where he wanted them from the mark I selected, though. No one's perfect, I guess.

*

I came out of my room one afternoon and saw Ron Marzano walking past with some papers in his hand and his head down. "What's the matter, Ron?" I asked.

He stopped and said, "Rick Chorlins' mother has written a letter to the wing commander asking about what happened to Rick, and he passed it to the squadron commander who passed it to me, and I have to write the reply."

"That's a tough assignment."

"For example, here is some of what she says," he continued. "'A piece of paper isn't much of an exchange for a son. I would like to know more about the circumstances of the mission he was on, exactly where he was, who was with him, and how he died.' How do you write a letter like that?"

Even though I had gotten to know Rick fairly well and had flown with him several times, it was not like he was a part of my family. I felt badly about him getting shot down, about losing a friend. I had just flown with him and had been in the same airplane the night before. It renewed the fears I first felt way back when Jim East was killed; but I forced myself to put them out of my mind as much as I could.

Those fears were never far below the surface, but somehow a pilot had to take on a feeling of invincibility when facing the guns over the Trail. He had to tell himself, "They're not going to get me tonight. I can thread my way through the shells. It won't happen to me." Maybe Rick thought the same thing. He probably did. But it *did* happen to him and now there were questions to be answered. Tough questions—and I didn't envy Ron the task of trying to answer them.

It brought me back to the basic question, "Why are we here fighting a war that we aren't going to win and that our government isn't really trying to win?" To lose a young man with as much potential as Rick essentially for nothing was an awful waste.

The letter gave me the perspective of our involvement in the war from the point of view of those waiting at home, and it wasn't a very pleasant picture. For someone like Rick's mother to receive a letter saying her son wouldn't be coming back must have been an awfully empty feeling, especially when she could only guess at the details of what might have happened. His body has never been recovered, so there was no military funeral service, no finality. Just a message and the return of some personal effects a few weeks later. That feeling could be multiplied by the families of the tens of thousands of American sons, brothers, and husbands who died in this miserable war.

We who were taking the fire had questions: "What would happen to our families if we didn't make it back? How would they react?" We would never have the opportunity to tell them what happened. They would just have the empty fact that we weren't coming home. The letter made me realize why my mother was trying so hard not to cry that morning nearly a year ago at O'Hare

International Airport when she and Dad and Emily saw me off. She had said, "Be careful, Dick."

"I will, Mom. Don't worry."

I knew I was well trained, and I could only imagine the hazards that lay ahead. Now I knew about those hazards first hand, and thanks to Rick's mother's letter, I could see a family's side, the ones left at home, a little more clearly, and that may have been the more difficult to handle.

I have had it said to me, "I don't know if I would have had the courage to do what you did—to face danger without flinching. You're lucky because you know you've got what it takes."

I never know how to reply to that because I don't know if I could do it again. All I know is I did it then and I was one of the lucky ones who survived. That feeling of invincibility is essential to anyone who looks danger in the eye and keeps going.

But the tragedies of Rick Chorlins and J. B. East and Clint Ward and Bob Moore and Dick Lytle and Jim Herrick and all my other friends who had been killed—and the sadness of their families—brought me back to the reality that we were playing for keeps and no one is invincible.

*

March 11, 1970. Wednesday. Took off at 6:50 p.m. in aircraft #609, a Zorro H model with Lieutenant Colonel Michaud leading. Candlestick 41 had spotted some trucks just west of the T intersection in Ban Ban Valley and had some marks down when we got there. We each had two funny bombs. Colonel Michaud missed the target, but got two trucks on his first pass anyway. On his second pass he missed again, but got another truck. They must have a lot of trucks. I couldn't hit the target tonight any better than Colonel Michaud. Mine landed right next to his, but not on the target, and I wasn't as lucky as he was—I didn't get any trucks.

*

Pilots had been scheduled for their last flight ten days before their DEROS since long before I arrived, but a move was afoot to change it to seven days and I was the first to be caught in the change. I objected and a decision was finally made about when my last flight would be. Jim Monk's DEROS was March 24 and he was to leave NKP on the 21st because he had a project in Bangkok. So his going-away party was to be the 20th and a decision was made to combine his party and mine. The party was always after a pilot's last flight, which means mine will be the 19th, the date I'd expected all along.

After nearly a year of flying mostly nights, I was tired of it and looked forward to flying day missions.

*

March 12, 1970. Thursday. The temperature was 102° F again today, which reminded me of one of the reasons I wanted to fly nights in the first place. I took off at 4:00 p.m., an hour and forty minutes late because an F-4 diverted in and closed the runway when his gear collapsed on landing. I was in the left seat of aircraft #448 with Major John Waresh who was on his first combat ride in the right seat. The flight leader was Lieutenant Colonel Don Fincher who was on his second lead qualification ride, so I had double IP duties. I wondered if they thought about me the same way I thought of Jerry Jenkinson so long ago. I hoped so.

Colonel Fincher's father died recently and he had just returned from emergency leave to attend the funeral. He was authorized to be gone three more days, but returned early.

The airplane was right at max gross takeoff weight, and in the very hot air it was a real dog, slow to climb. I told John I was glad it wasn't night because at least in the daylight we could see we were going to clear the tree tops at the end of the runway.

We struck with a Raven fac on the southwest slope of the 7,247-foot mountain northeast of the PDJ. The haze was really bad again, but I managed to put my bombs right where I wanted. Because of the haze and the proximity to the mountain, I released the ordnance high and luckily was accurate.

This Barrel Roll mission lasted only two hours and forty-five minutes. Maybe the guys who don't want to fly nights have a better idea after all.

*

When I got back to the hooch, I started to pack my personal items to be shipped home tomorrow.

March 13, 1970. Friday. I borrowed a truck from the squadron to take my things to Transportation for shipment home. I had no idea I had that much stuff. The weight was 980 pounds, 80 pounds over the maximum allowed, so I had to get approval from the base commander for the extra weight.

Flew an afternoon FCF on #448 for a prop regulator change. It was still in poor condition with low torque and high RPM on takeoff. What a miserable flying airplane! I was off the ground for only about five minutes.

*

I was scheduled for a 9:00 p.m. takeoff with Captain Bob Skelton in the right seat on his first night mission. Just as I released the brakes, sparks flew out the right side of the instrument panel and the console lights went out.

So we tried another airplane that needed a tire change. When the tire was changed, the right brake hydraulic line needed bleeding. Then the #2 inverter failed, so we called it a night.

<u>March 14, 1970.</u> Saturday. At 2:25 this afternoon Don Fincher's engine failed just after he took off and he crashed off the end of Runway 15. He was unable to get out and was killed. If he had returned from his emergency leave when he was scheduled to return, someone else would have been in that airplane. He was Jim Monk's roommate in the room right next door to mine. I flew with him just two days ago. It doesn't get any easier.

*

I was on stand by for FCF all day, but none came up.

<u>March 15, 1970.</u> Sunday. A-1s were launched on a first-light SAR this morning for a navy A-4 pilot who was shot down southeast of the base. I was in a flight of four gas birds, with Jim Costin leading Colonel Morris, Pete Williams, and me. We orbited about one hundred miles southeast of the base, but the survivor was picked up before we were needed. My call sign was Apeman 43, and I was in a Zorro E model, #878. A-1s from Danang ran the SAR. Weather visibility was down to three-fourths of a mile because of haze when we landed. The mission lasted two hours twenty-five minutes.

In the late afternoon, I had an FCF in aircraft #206, but ground aborted it because of a bad generator.

<u>March 16, 1970.</u> Monday. Another SAR was launched this morning for Nail 53, an OV-10 who went down to the southeast. He was picked up unharmed.

Took off at 8:55 p.m. in aircraft #621, an H model, call sign Firefly 50. Bob Skelton and Noel Frisbie were 51. We struck with Candlestick 41 who had a couple of trucks for us in the eastern end of Ban Ban Valley. Gunners shot at us as we were on the way out of the target area. This was my 200th mission; it lasted only two hours and ten minutes and was an easy one.

Fris and I played ping-pong for over an hour when we got back.

<u>March 17, 1970.</u> Tuesday. Took off at 9:15 p.m. in aircraft #058. We were twenty-five minutes late because a Hobo took the barrier and closed the runway. A Zorro, First Lieutenant Steve Howard, was my wingman. We struck with Hornet at Lima Site 72, south of the PDJ not far from Lima Site 98. Hornet wasn't a very good fac. The terrain is really high in that area and we had to be very careful about our altitudes.

I found out today my last flight will be Friday, nine days before my departure.

<u>March 18, 1970.</u> Wednesday. The American public was beginning to get more information about the war in Laos, but our involvement and specifically the role Skyraiders were playing was still not getting out.

I went to a memorial service for Don Fincher.

I was duty officer in the afternoon then took off at 9:15 p.m. in aircraft #314 with Frank Monroe leading. We flew around Barrel Roll awhile then jettisoned our ordnance because the weather was so bad. This mission lasted three hours and fifteen minutes.

The bad guys had really been pushing at LS 20, Sam Thong, and Vang Pao's HQ at LS 98, and it looked like they were going to capture them. Channel 113 was off the air today and things were deteriorating rapidly for the good guys. It was a shame we couldn't help them out tonight.

March 19, 1970. Thursday. Took off at 4:50 p.m. in the right seat with Bob Skelton in the left and Daryl Heusinkveld leading. The weather was bad with a lot of haze, so we had to jettison our ordnance again. This was my 203rd mission.

Final approach to Runway 15 at NKP

*

Loren Evenson's airplane was hit near Ban Ban this afternoon and he couldn't quite make it back to NKP. He ejected twenty miles west of the base and made friends with some locals before he was picked up.

An F-100 Misty fac was shot down in Steel Tiger this afternoon and picked up.

An F-4 crew, Wolf 6A and 6B ejected and a SAR will be underway for them first thing in the morning.

March 20, 1970. Thursday. Wolf 6A and 6B were just north of where Boxer 22 was in December in a very dangerous part of the Trail. I was scheduled to fly a gas plane in the SAR, but an FCF came up that needed to be flown for an engine change. The squadron operations officer Major Pete Williams asked if I would like to fly the FCF and let that be my champagne flight. I accepted his offer because it beat going to Ban Phanop on the SAR.

I took off at 10:20 a.m. in a Zorro H model, #575. The engine was running smoothly, so I flew around the local area awhile and did some sightseeing. I landed after an hour and five minutes and came in to the fire hose and champagne.

After being hosed down on my champagne flight. DeWan Madden is on the left.

*

Meanwhile, the SAR wasn't going well. Wolf 6B was captured or killed and 6A was in a poor location. Dale Townsend of the 1st SOS had to bail out and was recovered.

In the evening, Jim Monk and I had our going-away party and nearly everyone in the squadron was there because no one was flying night missions due to the SAR. Jim and I were former F-106 pilots, had been in the same class at Hurlburt for our A-1 training, and now we finished together. It was a good feeling, but we were still saddened by the death of Jim's roommate, Don Fincher, just six days ago, and we were distracted by the ongoing SAR.

I finished with 203 missions and 700 hours of combat time. (My DD 214 credits me with 204 missions, but that is incorrect.)

March 21, 1970. Friday. Even though I had completed my combat missions, the war went on and I was pressed into service to fly another FCF for a prop regulator change because the base was so short of A-1 pilots.

Wolf 6A was finally hauled out of the woods about 1:30 this afternoon. He had been holed up in a cave and had no broken bones, but was dehydrated, was in psychological shock, and had second degree burns around his neck.

After the successful pickup, Sandy Two, Major Ed Hudgins of the 22nd, was shot down and killed as he was exiting the area. He had only ninety days to go until retirement, and he was almost out of there when they got him.

About the same time, a Nail went down along Route 7 in Barrel Roll, and that turned into a full-blown SAR. Jim George was Sandy One and the survivor was picked up by an Air America helicopter.

During the SAR in Barrel Roll, two MIGs got within eight miles of the survivor before being chased away by an F-4. When the survivor was picked up the helicopter received ground fire just after he got in the hoist, so the pilot took off and flew about twenty minutes with him dangling about a hundred feet over the trees, but he was uninjured.

*

Jim Matthews was shot down and recovered while working a SAR near Ban Ban on April 6.

On April 21 an OV-10 was shot down on the Ho Chi Minh Trail and the efforts to recover the crew resulted in two more A-1s being lost. First was a Zorro, Captain John Dyer, and about thirty minutes later, Major Ed Whinery of the 602nd was shot down.

The next day, April 22, another A-1, this one flown by Dave Friestad, was shot down near where the two had been lost the day before. It was Dave's second ejection. All three A-1 pilots were recovered safely.

And so the war continued.

*

It was a relief to know that I was never again going to have to take off at maximum gross weight in a Skyraider or go over the Trail and watch 37mm shells come up or have to dodge the mountains in Barrel Roll in bad weather.

I had made my last trip across the Mekong where so many bad guys were waiting with their big guns and had come home. Part of me will always be affected by my experiences over Laos and by the loss of my friends who will never come home.

Many, but not all, of my contemporaries at Delta were Vietnam combat veterans both air force and navy. Some had flown jet fighters and some C-130s. Others were in O-1s, O-2s or bombers—very few were A-1 pilots—and we all had our stories. We almost never talked about it to one another, and so our stories were tucked away in many cases never to escape the thoughts of the veterans who lived them.

My biggest regret is that I never told my parents or older brother my story before they passed away. They could only guess at what my life was like and the challenges I dealt with. But now it was time to move on, to start and raise a family and build a life with Emily. So I did and put it aside for many years. Life is good.

Epilogue

My trip home was uneventful. The DC-8 flight to Travis AFB was full of soldiers, sailors, and airmen who had just completed a year of service in the war, and we were glad to be on the flight we had been dreaming of for so long. During a short orientation session at Travis, we were advised that when we flew out of the San Francisco airport it might be a good idea to wear civilian clothes in order to avoid potential confrontations with war protesters. Either uniforms or civvies were allowed, and to my regret at this late date, I complied with that suggestion. Welcome home!

Emily met me at O'Hare International Airport and the next day I boarded a Delta flight to Atlanta to interview for a pilot job. Emily was caught in a freak April snowstorm as she drove the one hundred miles back to her parents' home in Spring Valley.

I spent the night at Dick and Alice Colby's house in Atlanta. After the Delta interview I boarded a Northwest flight nonstop for Minneapolis to interview with them. Emily met me at MSP and we stayed a couple of nights with my brother Bob and his wife, Shar, at their house in River Falls, Wisconsin. On my birthday, June 2, 1970, I received a letter from Delta advising me I had been hired and I would be starting June 19. That's the best birthday present I ever received!

*

The 602nd Special Operations Squadron was deactivated in December, 1970.

Daryl Heusinkveld said that in his year at NKP, for the entire base, out of one hundred airplanes, forty crashed or were shot down resulting in twenty pilots killed. He was a lieutenant just out of pilot training and had a total of 290 hours of flying time when he arrived at NKP. The A-1 and its mission were a real handful for new pilots, but they were talented and learned fast.

*

After five years and a lot of therapy, Don Combs regained flying status and lives in Florida.

Aircraft #076, Kawliga, was destroyed by combat damage in 1972.

The air force lost 104 men and the navy lost 40 who were killed or missing in action while flying A-1 Skyraiders during the war in southeast Asia.

According to Chris Hobson in his book, *Vietnam Air Losses*, a total of 201 A-1s were lost by the air force in the war.

*

In August, 1970, the air force had an award ceremony at Dobbins Air Force Base in suburban Atlanta to present Jack Hudson with the Air Force Cross he earned on October 6, 1969, and Emily and I attended. The Air Force Cross ranks next to the Medal of Honor and is a very big deal.

*

Colonel Robert Sowers, who was the commander of the 95th FIS the last few months I was there, was killed in a helicopter crash in Vietnam on April 27, 1972.

Major J. B. East's remains were recovered and identified in 1994. He was laid to rest at the Sam Houston National Cemetery in San Antonio in August, 1997.

*

When the moveable Vietnam Wall came to Rockford during the last week of June, 2000, I volunteered to help people find names. Few showed up the first night, and as I was leaving, I noticed a couple in motorcycle clothes standing by the wall. I stopped to ask if they needed help finding a name. The man said, "No thanks. We're familiar with the wall. My brother was killed in Laos."

I replied I had more than 200 missions over Laos and asked what part of the country he went down in, never dreaming what he would say next: "We don't know, but his name was Jim Herrick."

Immediately I said, "I flew with Jim the day before he was killed."

We were both astounded at the long odds of our encounter as Roger Herrick was in Rockford temporarily as a contract engineer working for a local company. If they had spoken to any of the other volunteers at the wall that evening, they would not have known to introduce us. Very few people in the world could give the Herrick family as much information about what happened to Jim as I could.

As a result of our meeting, I was able to tell them what life had been like for Jim on the base and what he would have seen as he flew missions over Laos so long ago. I was also able to help them meet Jim George, who was his flight leader the day he disappeared, so Jim could tell them first-hand what happened. The family is still mourning the loss of Jim, but now they know a lot more about his disappearance than they did before.

*

The remains of Captain Ben Danielson, the pilot of Boxer 22, were recovered and identified in 2005. His son, Commander Brian Danielson, who is a navy flight crew member, was one week past his first birthday when his dad left for the war. The family held a memorial service in his hometown of Kenyon, Minnesota, on June 15 and 16, 2007. Jim George, Woodie Bergeron, some of the Jolly crewmen, and I were there.

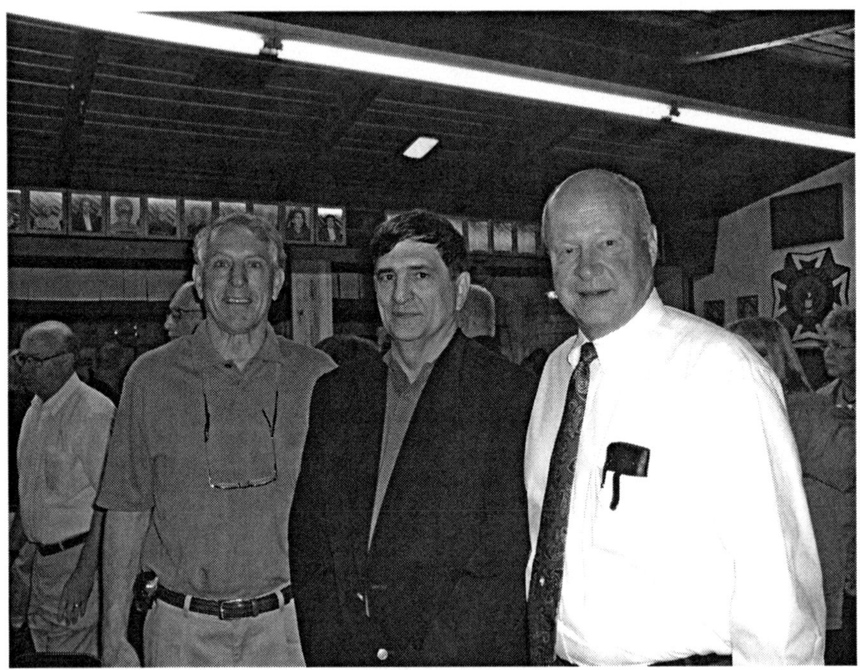

Jim George, Woodie Bergeron (Boxer 22B), and Dick Diller at Kenyon, Minnesota, June 15, 2007.

Ben was a graduate of the ROTC program at St. Olaf College in Northfield, Minnesota, where one of the instructors was then-Captain Bob Lambert. Captain Lambert was the tactical officer of my flight when I attended ROTC summer camp at Ellsworth AFB, South Dakota, in late June and early July, 1962. In 1969, he was Lieutenant Colonel Lambert, and as chief of intelligence at NKP, he was the officer who debriefed Woodie when he was rescued. Bob retired as a colonel and spoke at the service in Kenyon.

During his time at NKP, Bob Lambert met the wing commander and deputy wing commander in their offices on a daily basis. Deputy wing commander Colonel Pat Fallon had a picture of his wife on his desk and she was beautiful. (See July 4 entry.) Years later he was at a meeting in a hotel near the

Pentagon where in an adjacent room a conference of POW/MIA families was ongoing. He looked in and there she was, the woman whose picture he had seen. He recognized her immediately because she was so striking. He introduced himself and asked why she was attending the meeting. She said she was hoping Pat was still alive and she would find out more information about him. Bob had to tell her the sad truth that Pat wasn't going to come back and she should get on with her life.

The lives of MIA or KIA families are never the same and most never have full answers to their questions.

*

Jack Hudson, Daryl Heusinkveld, Jim Matthews, Jim George, and I all continued our flying careers with Delta Airlines. Jim George did so after retiring from active duty in 1987.

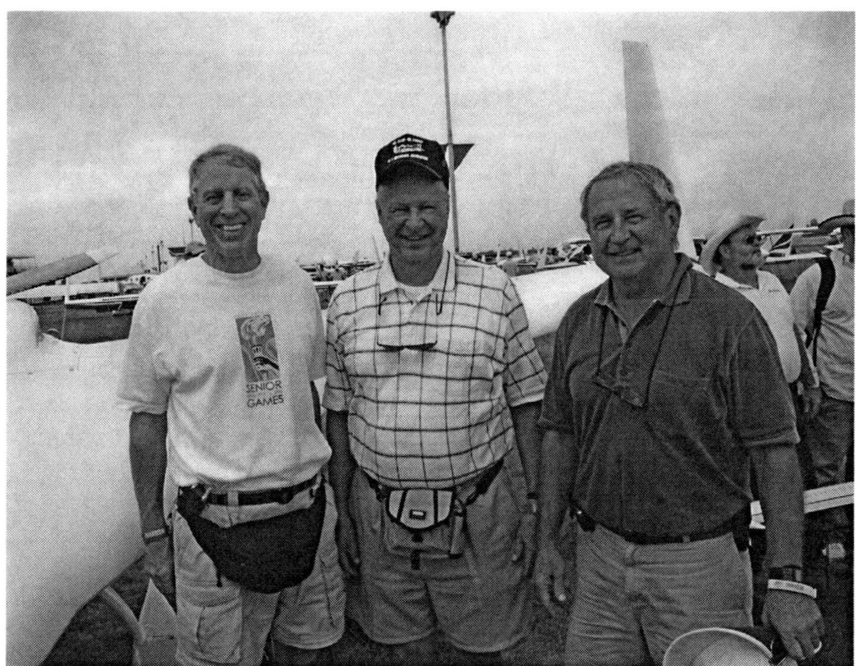

L-R: Jim George, Dick Diller, and Daryl Heusinkveld at Oshkosh in 2007

Jack Hudson died of a heart attack on March 15, 2002, seventy-six days before he would have retired from Delta at age sixty. Tom Coleman left active duty, joined the air force reserve, and ran a security service company in Atlanta. John Waresh continued with his tour and was one of the Skyraider

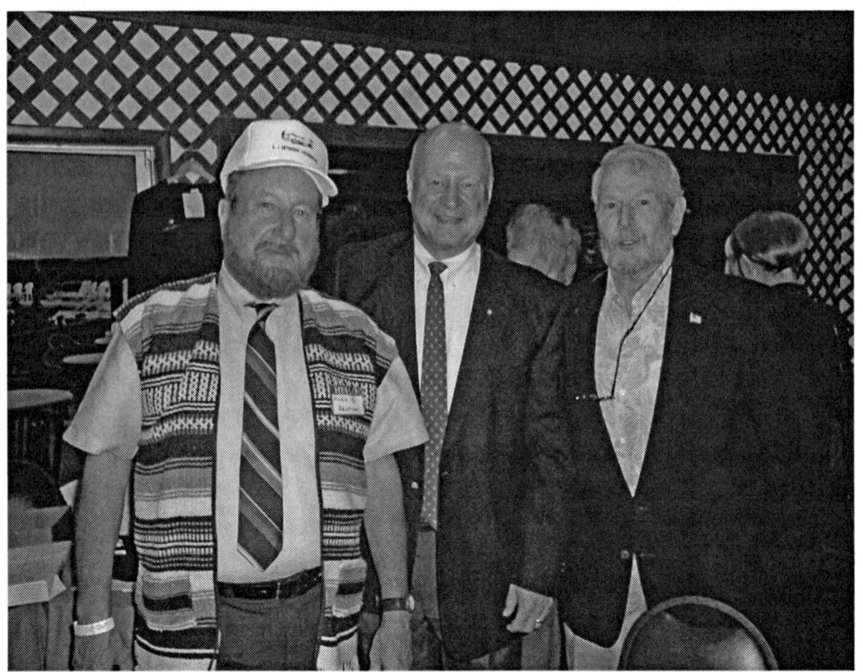

Jim Beggerly, Dick Diller and Jim Monk at a reunion in San Antonio.

pilots selected to participate in the Son Tay raid that attempted to rescue POWs in North Vietnam in November, 1970. Daryle Tripp retired from the air force as a major general. Jim Anderson completed his air force career and lives in New Jersey. Norm James, Larry Dannelly, Jim Beggerly, and Jon Ewing all retired from the air force. Norm lives in Hawaii. After retirement, Larry flew for American Airlines, Jim flew with United Air Lines, and Jon became an FAA inspector based in Miami. Jim Monk, Dan McAuliffe, Harry Dunivant, and Loren Evenson were promoted to colonel before retiring. Jim lives in Colorado and Dan lives in Florida. Harry died May 24, 2006. Rex Huntsman separated from the air force and worked as a banker in Idaho before he died in 2006. Jim Jamerson, with whom I flew on April 23rd, continued his air force career and was promoted to four star general.

*

Beverly Kasbeer's brother, Chuck, flew A-1s at NKP for a few months at the very end of the deployment of the airplane. He was a career officer and retired as a colonel after thirty years on active duty.

Doug Scroggs returned to Princeton with Bonnie where they still live.

*

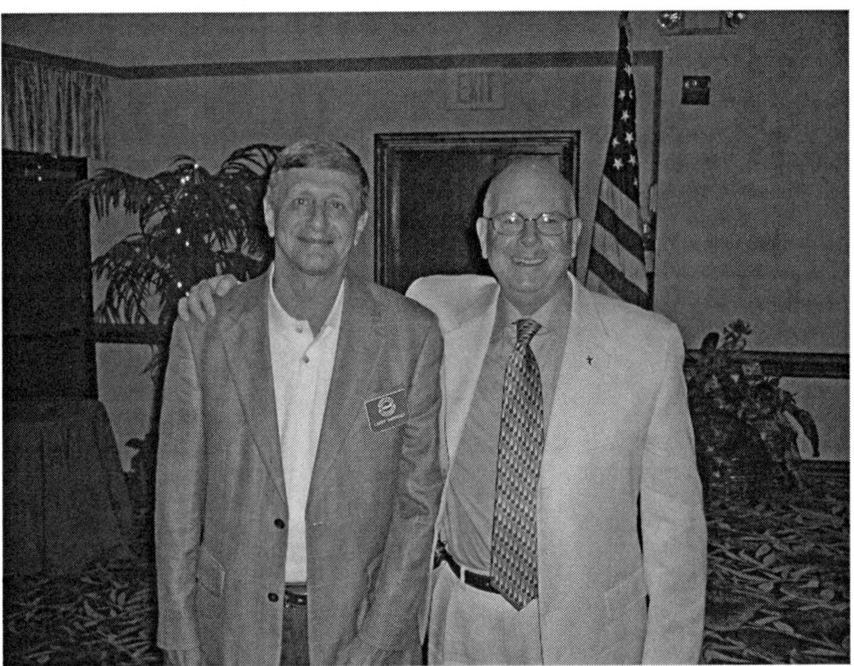

"Good Old Dan" Larry Dannelly and "Just Plain Dan" McAuliffe at an A-1 Skyraider reunion, September 29, 2007

In preparation for writing this book I contacted Rick Chorlins' sister, Toby Keene, who lives in suburban St. Louis. She said she and Rick had been especially close and their mother never recovered from his loss. Prior to my call no one from the air force had contacted the family after the first official notification, although they had been in contact annually with JPAC (Joint Prisoners of War, Missing in Action Accounting Command). Their mother attended POW/MIA family meetings for years hoping to find out more information or establish contact with someone who knew Rick, to no avail. Rick's loss is still difficult for Toby to talk about.

In about 2003, a crash site and human remains were found in isolated high terrain of the Annamite Mountains in Laos near Mu Gia Pass, very close to the border with Vietnam. DNA testing was not advanced enough to determine identification until about 2014, when the remains were found to be those of Rick Chorlins. The aircraft parts were identified as belonging to #570, the plane Rick had been flying when he disappeared.

Like the Herrick family, the Chorlins family knew very little about Rick's life as an A-1 pilot. His sisters, Toby, and Cheryl Spalding, invited me to Toby's home in suburban St. Louis when the mortuary affairs officer came from Dover to brief them.

Prior to combat, pilots were asked about personal preferences in case they might become missing-in-action, and Rick had expressed a preference to be buried at the Air Force Academy, so a memorial service was held there on April 14, 2015, and Toby and Cheryl asked me to give a eulogy. The Jewish Chapel was filled to overflowing with many of Rick's AFA classmates and family members in attendance.

And so, another sad story of the war came to a close, at least for the Chorlins family, who now have some degree of resolution to their terrible and tragic loss.

GLOSSARY

ABCCC	Airborne Command and Control Center.
ADC	Air Defense Command.
AFTN	Armed Forces Thailand Network, the local radio station.
AGL	Above ground level (See MSL).
Alleycat	The night ABCCC control ship for Barrel Roll.
Arc Light	Code name for B-52 bombing missions over Laos.
Armed recce	Armed reconnaissance. Looking, while armed with weapons, for targets of opportunity (usually trucks) that might be attacked.
Ban Ban	A valley in northern Laos northeast of the PDJ.
Barrel Roll	The USAF name for the northern Laos operating area.
Base altitude	An altitude that changed every day from which we made references in order to conceal our true altitude.
BDA	Bomb Damage Assessment—an estimate of how much damage we did to the enemy on a mission.
Bingo fuel	Fuel level at which it was necessary to RTB.
Bird Dog	See O-1.
Blind Bat	Call sign of C-130 night facs.

BOQ	Bachelor officers' quarters—living area for single officers on a base.
Brown bar	A second lieutenant.
Candlestick	Call sign for C-123 night facs.
Care package	A box of goodies from home.
CBU	Cluster bomb unit. A cluster of six tubes mounted on a wing station. Each tube contained nineteen bomblets. CBU-14 were anti personnel bomblets. CBU-22 was smoke. CBU-19 was gas.
Channel 89	The frequency of the NKP TACAN.
Channel 113	The frequency of Skyline, the TACAN for northern Laos.
Combat sky spotting	Ground-based radar-controlled bombing.
Cowl flaps	Flaps around a large radial engine used to regulate engine temperature.
Crew chief	The maintenance man assigned to an airplane.
Cricket	Call sign of the daytime ABCCC ship in Barrel Roll.
Crispy critters	Bad guys after we nape them.
CTO	Crew time off. Four-day trips to Bangkok.
Daisy chain	Skyraiders flown in a circle to dispense ordnance (usually smoke or incapacitating gas) to protect a survivor and rescue helicopter while a pickup attempt was made in a high threat area.
Dead reckoning	A navigation method, utilized when there are no other references, using time, speed and heading from a known location to arrive at another location.

DEROS	Date effective return overseas. Military jargon for Freedom Day.
DNIF	Duty not involving flying. A pilot's status when sick.
Dollar ride	The first flight for a pilot in a new airplane.
DOR	Date of return (from overseas duty).
DOS	Date of separation (from the air force).
DOSA	Department of Special Actions.
DR	Dead reckon.
Duty Officer	The officer assigned to answer phones at the squadron for the day.
E&E	Escape and evasion. Tactics used to avoid capture if on the ground in enemy territory.
Emergency egress	The act of leaving an airplane in a hurry while on the ground.
Ethan	Call sign for EC-121 radar picket ships.
Exfil	Exfiltration. Removing troops from an area.
F-4 Phantom	A two-man two-engine fighter/bomber used in Vietnam and Laos.
F-105 Thunderchief	A single-engine single-seat airplane mostly used as a bomber in Vietnam and Laos. Sometimes known by pilots as The Thud.
Fac	Forward air controller. An airborne or ground based observer who directs attacks from the air.
Fast mover	A jet strike airplane like an F-4 or F-105.
Fat face	Side-by-side two-seaters. A-1E or A-1G.

FCF	Functional check flight. A flight made to determine that maintenance action has been accomplished correctly.
Fence	An imaginary line just north of the bend in the Mekong where it turns west where we kept going straight.
FIGMO	Fooie, I got my orders.
Firefly	Call sign of the 602nd Special Operations Squadron (SOS).
Fragged target	A target assigned to a flight based upon intelligence gathered from reconnaissance photographs.
Front Snap	A head-on intercept procedure used by ADC pilots.
Funny bomb	Official designation was M-36. It had 182 magnesium bomblets wrapped in thermite.
G	The force of gravity.
Gas bird	An A-1 loaded with CBU-19.
Goat skins	Flight suits.
Gomer	Bad guy.
Hmong	The name of the ethnic group who were friendlies in northern Laos.
Hobo	Call sign of the First SOS.
Hooch	The name given to pilots' living quarters.
Intervalometer	A dial on the cockpit panel used to select the wing station from which ordnance was to be shot or dropped on a pass.
IP	Instructor pilot.

Jolly Green Giant	CH 3 or CH 53 helicopters used to recover downed crew members. Also known as "Jollies".
JUSMAG	Joint United States Military Advisory Group.
Karst	Limstone cliffs that rise nearly vertically out of the ground in souther Laos
KBA	Killed by air.
KIA	Killed in action.
Klick	Kilometer. 1,000 meters.
Klong	Open canals in Bangkok. The call sign of daily C-130 flights to BKK.
LAU	Rocket pod designation. LAU 32 had seven rockets. LAU 3 had nineteen.
Lima site (LS)	Laotian military outposts. Lima stands for Laos.
Log	Name given to LUU-1/B ground mark used at night.
Mark 82	Designation for 500 pound bombs.
METO	Max Except Take Off.
MIA	Missing in Action.
Mil setting	Gun sight setting.
Mobile control	A duty assigned to pilots that involved watching take-offs and landings.
Moonbeam	The night ABCCC control ship for Steel Tiger.
Movers	Enemy supply trucks on the move in Laos.
MSL	Mean Sea Level. Aircraft altitudes are usually given in reference to MSL.

Nail	Call sign of the O-2 fac squadron at NKP.
Nape	Napalm.
Navaid	A broad term referring to any radio navigation station.
Nimrod	Call sign of the A-26 squadron based at NKP.
Nine level gunner	An antiaircraft gunner whose shells came close.
NKP	Nakhon Phanom. A city in Thailand after which the base was named.
NOD	Night Observation Device, aka starlight scope.
NVA	North Vietnamese Army.
O-1 Bird Dog	A single engine tail dragger light plane used by facs in Vietnam and Laos.
O-2	A twin engine Cessna Skymaster used for faccing in Laos.
Ordnance	An all-encompassing name for bombs, rockets, napalm, guns and CBUs.
Palace Cobra	The ADC code name for a list of pilots who were most eligible for combat duty in Southeast Asia.
Party suits	Brightly colored flight suits that had rank insignia and squadron patches sewn on which were worn to parties.
Pass	An attack consisting of one trip over a target usually involving a forty degree dive angle in which ordnance was dropped or shot.
Pathet Lao	Laotian communist forces. The bad guys.
PCS	Permanent change of station. In the USAF, a six months minimum assignment.

PDJ	Plaine des Jarres. French name for the Plain of Jars in northern Laos.
Pickle	Pushing a button on the control stick to release ordnance.
PJ	Parajumper. Crew member on rescue helicopters.
PSP	Pierced steel plank used for the ramp and taxiways at NKP.
Raven	Call sign of O-1 facs with whom we often worked in the daytime in northern Laos.
Recip	Reciprocating engine (as opposed to a turbo, or jet engine).
Roll in	A sharp descending left turn to initiate a pass.
RPM	Revolutions per minute.
RTB	Return to base.
St. Elmo's fire	Static electricity buildup on leading edges of the airplane and ordnance.
Sandy	Call sign of an A-1 being used in a SAR.
SAM	Surface to Air Missile.
SAR	Search and rescue.
SEA	Southeast Asia.
Skyraider	An A-1. Trouble to the bad guys.
SLIJO	Silly little insignificant jobs officer, of which the USAF had many.
SOS	Special Operations Squadron.
Sport model	A single-seat Skyraider, either an A-1H or A-1J.

Station	An ordnance attachment point on the wing of an attack aircraft. The A-1 had seven on each wing including the stub.
Steel Tiger	The operating area of southern Laos east of NKP through which passed the Ho Chi Minh Trail.
Stub	A heavy duty ordnance attachment point on the wing that was just outboard of the landing gear and inboard of the other six stations.
Sump light	A red light on the instrument panel that meant metal shavings were being detected in the engine oil.
TACAN	Tactical Air Navigation. A radio beacon used by pilots for navigation.
Tail dragger	Any conventional landing gear airplane with a wheel in the tail.
TDY	Temporary duty. In the USAF, any duty assignment less than 180 days.
Thud	Name given by pilots to the F-105.
Tracer	A gun slug that has material inserted into it that glows after it is shot so the shooter can see where it is going.
TUOC	Tactical Unit Operations Center. Operations headquarters for the base.
UPT	Undergraduate pilot training.
Vang Pao (VP)	The Laotian commander of friendly troops in northern Laos.
Willie pete (WP)	White phosphorus. Usually used on rocket tips to mark a target because it produced very visible smoke.
Winchester	Out of ordnance.

Yankee system	The A-1 ejection system so named because it was designed to yank the pilot out of the airplane if he ejected.
Zorro	Call sign of the 22nd SOS.

CPSIA information can be obtained
at www.ICGtesting.com
Printed in the USA
FSOW01n2350190218
44626FS